MARTIN SMITH

Managing the Training and Development Function

Second Edition

To
Walter Evans

MANAGING THE TRAINING AND DEVELOPMENT FUNCTION

SECOND EDITION

Allan D. Pepper

Gower

First published 1984
Second edition published by
Gower Publishing Company Limited
Gower House
Croft Road
Aldershot
Hants GU11 3HR
England

Gower Publishing Company
Old Post Road
Brookfield
Vermont 05036
USA

ISBN 0-566-02977-4

Printed and bound in Great Britain by
Billing and Sons Limited, Worcester.

Contents

Acknowledgements

My thanks to many people for information and help in preparing this edition, particularly to Wendy Hirsch of IMS, Paul Banks and Kate Owen of BP, Bob Dorries of Shell (USA), and, once again, to Muawiya Derhalli of the Centre for Overseas Briefing. Special thanks to Bryn Roberts for his help in sorting out the booklists, and to John Nye for his organisational insights.

ADP

Preface

During the past decade a number of factors have emerged in the field of training and development that are of prime importance. The most obvious of these is that training and development for today and for tomorrow must not be neglected. If it is, then sooner or later the employing organisation will be in deep trouble. Hence training is seen more and more as a direct management concern and responsibility; not merely because managers are the bosses of employees and are in the best position to identify their training needs, but because the company depends on employee capability and motivation for the quality, quantity and cost of products. So standards and rigour of training have a place on management's agenda, alongside the quality of products and services.

It has also been recognised that human beings spend a large portion of their lives at the workplace. They live there, one might say, just as much as they live anywhere else. So the workplace, and the company, should be a place fit to live in. Moreover 'work' should be an activity that is compatible with the health and development of the human being.

Equally apparent is that companies are becoming increasingly international in their trade, their organisation and their staffing. The implication, the obligation, is to work towards international understanding of political, economic and social matters, in both national and individual human terms.

Of no less importance is the fact that any company may be obliged to make radical changes to its organisation structure, to its production line, to its management style or to its employee relations practices. These changes may be for the sake of survival, or for improvement, or to meet legal, social or environmental obligations. The larger the scale, the greater the need for close management attention and employee cooperation.

All of the points raised above featured in the first edition of this book. However for this second edition I have amended the text to place greater emphasis on these and other current issues. In addition there are three new chapters: 'The International Context', 'Corporate Change' and 'Continuous Development', exploring more fully the roles of the Training and Development (T&D) function and of line management.

It is my hope that this book will continue to help T&D managers and personnel managers to develop their roles not merely as a service *to* management, but as an integral part *of* management.

ADP

Introduction

All those activities which demand planning, control and evaluation in addition to their actual execution need to be managed. We are familiar today with the necessity for the good management of the whole company and of the separate functions and activities which make up the total. During the past quarter of a century, at least, the body of knowledge on company management has grown considerably and is well presented in a formidable array of publications. The knowledge and teaching on the management of the component functions of a company is less well developed although it is now growing rapidly. Operational management, project management, the management of technology and other topics have emerged to serve the purpose of those whose immediate concern is not the conduct of the enterprise as a whole, but of one part, or specialisation or function.

One such specialisation is the training and development of manpower, and this book presents and discusses their management within the total enterprise. It is as well to clarify certain points on the subject matter and its treatment at the beginning if the book is to have the value and the usefulness intended.

First, it is not a book on training methods. The techniques of teaching and instruction continue to be described in books and professional literature and much of this is readily useful to those searching for methods suitable for industrial, commercial and other comparable organisations. Nor is it a book on management principles and techniques in the general sense. There exist already ample reading and teaching in the essential principles and practices of management of any organisation, large or small, in which objectives have to be defined, resources assembled, methods decided on and planned, and the results subjected to some form of assessment and accounting procedure. It is assumed that most readers will have experience or knowledge of these, in a general sense. We aim, in this book, at providing the bridge between the general skills and theories of management, and their special use in training, taking for granted that the reader is already aware of the techniques of planning, costing, and other analysis typical of modern management.

It is probably true to say that no book can describe exactly how to manage well.

At best it can present certain concepts and techniques which, if suitably chosen and adapted, may help improve the capability and performance of the manager and of the function for which he is responsible. Hence in the following pages a number of ideas, all concerned directly or indirectly with training and development, are presented in the belief that they contain potential material for use by those people who already have some orientation in management thinking, and are concerned with bridging the gap between their knowledge of training practices and of personnel data, and the complex, and much less clear requirements of the organisation, the company, the department, in which they work.

There was a time when only a few companies had training officers, and they were responsible mainly for the apprenticeship and new entrant training schemes, within which there was a great deal of craft and clerical instruction to be organised and given. As time went by more ideas, books and courses appeared, dealing with supervisory, management and communication skills, and the scope of the training officer was enlarged. Later, it became recognised that virtually any human learning need could be met by some type of training effort, perhaps in a package form off-the-shelf, perhaps home made. The training officer, now probably called the training manager, found himself faced with the entire company and its defined and undefined training needs, and not merely with certain traditional groups of 'trainees'.

This change alone posed problems of priorities and decision-making but more recent events have made the problems even more profound. The idea that the sequence of moves of an individual, from his first to his last job, can be seen as a development process, is as old as the hills. The ambition of some personnel managers has been that this could become a planned and controlled process – but too often extraneous factors and circumstances made it almost impossible to achieve results in more than very few individual cases. Nevertheless, the idea has been pursued, and analytic concepts and techniques are now available which make it possible, perhaps imperative, to look into the future, not of the individual, but of all employee groups, of the company, and of the environment in which it operates.

Within this theoretical framework, provided by manpower analysis and planning, the need for development of capability of employees, and the possibilities and limitations of their future careers, becomes clearer – but only if the analysis and planning is understood. The training manager, now sometimes called the training and development manager, has a vital role to play in this new scene, provided he can rise to the occasion.

Traditionally, many whose jobs are to look after training have been appointed to their jobs, or have risen to that level of responsibility, because they have shown themselves as 'good trainers'. This meant often good instructors, or lecturers, or good supervisors of a particular training scheme, such as an apprenticeship. Or they may have been transferred from another function such as recruitment, or finance, or organisation and methods because of technical skill, a way with people, and an interest in education. Very rarely are they selected on the basis of their ability in the management necessary for training, and, more recently, necessary for manpower development.

Above them are, typically, the personnel managers and administration managers, and sometimes the departmental or works manager who takes the training function under his own wing. Here we also have people who may be well versed in management practices and in personnel work, but whose need is to understand better the scope and possibilities of the training and development for which they carry ultimate responsibility, to see clearly its relationship with other functions and activities in the enterprise as a whole, and to supervise in a satisfactory way specialists who work for them. It is hoped that this book may contribute to this understanding; many pages are devoted, throughout, to an examination of working relationships, and of the role of managers who work outside the training function. These need to be clearly defined and understood if training is to proceed successfully, and if longer term development schemes are to bear fruit and avoid unnecessary problems.

Is there anything about this specialisation that makes its management different from that of other functions? The answer is 'yes', although the difference is to be found in all functions which are more concerned with the future than with the present. In many companies today it is a fact that the training function concerns itself with a wide variety of activities: courses, seminars, projects, inside and outside the premises, on-the-job and off-the-job, at all levels from the top to the bottom of the organisation. It is a matter of good housekeeping – one aspect of management – that at any one moment all of these tasks, often widely varied, are successfully designed and carried out. But the question that must be asked of the training manager is 'What *should* you be doing?', as well as 'What *are* you doing?' In a big company it is relatively easy to find opportunities for training action. How do you find the important ones? The identification of training needs is a prime responsibility of the training officer, and has become a too readily used cliché in many parts of the world. It is, however, a prerequisite also of good training *management*, for the *full* identification of training needs provides the basis for further planning decisions and objective settings. The immaculate management of those training activities *already launched*, based on decisions made yesterday and last year, may merit praise for good performance, but not necessarily for best contribution to the continuing well being of the company, which lies in the future.

So the main distinction that has to be made, in managing the training in any enterprise, is between, on the one hand, the training which is performed today, for today's and tomorrow's requirements; and, on the other hand, the training which is yet to be started, to meet the requirements of the near, middle and long-term future. In the second and third cases, clearly, we are in the domain of corporate longer term objectives and plans, and of manpower planning, and perhaps of career development. In this book we shall be examining decisions and actions under all of these headings, and for convenience have divided the book into two parts – the Management of Training and the Management of Manpower Development.

One particular question which has to be dealt with by managements, and which demands good training direction, is that of 'changes'. Changes are imposed on organisations by environmental influences of economic and social nature; and some are self-imposed by the organisation itself for its own internal purposes. The processes of training can therefore never be static, never regarded as meeting tomorrow's requirements fully, even if today they seem very adequate. It is clearly unsatisfactory to have a training function which is insensitive to, or only partially aware of, those changes which are actually taking place, and those which are predicted to take place in the future.

The communication problem, of keeping the training and development function sufficiently in the picture, and of enabling it usefully to express its views on what actions need to be taken, is a recurrent one and demands careful consideration. It is a problem which is often coupled with that of the position and status of the function in the company, and the access which it has to 'confidential' information. If the integrated view of training and development, as presented here, is adopted, then, in all probability, much of this communication problem will not so much be solved as simply not occur.

Throughout the book frequent reference is made, for simplicity, to the 'training manager' of the company. This should not be taken as implying that all companies have to have training managers, or training officers, in order that training and development work can be done. It is hoped that the principles and practices described in the book will be of value to those companies in which there is no special training function, and in which everything is done by managers and super-visors and their personnel assistants without outside servicing. It should be of value also to those companies which have both a training *and* development function, between which there needs to be close understanding and co-operation.

The training manager does not work so much with a company, as with all the people who make up that company. He does not sit in the middle of a complex conceptual structure of information, decisions and evaluation. He is, in fact, in the middle of a lot of people, processes and activity, some visible and a lot invisible, and this, and information about it, is what he has to deal with much of this time. Because of this, there are included in this book many examples which describe not only the training or development problems in conceptual and technical terms, but also the organisation, the people, and the relationships out of which the problems have arisen. It is hoped that this will encourage the reader, particularly if he is a training manager, to go on looking at and dealing with the wider situation, no matter how mundane it may appear, in his treatment of the more central training problem. It is hoped, too, that he will be comforted by reading of universal problems in organisation and relationships, with which he may identify himself, and recognise that these problems are not only his but are shared by many. The student, too, may find that the examples and situations described help bridge the gap from the theoretical to the reality.

Finally, the book does not set out to treat exhaustively the subject matter under any one chapter heading. Instead points have been selected which, to the writer, appear to be basic to good management, often giving rise to difficulty in compa-nies, but concerning which there is too little reading available in the literature. Particularly in the chapters describing manpower analysis for planning purposes, there is reference to mathematical techniques and to the use of mathematical models and computers. No attempt is made to present any of this in technical detail. Instead the basic concepts are discussed in non-mathematical terms, with some simple examples that all readers will take in their stride. The concepts, we suggest, are more important to grasp than the details of mathematical method. The bibliography at the end of the book provides a guide to reading that will enable the reader to build on the concepts in this and other main topics.

Part I
THE MANAGEMENT OF TRAINING

1 Some definitions

It is as well to establish first of all some of the parameters which are inevitably present in any discussion of training and development, whether of training methods or training management. We shall start with the word 'training' itself.

Training is that organised process concerned with the acquisition of capability, or the maintenance of existing capability. There are several notions embedded in this statement that need attention if we are to turn a somewhat abstract statement into something practical and useful.

Let us consider the word 'process'. We are today aware that the whole range of things which have to be done in order to bring about improved employee performance is considerable. The first use of this word process is in connection with that range. They normally take the familiar form of the

1 Identification of the training need
2 Specification of the steps to be taken and the training methods to be used to meet the need
3 Detail design of the specific training activities
4 Conduct of the training so designed
5 Evaluation of the impact of the training on the trainees and on the organisation.

All of this represents the training process. It is a process with well defined phases of decision-making and action. Such a process is characteristic of management today in any field, and one can see that the effective pursuit of training in the modern enterprise embodies, by virtue of these features alone, the exercise of some basic management skills. It will be noticed that in the above list the word 'training' could be replaced by 'transport', or 'marketing', or 'computing', and with very little alteration to the other words we would have a valid statement about the management of those functions too.

There is another respect in which one can correctly speak of training as a process. This is in connection with the teaching and learning process, by which we refer to the complex of events at the centre of which the learner perceives, digests, comprehends and later utilises the material available for learning. This is yet again an abstract definition, and is necessarily so to start with because of the wide variety of situations in which teaching takes place and in the equally varied ways in which learning is effected. The full treatment of this is given in other publications, but for us it is important to fix in our minds:

1 Learning can take place in any situation confronting an individual. If the situation has been set up deliberately by management or supervision then one refers to the action taken as training. In this is the process of perceiving, practising and remembering which we call the learning process. If the 'learner' has merely to perceive for himself the machines, the vehicles, the sort of people working, then there is no actual teacher, at least not in the formal sense. Nevertheless, it may still be part of planned, organised training.

The introduction of a teacher, more and more the case in industrial situations today, does not in itself make the difference between training and non-training. The teacher, or instructor, or manager or supervisor, is there to try and ensure that the right things are learnt with the understanding and accuracy considered necessary. But the learning process is still there, much the same, but more focused and more sustained, or more highly motivated – if the teacher is a good one.

2 The accent being on learning, it must then be recognised that of *all* the things learned by a person, only a small percentage are obtained through organised courses, a somewhat larger percentage through organised on-the-job instruction, and the great bulk is acquired through casual, random, personal observation, and through working communication and contact from day to day. This is an important aspect of learning to be a manager. Managers can be taught the current uses of information technology, and budgeting principles as well as many other company methods and rules. But less tangible things, of great importance to managers, can be learnt effectively through experience, provided the manager is a good 'experiential learner'. We return to this in Chapter 26, 'Managers as learners'.

3 Job training is that training needed to enable a person to do his present work satisfactorily. It may be given on-the-job, i.e. at the bench, at the desk, or on the process unit itself; or it may be given off-the-job, i.e. in a separate training bay, or in a classroom in the administration building, or in a local technical college.

4 Background training is that which supplements the job training by giving information which illuminates and gives meaning to the work undertaken. Experience and research have shown that a machinist works, in most circumstances, rather better if he understands the reason for the inspection system to which his work is subject; that people are more likely to observe safety rules and regulations if they understand the nature of the danger that toxic substances and malpractices expose them to. This sort of training can take place off-the-job, which is becoming more the case in the larger organisation with classrooms or office space to spare; or it can take place on-the-job, as information presented by, say, the supervisor in an organised way.

The above have been defined first not only because they must apply to *all* people who work in a company, but also because job training is such a vital ingredient of many training schemes which have as an objective the provision of more widely skilled people in the future. We shall refer to such schemes as development schemes. The appearance of personnel development, career development, and manpower development during recent years has been one of the striking and impressive features of both modern personnel management and modern corporate management. In later chapters there is discussion of these but in order to get them into immediate perspective we shall extend our definitions and illustrations.

TRAINING AND DEVELOPMENT

These two words are frequently used side by side. How do we distinguish between them? Where the objective is to acquire a set of capabilities which will equip a person to do a job some time in the predictable future, which is not within his present ability, that person is often said to undergo a process of development. Of course straight forward job instruction or rather job learning, is by this definition, a development, but the term has become associated with longer term and more complex arrangements for learning, often with job moves included in the plan for the individual or for groups of individuals. Some examples will illustrate.

(a) The apprentice undergoing a three or four year apprenticeship is, in fact, on a development programme. A series of attachments enabling him to work on essential skills of his craft or profession, plus academic studies on a planned and regulated basis, provide the organised structure of the total programme. There is a lot more to it than that, for he also learns about people and management and working conditions; and about taking responsibility and about integrity; and during this time he is growing up – physically, mentally and spiritually – and learning to see situations as a whole and not as fragmented and dissociated parts. The bits of the entire programme which have to do with learning specified skills and knowledge, and with its integration into a whole, are unarguably a training matter. But the other bits, to do with growing up, and social behaviour, are not usually subject to the same planning. But it is the same person, mechanical skills or social skills, and traditionally he has been 'looked after' by the training officer, and is regarded as a 'trainee'.

(b) The potential manager, undergoing a several year programme, will also be placed in a range of work situations and responsibilities. He may also be obliged or encouraged to undertake academic studies, and in some companies he will be sent on courses in order to accelerate his learning of some skills and knowledge. At the end of the total programme, or before, if his progress is rapid, he will not only have obtained for himself appropriate technical ability but may, in addition, have gained in human and organisational sensitivity and judgement, and in the courage to support them.

So we see that the management development programme, like the apprentice programme, has a large ingredient which is unquestionably training, according to our definition. But in both there is this other consideration, relating to the emergence of personality and character, for which there is no acknowledged creditable training method, and a very difficult set of characteristics for rigorous appraisal. The training and development specialists, and others, have to acknowledge these factors. Programmes should not be seen as a mere series of skill acquisitions, nor an engrossment of character without the gain in specific and necessary skills.

5

A further factor which has to be taken into account is that the person undergoing a management development programme is a mature adult whose placements in various jobs for development purposes require, nevertheless, that he does a fully responsible job wherever he is placed – it makes for lack of confidence all round if he is seen to be not contributing to the work effort in a way that is commensurate with his status and potential. This will be dealt with more fully in a later chapter, but here it should be noted that an exceptional constraint is placed on the planning of his development programme, which is nothing like so severe in the case of the apprentice. But in essence the processes of the two are the same; as well as for executive development, supervisor development and any other development programmes which are based on the concept of capability acquisition in the longer term, through planned work and study.

The above instances are all of personnel development, for the apprentices, managers, executives and supervisors are all personnel in the company, but with different titles and different status.

Career development is a similar set of processes, but has distinctive and important further features. During the whole lifetime of employment, an employee grows older, gains experience, probably improves in ability, and is moved on occasions from one job to another, sometimes with a promotion. The total pattern of employment and job moves, as long as they relate to some thread of logic or ambition, we refer to as a career. Career development, as increasingly practiced by companies, is the planning and execution of moves over a period of years so that an individual is presented with present work and future work moves or reasonable prospects of moves which are both motivating and satisfying. That is the object of career development from the company's point of view; for it can bring with it the rewards of lower turnover, more highly sustained work effort and greater contribution from the employee.

Naturally there are problems to be faced of opportunities, ambition and capability, and not all of them can always be dealt with to the equal satisfaction of employer and employee. This topic is also dealt with later, but here we must distinguish between the career development activity which attempts to provide progressive employment, which suits both the company and the employee, and personnel development which attempts to produce greater capability in a planned way. The two look very similar, in terms of practices. They are sometimes confused. They frequently are both undertaken at the same time, and rightly so. But their objectives are not the same, although they are likely to be complementary.

Manpower development is yet a further expression which is used for activities of a nature similar to the above, but, again, with an important difference. We can envisage an enterprise in which the management are examining the present total workforce, from the top to the bottom of the company. The numbers, types, ages and wastage rates are known. Attention is then turned to the requirement for, say, five and ten years ahead. One thing is clear – the *present* workforce will then be older, and, because of losses, smaller. What is needed, it is realised, is not merely a larger workforce in the future, but one with some specialisations which barely exist at the present, and more supervisors and more managers, and better ones at that.

The statement then produced of what manpower is required is a statement of the manpower objective. The general way in which this is to be achieved constitutes the manpower strategy, referring to the general decision to train employees in new skills, promote employees to new levels of responsibility, and to recruit certain types at certain levels of seniority or juniority into the company. The detailed statement of actions to be taken, on a time scale, in recruitment, training and internal movements and promotions are shown in the manpower plan, and that part which is concerned with the total production of capability in the employees, is manpower development. Obviously manpower development will either include or take account of both personnel and career development; one would expect to find that manpower development establishes the greater framework at a corporate level within which any personnel and career development find their place: if not there will be conflict.

RESPONSIBILITY FOR TRAINING

Who is responsible for training and for development programmes?

The manager of any work area is responsible, amongst other things, for producing a planned volume of work to defined standards. This work is done by the employees in that area, or by machines or equipment operated by the employees. The manager must, for purely practical reasons of control of standards and quality be responsible for the work done by the employees, responsible for supervising them in doing this work and responsible for ensuring that anyone who needs correction or basic instruction gets it, and gets it to a level consistent with the quality and safety requirements of the actual workplace, the equipment and the product.

Now such training may be given outside the work area, by some independent party appropriately skilled. But to ensure that the instruction is satisfactory from the point of view of that manager, in all specific details, the manager should carry some sort of authority over the outside instructor. It goes without saying that the instructor might well be a supervisor or another experienced person drawn from inside the work area, reporting automatically to the manager, in which case the question of authority would not readily arise.

Industrial history over the past years is full of instances in which the above self-evident requirement for managers to assume responsibility for the training of those employees who work, or who will work later, for them, has been by-passed or replaced by some other arrangement for authority. The result has sometimes been conflict, sometimes a neglect of training, and sometimes a waste of human resources.

The importance for us in this book is to see from this simple principle that the management of training is something for line management consideration, not merely to enable them to call their training specialist to account, but to ensure that they can fully meet a complex responsibility with the same effort and dedication that they give to other management activities.

It is an over-simplification, but nevertheless a useful guideline, to say that clerical and operator training is the responsibility of the foreman and supervisor; supervisor training is the responsibility of the manager, and management and corporate training of the whole enterprise is the responsibility of general management and the directors. Where then does the training manager and the training officer fit in to the picture as far as responsibilities go?

Training is to be seen as a service function in the same way that accounting, computing, recruiting, office management and other functions of a similar nature are seen. The training manager is there to assist line management to meet its training responsibilities; to help them meet the highest professional standards; to help at all phases of identification of needs, formulation, execution and evaluation. This is done either with advice or by providing an actual physical service; or with both, as is often the case. The responsibility of the training manager is therefore to provide this back up; and to make sure that it remains a back up to a real management acceptance and commitment and not a substitute or a replacement for it, nor an interference with it.

The reason is a practical one. Although it is sometimes expedient to move towards the seeming independence of the training function, this runs the strong risk of decreasing the quality and relevance of training. Independence can lead to the neglect of those things which lie in management's inner thoughts and plans and to the rejection by management of training activities in which it has no deep interest, particularly in times of economic stress.

However, developing the best and most fruitful relationships between line management and training is not the easiest of tasks, particularly if there already exists misunderstanding, or mistrust. It is hoped that the following chapters will help in producing such an approach to the management of training and of complementary development activities that the right roles and relationships between the specialist and his management will be created.

2 Policies and practices

The modern company will have a range of training practices. It may take the more prominent of these and describe them and their purpose in a company publication such as the 'Employees Handbook' or the 'Manual of Personnel Practices'. It must be in everyone's experience that from time to time questions are asked, beginning with the words 'what is our policy on . . . ?' or, on the other hand, 'what do we do in the case of . . . ?' One question is on policy, and the other is on practice. At least that is how it seems at the start. When the answer is 'well, I don't know what our policy is, but what we do is . . . ' then we realise that distinction between policies and practices does not exist as clearly as it might. Does it matter?

There are different sorts of statements which describe management decisions and intentions, whatever we call them . . . policies, practices, objectives, strategies, and so on. The distinction that has to be made between policy and practice is that a statement of policy on any matter is a general statement by management of how it wishes all questions and problems of a certain general type to be approached; a statement of practice tells you what to do. For example, a policy statement relating to the continuation of personal studies by mature adult employees might read

> . . . the company recognises the importance of continued education for all adults
> . . . and encourages its employees in their pursuit of studies and qualifications.
> . . . and is prepared to give assistance to those on approved courses of a financial nature and by allowing time off where this is regarded as necessary and where it does not significantly lower the effectiveness of the unit in which the employee works.

Nowhere in the above carefully guarded wording is there any statement on exactly what the rules are to be or what they may be at this moment. These have to be worked out in detail, and thoroughly examined and tested before they are made public. They constitute the practices; they are not the policy statement, although they are the means of getting the policy enacted.

One can see immediately the importance of policy-making. It must reflect management's general decisions, it must lend itself to the formulation of really practicable rules. It indicates the position management adopts in the various situations and challenges with which it has to deal. In training terms the policies constitute the mandate under which the training specialist works; they define not only the areas and situations in which action has to be taken, but also the authority which is given to the training specialist, to managers and supervisors and to employees in taking that action.

It would be wrong to suggest that every new action for which there is no present policy coverage requires a written or printed policy document, but it is suggested that when such new situations arise attention is paid to the question of whether they merit new policies. Over the past years in many organisations this attention has, it would often appear, not been fully given and the result can be a bundle of practices with little guidance for later necessary change, constraint where there should be permissiveness, and the inevitable complaint from line management that 'Training needs to get its priorities right'. Inevitable, because if line management are not frequently consulted on policies when the circumstances demand, then training may take a wrong direction, but unnoticed because of the ease with which a well performed training *action* is mistaken for a good and essential training policy.

In the absence of a declared policy it is not always to be assumed that it does not exist. It may be tucked away in the mind of the creator of the particular scheme or practice; it may be so self evident as to seem not worth mentioning formally; it may be written into the statement of practice, as a separate paragraph or buried in the other wording. As long as the creator or author remains in a position of authority then little harm may be done, for he is always there to be appealed to personally, although the personalisation of power is not necessarily to be encouraged. But as soon as he moves away from that position the chances of mismanagement increase unless, of course, the newcomer insists on policy-backed practices.

We shall now look at a sample set of policy statements. Each one is designed to cover a specific issue, as in the example at the beginning of this chapter, but they are not offered as the particular set for the purposes of the companies in which readers may be employed, although some items may be readily transferable from book to company. The whole set can be imagined as representing the total policy requirement of a hypothetical company. The energising effect of this is readily appreciable, for the total area covered in the set is that in which the training function is authorised and expected to work, and the form of the statement is sufficiently 'open-ended' to permit the development of new training practices as distinct from the mere continuation of the present ones. One could add that in a progressive firm the training manager is expected, quite specifically, to develop training to keep up with changing internal and external circumstances. With the right policy package he can do this, in conjunction with the departments and functions he is servicing, with well based confidence. He will, of course, have to keep his eye open for those changes of circumstances which make even the policies out of date, and when this occurs work with management on the reformulation of policy.

EXAMPLES OF TRAINING POLICY

Each item below is offered with an accompanying 'Note' which enables the essential policy statement to be made in the shortest and crispest way in its own paragraph. The note provides some further information which helps the reader – employee, manager or personnel officer – to understand the reason why that particular policy has been formulated, or the way in which it should be interpreted where there is reasonable possibility of misunderstanding. It will be noted that several are virtually 'permission to act', although the exact form that the action is to take still has to be expressed elsewhere.

1   It is the company's policy to provide training for any employee faced now, or in the foreseeable future, with new work or new organisation or a new work environment, to enable him to deal competently with his work.

Note: the training given must be to certain standards; there must be sufficient prior planning, the instruction must be given by a competent person, and the training must result in work performance of a standard acceptable to management.

New jobs, tasks or techniques are clear reasons in themselves for providing training for the employees concerned, but equally important are changes in organisation, relationships, communication systems, standards and objectives etc., which merit systematic training.

Although the employee may learn spontaneously from supervisors and colleagues, the company does not accept this fortuitous process as a satisfactory sole means of raising the competence of its employees to a suitable operational level.

2   It is the company's policy to provide such further training as may be required to maintain the necessary standards of performance over a period of time.

Note: a number of factors make for a loss of effectiveness and a lowering of standards over a span of months and years, such as the expedient adoption of undesirable short cuts, the relaxation of supervision, the effect of overlong work monotony, misinformation on work from outside sources. As the maintenance of high work standards is as important as reaching these standards at the outset, continuous training must be given consideration and implemented as needed.

3   It is the company's policy to provide opportunities for employees to maintain their flexibility and potential, with a view to making any later changes in work content or work environment easier to accommodate.

Note: the maintenance of job performance and product standards does not in itself ensure that individual adaptability and learning ability are sustained or developed. This is important particularly where people work on unchanging tasks for a long period of time. Where relevant, opportunities must be provided for people to deal with new ideas and practices, either on or off the job.

4   The responsibility for training any group of employees lies with the management of that group. The time and effort given by managers to the planning and conduct of that training is to be regarded as a correct pursuit of their responsibilities. The training function provides a service to management, to assist them in discharging their training responsibilities.

Note: line management's responsibility is positive and active. A wide range of important issues, such as loyalty, standards of performance, economy of training effort depend on management's full acceptance. They are doing their job when they devote their time to this, although it may not appear to contribute much to the main work effort. Training officers or personnel officers may help with analysis, programming and organisation as required by management, but they do not alter line management's responsibility; neither should they detract from the rapport between management and employees.

5   The time and effort, in working hours, devoted by an employee either on or off the job to raising the level of capability through approved training, is to be regarded as a correct use of his services.

Note: although an employee may not contribute to the work effort of his unit during a period of training on the job, or away on a course or a visit for training purposes, this should be considered as part and parcel of his employment. He is not only employed to 'do' but also to 'learn to do'.

6   The employee must be involved in the planning, the progressing and the evaluation of his own training.

Note: although line and personnel management will undertake the bulk of the planning of training and development programmes and moves for their employees it is rarely fully satisfactory to make all decisions without some early discussion and some consultation with the employee concerned. Unilaterally designed programmes cannot make use of the knowledge and motivation which the employee might contribute; they may be counter to the personal interests of that person; they are least likely to produce a sense of participation and responsibility.

7   The company will encourage and provide some support for each person's own education interests.

Note: it is likely that the mainspring of a person's work effort lies in the interest in the work that has to be done. This particular interest is more likely to be fostered if they are sustaining generally an appetite for 'learning and doing' new things. Educational studies undertaken voluntarily make a marked contribution to this. Further incentive and satisfaction to the employee may accrue if the studies are in subjects which lead to useful career qualifications.

8   Any department or function will be prepared to take members of other departments or functions into their work for agreed periods of time, as part of an approved training scheme or programme.

Note: properly planned attachments or visits not only enable employees to acquire valuable skill and insight, but also build up personal relationships and mutual confidence essential in a complex organisation. Such attachments will normally produce no significant interference or real cost in the host department.

9   Any department or function will be prepared to take apprentices or members of other company training schemes, where it is agreed by management that such work placements contribute to the achievement of the objectives of the schemes.

Note: the success of these schemes depends almost entirely on the provision of a sufficient number of properly supervised and otherwise suitable workplaces throughout the company. The trainee should make a real contribution to the work of the unit to which he is attached and be subject to the normal work rules and disciplines of that unit.

10   Provided that there is no significant interference with work and output, and

provided that there are no restrictions due to security or confidentiality, managers will be prepared to take trainees or other members of other companies into their departments on agreed training programmes.

Note: there is a small movement of people for training purposes, within and across national boundaries, to which we contribute and from which we can benefit.

11 The company will accept into its departments for visits or work, students, teachers, researchers and administrators from educational establishments wherever this will assist in the progress of their educational programmes. The company will also nominate employees at any appropriate level to visit educational establishments to provide information in response to reasonable requests.

Note: education turns to industry increasingly for co-operation in a variety of forms. We accept it is industry's responsibility to respond sympathetically and to encourage the educational world to approach industry for whatever help can be reasonably given.

The above collection of policy items is not intended to be exhaustive; it would be impossible to construct such a list, for the policy requirements of any company or other institution will depend on the political and social environment, on the structure and organisation, as well as on the particular training ideology which the management favours. However, it would seem that the above do represent a fairly common set of considerations with which very many companies have to deal in many parts of the world, and they may be therefore of practical value to some readers.

The purpose however of presenting them is to illustrate the value of such a package to whoever is responsible for the management of training. It will be clear that each clause identifies one area in which positive training action is acceptable and is to be encouraged. It indicates that there are certain roles and responsibilities for both the line manager and for the training specialist, that they must observe. It does leave unstated exactly what is being done, or will be done in the future. This may appear to be a weakness of such open-ended statements, for no particular actions are specified. Indeed, should there be a company in which there was little creative or executive competence, then it might be better not to have such seductive but inconclusive statements.

But where there is reasonable competence in both management and training specialist, this type of policy statement acts as a mandate for action bestowing purpose and some authority on those responsible for conducting and developing training. With this in mind we can now turn our attention to the consideration of what actually has to be done in training, in the sort of detail that is omitted from the policy statements.

3 Intentions and objectives

OBJECTIVES

The subject of objectives, and the study of the way in which management needs to establish and adhere to objectives, has featured in a great deal of management teaching and literature. It is a subject also of vital interest to those concerned with the management of training and we shall therefore pay some attention to this, looking first at the most useful definitions.

A 'training' objective' is that state or achievement which the training helps bring about. A training objective is not the training itself, but something beyond the training, as it were. This is our definition, and it is a very important one. It is indeed a very important form of definition for any type of management, particularly service management. Thus, computer management would state as the objective beyond the installation of new equipment, 'the high speed provision of certain new marketing analyses to members of marketing management'. The objective is not, and obviously cannot be, merely the 'updating of equipment'. It is only by examining the objective beyond the purchase that one can satisfy oneself that any action needs to be taken at all, and that the particular purchase is the right one to make.

Similarly, the objective beyond the practice of vehicle preventive maintenance in a transport maintenance department, say, is not merely maintenance to 'prevent wear or failure'. It is, normally, to bring about net economies in maintenance, vehicle and part replacement and in product distribution. An economic objective, not an engineering objective. One might say that the pertinent question to ask when one is examining objectives, or indeed when one is considering the justification for any action, is 'what are you trying to achieve?' or 'why are you doing it, beyond the provision of work for your unit?'

Training managers have to face this question, as do line managers, with as much 'objectivity' as can be summoned. As we examine the implications of objective setting for the training function, we see how it inevitably brings the management of training into the closest working relationship with the management of other functions and ultimately the corporate body as a whole. We shall also find our-

14

selves in a better position, as a result, to deal with the question of 'who is responsible, and for what' when such a question is raised in discussion between the training and the line functions.

INTENTIONS AND OBJECTIVES

We introduce the word 'intention' because of the fact that, within an organisation of complexity and interdependence between functions, the objective of one function may not be the objective of the next function, which benefits from the action taken in the first function. This is best illustrated by an example, and shows the usefulness of the additional word intention.

The training manager is advised that the setters in the machine shop need to be given a course in the use of multi-point tools, their setting, replacement and requisition from stores, in accordance with the new practices shortly to be introduced into the company. The training manager learns, during the discussions which follow with production management, the intention behind the introduction of this new system of tool control. It is, from the production engineer's point of view, to bring about financial economies in tools and also to achieve a reduction of machining time-loss due to occasional machine/tool breakdown.

The training manager's intentions, which he would call his objective, is to have the setters acquire a capability in knowledge and skill, which they can then use on the job in the future. There is here an immediate question to ask – is the training objective, that is to say of the training manager himself, to have the setters skilled, or to have them use that skill in the machine shop? Or is the use of the skills in the machine shop an objective of the machine shop foreman, for it will certainly be his intention? So we find that because we are using the word objective in accordance with definition, and because the actual allocation and acceptance of responsibilities for action and results hangs on this, it is important to be as clear as possible about terms and what they represent.

It is clear that many actions in organisations in which there are departmentalised service and operational responsibilities, are a long chain of contributory actions which lead to some end result of benefit to the enterprise as a whole. The example above illustrates the chain in the training/machine shop corner of the company. We took the illustration no further than that, but the full chain of intentions, events, and consequences would not stop there. We are in a position to generalise and establish a few rules.

We shall put the word objectives to one side for the moment and talk in a more general sense about intentions. Let us start at the beginning of an action chain and identify the sequence of intentions of those concerned, in a simple hypothetical example.

Intention 1   A group of salesmen are to be given an internal course on a new product, covering its properties, uses, hazards; prices, discounts; availability and distribution; advertising campaign, product interaction and major competitors; start date and targets.

Intention 2   To ensure that the salesmen are completely informed and competent to use this information at the moment of leaving the course.

Intention 3   Each and every salesman will return to his job and in the course of the day's work use the new capability.

Intention 4   The result is the placing of customers' orders for the new product.

Intention 5   This will lead to an increase in the revenue of the sales division for which any particular salesman works.

Intention 6   This will boost the total revenue of the company.

Intention 7   This will improve the total trading position of the company, not only in terms of net profit, but in terms of image, dividends and future share issues.

All of the above, necessarily a picture in miniature – for the full set of intentions is more complex – is commonplace but gives us now the introduction of the rather more specific term 'objective'. We have in this chain all the intentions of management from start to finish, and we call this the 'chain of intentions'. The objective of the training manager corresponds to Intention 2, i.e. his objective is to have the salesmen competent and ready for action. This is his objective, and it is also his *responsibility*. His responsibility is also to design and conduct the training in Intention 1, but that, the mere training activity, is not his objective.

From then on the other executives and managers work towards their objectives which can be identified in the chain of intentions. The salesman did not go on the course for the sheer pleasure of learning interesting things, but with the objective of getting orders in the new product, when back on the job, according to the selling tactics laid down. The divisional sales manager has as his objective the new sales and revenue targets for his division, not the mere exercising of the new capability of his salesmen as and when it fits in with any other business they are doing.

Each person in the chain has, therefore, his personal objectives at a certain level, and we can call this the personal 'objective level' in the chain. It may appear that by producing this view and definition of objectives we are limiting the outlook of the executive concerned, and in effect blinkering him when, surely, we should be encouraging wider involvement and responsibility. Should not the training manager have as his objective the increase in revenue in the divisions from which the salesmen are drawn? A moment's reflection will show that this, in terms of responsibility and those actions which the training manager can himself take, is an impractical target. He can only be held responsible for those things which he can directly effect, and these lie within his scope as a training specialist. His objective must be located, then, somewhere at the end of the actual training process, in the quality and enhanced ability of those who have been through the process. The same principle will be true in searching for the objective of others further up the chain, as long as we stick to the idea that objectives and effective authority are essentially linked together.

However, management effectiveness is not dependent solely on the pursuit of personal and specialist objectives. It is equally important that each person in the chain is aware of the *full* chain of intentions, as far as this can be seen. Although, by definition, different executives cannot have the same objectives. But, it will be clear, this understanding of the chain of intentions is a prerequisite for the establishment of compatible personal objectives and the harmonious interaction of all functions towards a common end.

The training function is not therefore constrained in its outlook and its view of the full range of corporate and functional activities and problems as a result of this use of objectives; and nor should this be case for the management of other functions. There is a particular reason why training management should exploit all the insights given by examining the full chain of intentions. First, if we return to our salesman training example, we can see that in designing the course, its content, methods and duration, it would be very difficult to do justice to the wishes of marketing management without knowing a great deal about all the intentions and likely consequences connected with the new marketing proposition. The factors likely to hinder success, the relationship between the sales effort and the efforts of the accountants, transport personnel and others who contribute directly or indriectly, need to be taken into account. The salesman does not work in isolation from the company, and needs to know how other people's efforts affect his work and how his efforts affect their work.

Second, and this is a point at which the training manager penetrates the company as a whole, the fact that the intentions constitute a long chain, from classroom to balance sheet, demands that the learning requirements of all those who have to make some sort of adjustment at all points on the chain need to be investigated and actioned. Thus the training manager is going the full length of the chain of intentions (and branching off at the sides too, as we shall see), but he is doing this in his training capacity, and not assuming or interfering with others' responsibilities.

Had our example dealt with training that has to take place on-the-job, and not in the classroom, the question of objectives would be dealt with in the same way, although it might appear that the training manager is moving into the work area for which another manager, a line manager, is responsible. Let us look more closely at this equally familiar situation. We are still dealing, let us assume, with the salesmen who have to be taught a range of facts and skills in connection with a new product.

The fact that they are to be trained on-the-job, by sales supervisors who have already received information on the product and the desired marketing effort, is due to a decision to which the training function was party. It seems, in this instance, to be an economical and practical approach to the training. The contribution of the training function is to provide analytic help for the information which has to be taught, advice on check lists to be used for recording and controlling individual learning progress of the salesmen, and an *ad hoc* inspection and help as and when called for by the marketing manager. The objective of the training manager is to produce a salesman who is competent in a specific way, as was the case when the training was undertaken in the classroom. The big difference lies in that in the classroom, on premises run by the training function, it seemed that the training manager was much more in charge than when the training took place in the field. And in a sense this is true, but it is only because in the classroom the training manager had contracted to produce certain physical services and amenities, which he could not do for training which takes place on the job. Again, in the classroom the contracted service puts the training manager much closer, with advantage, to both the salesman under training and the supervisors who are teaching them, reinforcing the impression of authority, compared with that which he has in the field, away from the classroom. This is, in effect, the authority of the organising host and contractor.

17

On the job, the authority for giving the instruction lies with the marketing manager and his supervisors. The training manager, normally, cannot directly intervene; but he is nevertheless totally interested in the teaching/learning process as it actually occurs, should have reasonable right of inspection, should be entitled to a hearing if he wishes to express dissatisfaction to the marketing manager, and must be given the information he requires to satisfy himself that the finished product, the competent salesman, is being produced to the agreed standards.

This is clearly a much more difficult relationship to sustain than that arising from the classroom and is, in fact, one which produces countless problems of misunderstanding between training officers and line management.

Implementing what is learnt in training is also quite different in our two situations, in the classroom and on-the-job. In the former it is impossible for the new capability to be implemented in real work terms; in the latter it may happen immediately, and it then becomes impossible to distinguish between training and operational work, or between the supervisor as an instructor and the supervisor in his normal role. A little while later – hours or days – the new ability is embodied in the general day's work and has lost all apparent connection with organised training. This is a familiar matter for most but is nevertheless of some importance in determining objectives for the training function, objectives which can only have practical significance if they relate to those actions which the manager has authority to take. In our view, the objectives of the training manager can remain as clear, with reference to producing trained personnel, in on-the-job training as in off-the-job cases, but very close attention needs to be paid to specific authority, as described above, which he carries relative to training which goes on within the workaday situations of the company.

As a general rule, then, what is produced by one manager in reaching his own objectives is taken up by the next manager in the chain, and he then works towards *his* objectives. The justification for any one manager's own objectives, when he offers them to his superiors for approval, lies further up the chain, in the same way that the consideration of what his objectives and consequent actions might be arose in the first place from information up the chain, information on what the company was intending to do.

Whatever the difficulties inherent in stating and reaching objectives, there cannot be any limitation in the search for them, and the extent to which the ultimate benefits spread across the company. The breadth of this search and consequent impact will occupy much of the later chapters.

SIDE EFFECTS

We have deliberately used the word intentions because it expresses so clearly that management wants something to happen in a given way. But, even if these things do happen, there may be other consequences of the intended action which are significant, for better or for worse. These other consequences we call side effects; but they are just as real, sometimes just as powerful as the principal intention, and need just as much thought and attention. Unfortunately, whereas the events along the chain of intentions are supposedly predictable – at least they are planned to happen – the side effects are not planned, are speculative, or unpredictable.

18

Here we are not talking of the impact of the new sales effort on the work of the sales clerks, for this is predictable and should be allowed for in both the operational and the training planning, as would be similar impacts on stores, transport and recruitment. We are concerned with things which arise because of unexpected interpretation of training action, by employees whether undergoing training themselves or not. This is not something which is strictly a training matter, not therefore within training management's defined responsibilities. But, given the training manager's share in the full chain of intentions and, as a member of company management, his concern for the general well-being of the enterprise as a whole, it would seem that one of the things he should be good at is pointing out the 'unexpected' to management, when it arises, or may arise in the future, as a consequence of training.

For example, in the area of simple, organised, job training many companies have discovered that by introducing programmes of job instruction for those who are to do no more than teach new recruits their jobs at their workplace, they have led those newly trained tutors to assume forthcoming pay rises and promotions which were certainly not in management's intentions. But the situation has always had to be dealt with, and not always satisfactorily; for when people are taken out of routine work and given the opportunity to learn new things, and to rethink the old, this newly released motivation, interest and energy will spread in directions determined by the preoccupations and ambitions of those people, and will not be confined to the strict matter in hand as laid down initially by management.

This is not presented here in order that management, training or line, should learn to build up their defences in good time. The reverse is often to be hoped for. There is much in the side effect that is beneficial to the company and to the employees, provided it can be properly channelled; there is also much that can be done in using the side effect as an opportunity for establishing understanding and goodwill on matters which management had not previously regarded as important to the employees. It is, at the same time, for management to explore in advance all possible or reasonable interpretations, or misinterpretations, of their training decisions, in order to avoid employee disillusionment and cynicism.

4 Training opportunities

The identification of training needs is a prerequisite of training action. This is a point that hardly needs emphasis, yet in practice the actual identification of those people, situations and events which demand training attention is a much more difficult exercise than it might appear. Is there a technique which will enable the training manager, or the line manager, to find all or most of the opportunities which present themselves, as distinct from merely finding some of them? In a large organisation there may be a lot of training going on. The question to ask is 'is it the right training?' A close check of objectives and benefits may show that a high percentage of what is done is really worthwhile and should continue, but leaves unanswered the further question 'what about the training that you are not doing?'

This is a serious question, for it is not unusual to find that the pattern of training has grown up over the years without any organised attempt to search thoroughly for all real requirements. Instead, as things are thought of they are examined, and then accepted or rejected. The confidence which corporate management have in their training management, in the light of the above, should really be a confidence in the training manager's ability not to miss anything important, as well as a satisfaction with what he is actually doing.

Clearly a hit and miss approach is not enough, and we shall see that a systematic approach to the identification of training needs is both possible and practicable. Before we look more closely into this we must clarify what is meant by the identification process, for it has more than one meaning, and the action to be taken in order 'to identify' depends on which sort of identification is being attempted.

Let us look at some examples of identification. First, the training officer is approached by the machine shop superintendent, who asks that a course is found for his senior charge-hand who is not very good at handling employees, particularly when the employees express grievances. The request is legitimate; the charge-hand has indeed something to learn, whether by means of a course, or by reading the company's grievance procedures again, or by being more closely

20

supervised and coached by the superintendent; or by a suitable combination of all three.

The training officer analyses the problem and the detailed need of the charge-hand. He also specifies the best training action including the follow-up necessary if the new capability is to stick and be effective. Who has identified the training need, the superintendent or the training officer? The answer is both; each has contributed something vital to the total identification, and each has complemented the other. We should add here that a further important contribution to the total identification of need will have been provided by the charge-hand himself, for during the interviews and discussions he provides insights into his weakness and difficulties which modify both the diagnosis and the specification of the training to be provided. We are not at this moment so concerned about who does what in the identification process, important though that is, as with showing that there are two distinct parts to the process. The *primary identification,* i.e. perceiving that a situation exists which merits further need-analysis; and the *secondary identification,* i.e. looking then more closely at that situation to find out more precisely what the skill or knowledge shortfall is, and which can be made up by some suitably devised learning experience.

It will be seen that there are almost limitless examples of this division into primary and secondary. The works manager has become convinced that his maintenance fitters are ignorant of the dangers inherent in working on electrical plant and equipment, and that they need to understand more, they need to be taught. The training officer, or it might be the maintenance assistant manager, then looks into the existing understanding of electricity and existing practices and malpractices, eventually producing a schedule of training requirements; the training is launched. The works manager has made the primary identification; the rest is secondary. That is not to say that it is secondary in importance, for it is essential, but follows on from the primary identification.

Now the fact is that the primary and the secondary identification of training needs are almost totally different in method and in degree of difficulty. Whereas the secondary identification focuses on a subject already located and captured, the primary identification is something that arises as it were from the blank sheet of everyday experience and perception. One can see that there is a lot of difference between saying to a training officer, or to a line supervisor, 'look closely at this man and tell me what he needs to make him better at the administrative part of his work', and saying to him 'tell me the training requirements which are likely to arise in the administrative departments during the coming year'. The bulk of training officers depend, and not wrongly so, for primary information passed on to them from other managers and executives. The training officer then carries out his secondary analysis.

This is not offered in criticism, but as an observation of the arrangement that is almost inevitable; for the line manager is not only himself concerned with and involved in training, but he is uniquely and eminently well placed for the primary identification of training needs. And, by and large, the training officer is not.

We can see immediately that there are two major challenges for the training manager arising from the above. Even if there were no specialist training function, we must hasten to add, the following would still be a requirement, but handled in a

21

different way. First, it is necessary that the line manager has the personal ability needed for perception and diagnosis that will result in a correct primary identification. The training manager and his training function as a whole have a considerable interest in ensuring that the line manager has, or is able to develop, this ability. It is not to be taken for granted, as are, unfortunately, so many management attributes.

Second, the coverage of primary identification has sufficient breadth to give corporate management confidence that the actual training undertaken does not leave important needs undisclosed. This coverage has in some way to be established, and the perceptive skills of line managers have to be turned in the right direction. This is a fundamental concern for the training manager. Neither he nor his training specialists are in the front line alongside the line manager in action.

We shall start by focusing on the employee, at whatever level, at the workplace. The following are the most common situations which demand training action.

1   New recruits to the company

These have a requirement for induction into the company as a whole, in terms of its business activities and personnel policies and provisions; the terms, conditions and benefits appropriate to the particular employee, and the career and advancement opportunities available. The job training, in terms of the immediate skills needed and the background knowledge of surrounding and related functions, is vital to the new recruit, irrespective of what job he goes into.

2   Transferees within the company

These are people who are moved from one job to another, either within the same work area, i.e. the same department or function, or to dissimilar work under a different management. Under this heading we are excluding promotions which take people into entirely new levels of responsibility. Like the new recruit, the transferee requires job training. He may well need updating on terms and conditions, and is likely to require entirely new information on related functions. The fact that he has been employed elsewhere in the organisation does not mean that he knows all that he should know, even though he himself may believe that he does.

3   Promotions

Although similar to the transferee in that there is a new job to be learned in new surroundings, he is dissimilar in that the promotion has brought him into supervision or management for the first time, or has brought him to a new level of supervisory or management responsibility. The change is usually too important and difficult to make successfully to permit one to assume that the promotee will 'pick it up as he goes along', and attention has to be paid to training in the tasks and the responsibilities and personal skills necessary for effective performance.

The above deal with the training opportunities associated with the movement of people. We shall now take those which arise from changing the work itself.

4 New plant or equipment

Even the most experienced operator has everything to learn when a computer and electronic controls replace the previous manual and electro-mechanical system on the process plant on which he works. There is no less a training requirement for the supervisors and process management, as well as for technical services, production control and others. Any new feature in the machinery which people are responsible for has to be learnt and fully understood, each to his own need and requirement. Some of this can be dealt with by quick on-the-job re-instruction; some demands additional longer planning and teaching off-the-job.

5 New procedures

Mainly for those who work in offices in commercial and administrative functions, but also for those whose workplace is on the shop floor or on process plant, on any occasion on which there is a modification to existing paperwork or procedures, for, say, the withdrawal of materials from stores, the control of customer credit, or the approval of expense claims, there needs to be instruction on the change in the way of working. In many instances, a note bringing the attention of all concerned to the change is assumed to be sufficient, but there are cases, such as when totally new systems incorporating IT up-dates are installed, when more thorough training is needed.

6 New standards, rules and practices

Changes in any one of these are likely to be conveyed by printed note or by word of mouth by the manager to his subordinates, and this can be the most satisfactory way of dealing with the change from the point of view of getting those affected to understand their new responsibility. However, not all changes under this heading can be left to this sort of handling. Even the most simple looking instruction may be regarded as undesirable or impracticable by whoever has to perform it; he may not understand the purpose behind the change and lose confidence in a management which he now believes to be 'messing about'; or he may understand the purpose and have a better alternative to offer if it is not too late. Each change, or rather the introduction of each change, has to be examined and treated on its merits, in terms of what we have now called 'management intentions' and 'side effects'. From time to time a more thorough approach to the presentation of information to employees and supervisors may be needed, to ensure that not only are the new requirements met, but that general understanding and goodwill are sustained.

7 New relationships and authorities

These can arise, as a result of management decisions, in a number of ways. For examples, the reorganisation of the accounts department can result in a reallocation of responsibilities between the section leaders of credit control, invoicing and customer records, although there is no movement of staff between the section (i.e. no transfers). Although the change in work content for each clerk and supervisor is defined clearly for each person in the new procedures, there is nevertheless a need for each person to know where he stands in the new set up, who is responsible for what, and where to direct problems and enquiries as they arise in the future. Clearly this produces no real problem if these functions are all looked after by two or three people who all sit and work together with long established harmony in the one room. But it is a different matter entirely if the sections are large, in different rooms, on different floors even, and are separated by tension and rivalry, or by a long history of mutual indifference.

Hence we are concerned, under this particular heading, not so much with the actual content of people's work and the changes which arise in that, as with the scope of their responsibilites as they affect others, and the working and personal relationships which have to undergo adaptation and change. The working relationships gain clarity in the eyes of the employees and supervisors if they are able to see the work which they all undertake as part of a rational system. The personal relationships stand to gain if the role of each person, in turn, is more precisely understood by the others. This knowledge cannot be gained accurately in a casual fashion; some effort has to be made by management to supplement what the employee learns, accurately and inaccurately, in the course of the day.

So far we have looked at the training opportunities which arise as a result of the introduction of change into the work content or work context of any individual or group of individuals. The emphasis is on newness. There are two further items to consider as training opportunities which relate, not to change, but to the maintenance of present attributes, and which have featured in the example policy statement earlier.

8   Maintenance of standards

We are here concerned with maintenance of standards through training, for it must be remembered that supervision and inspection and quality control are continuously responsible for standards and exercise their own authorities to this end. Although it is generally agreed that some retraining from time to time, taking varied forms even for the one group of employees, does act as both a reminder and a stimulus, there is not much agreement on the exact frequency and form that such retraining should take, for there is as yet little 'scientific' knowledge on this subject which is of much use in industrial situations.

Most attention is given, not unexpectedly, where it is clear that a fall in standard of performance might produce human disaster. Hence the constant refresher training characteristic of petroleum, nuclear and some chemical plant; airline flight staff, airfield fuelling crews; firemen, and so on. In these cases the permissible error rate is zero, the cost of actual error very high in human and financial terms, and the cost of frequent retraining very small in comparison with both normal operating costs and the cost of disaster.

In other types of work the equation is not so clear, nor the impulse to avoid error at any price; but the matter still requires attention and an appropriate low cost solution worked out.

9   The maintenance of adaptability

Again, whilst there is little scientific study of the loss of ability to learn new skills in those cases where people spend a long time without change, and without the need to learn, there is increasing evidence in current experience to suggest that this is the case in industrial employment. And, of course, there is the inference arising from the laboratory experiments of psychologists. Adaptability would be of little importance if there were no reason ever to change the content and environment of a person's work, but changes do occur for many people with increasing frequency. The paradox is that those whose jobs do change with some regularity are likely to retain their flexibility, thanks to the exercise of their minds which is produced by the changes themselves. It is those who are not undergoing such frequent change who need special attention, to re-establish mental flexibility in anticipation of the time when they too have to learn new skills, work methods and relationships.

The method to be employed here cannot readily be merely a retraining in the present job. Sometimes a form of job rotation is provided in order to oblige people to learn and think anew; sometimes in-company courses designed to stretch and shake up; sometimes external courses in company or personal time to broaden outlook; but in each case an element of mind stretching is included.

10   The maintenance of management skills and standards

Skills in supervising, employee appraisal, communications, leadership etc. are important in all companies. Some of these skills are seen to be critical to major developments in company organisation, culture, employee empowerment, and so on. Initial training in these skills is not uncommon in the larger companies on appointment into management and supervision. But continuous training and performance monitoring is rare, despite the common knowledge that standards are as varied as human nature.

11   Retirement and redundancy

Employees of any position in the company who are heading towards retirement will benefit from learning about health, social life, work opportunities, money management etc. Internal or external courses are best attended a year or two before retirement date. In a few companies a member of Personnel will act as a counsellor as required.

Those made redundant may need a lot of help in overcoming shock, in restoring their self respect, and in finding new work. Individual counselling, and information about external agencies can be valuable. A delayed departure from the company, with complete freedom to job-hunt during that time, is sometimes possible to arrange and is, for some people, very valuable, particularly if there is continuous access to company advisors.

TRAINING OPPORTUNITY GENERATORS

In using the idea of training opportunities in a search for what needs to be done in a company, one needs to be aware of the factors and influences which make these opportunities real, as distinct from merely possible. These factors and influences we call training opportunity generators. Obviously the opportunity provided by the new recuits (No. 1) needs little further attention in this text; it is self evident. But the accounts department example (No. 7) describes a much more elusive need, from the point of view of both functional and training management. The accounts manager is preoccupied with getting the work through without upset, and gives little thought to any but the most obvious training requirement; the training manager does not know that the reorganisation has even taken place.

Had the training manager been forewarned of the impending reorganisation he might have said, 'What is the effect on the work and relationships of the people in that department and elsewhere, and does anything need to be done to help establish new capability and understanding?' If the answer had been positive it could have led, at least, to a briefing of the supervisors, not only on their future accounting responsibilities, but on also what they had to do to teach their subordinates their new tasks and relationships; at the maximum it might have produced small group meetings amongst the employees and supervisors to explore the proposed changes, to look for problems of implementation, suggest practicable improvements, plus the job instruction necessary for all with new tasks to perform. This is more elaborate but it is not training for training's sake. Every element has a clear future pay-off, from the accounts manager's point of view, and the new system will operate more effectively as a result. He will meet his own objectives and contribute to the whole chain of intentions.

But without the information on the proposed reorganisation, although the opportunity for training was there, it would not be taken. Hence the need to be aware of the general nature of opportunity generators and, in the event, their actual occurence. We shall list the most obvious ones and discuss their relationship with the opportunities already listed.

1 Basic manpower maintenance

In a company of little growth in size or activity there is nevertheless the need to maintain the strength of the manpower in the face of losses. The losses are due to retirement, death, those who are discharged and other leavers. Not only do they have to be replaced; their departure produces transfers and promotions, and these are all training opportunities. Obvious though this is it is important to realise that they do not occur spontaneously, and that there is usually in the personnel department short and long-term predictions of the size and pattern of these arrivals and movements which can act as a guide to planning and objective setting.

2 Development schemes

Under this heading we include those listed in Chapter 2, i.e. personnel development, career development and manpower development. They all are likely to specify transfers and promotions – already in our list of training opportunities. The overall pattern of moves for each person in such a scheme has to be designed, and this is of concern to the training function in so far as it produces a blueprint for the development of a new capability. The effectiveness of this blueprint depends very largely on the successful training and employment of the person under development in each job in which he is placed. Development schemes and their blueprints, in bringing about movement and promotion, are just as much training generators as manpower maintenance, and any assumption that the pattern of moves alone is to be equated with development is misleading and sometimes dangerous.

The difference between the transferee for manpower maintenance and the transferee for development lies in the objectives behind the moves, and what is likely to happen to the job holders later. So the two people are not to be seen in exactly the same way although each has to do the job to the standards required. The rate of learning, the response to upset conditions, the contribution to work improvement may well feature in the appraisal of performance with greater prominence for the person on a development programme. So he is not just another transferee. Apart from having been party to the design of the blueprint for the movement of the person concerned, the training manager needs to know that the move is pending so that briefings can be undertaken in good time.

3   Corporate growth

Recruitment, transfers and promotions accelerate in a specific and predictable fashion when planned growth, positive or negative, takes place. Again, although each particular arrival is much the same as those due to the training opportunity generators above, there is every reason that training management and functional management should anticipate the arrival and the reason for the arrival of an increased number of employees for training and employment, not merely in general terms, but in detail of numbers, location and dates. A small growth might pass virtually unnoticed, but the larger the growth in manpower the greater the problems in resourcing the training.

4   Corporate and functional objectives

Changes in these will normally have an impact on the responsibilities, standards, targets and other factors, many of which we have listed as training opportunities. An increase in manpower, the operation of a higher standard of product quality, the transfer of people from production control into sales are, in an example in mind, all the result of a change in marketing objectives, to raise the market share by $3\frac{1}{2}$ per cent. This has generated a host of other changes in the company right down to the point of producing specific training opportunities and, in this case, actual requirements.

It is not merely illuminating for the training manager to know what has brought about the step-up in training demand as and when he encounters it; his responsibility includes the *anticipation* of the training demand and the proposition of the measures to meet it, whether on-the-job or off-the-job. Indeed, if this responsibility is not fully accepted, then the corporate objective may not be fully met, for whatever training is then undertaken may only be that which is set up by the more thoughtful and energetic line managers, leaving a portion of it unattended to, not even thought of.

The chapter on corporate change (Chapter 23) is of relevance to this section and to sections 5 and 6 below.

5 Efficiency studies

From time to time in most companies a study is made formally or informally, by insiders or outsiders, of the effectiveness of some aspect of the systems, the organisation or the manpower. As a result, almost anything might happen; reorganisation with job changes for some and new relationships for many, new procedures, manpower cuts to produce savings, or the introduction of entirely new time- and money-saving office machinery. All these we recognise as training opportunities requiring closer examination, with the efficiency study, or rather the final plan of action, as the opportunity generator.

Again, it is essential that training management and line management should recognise the later training implications of the introduction of such studies, and the more definite requirements of the accepted proposals. An early warning system is needed if the most useful training contribution to ultimate effectiveness is to be provided.

6 Environmental changes

Some things outside the company can change and have no noticeable effect on what goes on inside as far as training is concerned. A change in early-closing day in the local shopping centre, a rise in taxes on industrial premises, the opening of a new town welfare centre: one can imagine no significant internal impact. But there are many environmental changes which are of real importance to the life inside the company and which generate situations and problems which require training attention. The most dramatic of these are usually those arising from changes in the law of employment. All things to do with employees' rights and employers' obligations, with pollution, with safety and health, and which appear in new statutes, are likely to produce new systems, standards, procedures, as well as demand new understanding and capability in management.

It is important to take positive action to enable the employee to appreciate fully the status, rights and responsibilities which he has acquired as a result of the last Act; and this, quite distinct from the more typical job training associated with the vast majority of employees, requires training suitable for gaining an understanding of rights within the law.

Less spectacular, perhaps, are those changes in fiscal and taxation law, some of which are merely of concern to the experts, but others bringing about changes in the relevant practices, or even in communication to all employees where there is question of deductions from, or additions to, salary.

Not all outside changes of importance are statutory. The construction of a large company in the neighbourhood, with its demand on scarce manpower, can force a revision of internal manpower policies and plans, as can the appearance of the first of a long succession of graduates from a new local high school. And, of course, the external economic environment and market-place, are primary influences on decision-making inside the company. All of them can generate training opportunities by virtue of the changes in internal decisions and practices which are found to be necessary.

It is not to be assumed that this is a comprehensive list of opportunity generators. There are others, some unique to the particular locality and the country of a company. Neither the list of training opportunities, nor that of the generators, is of use unless it reflects local circumstances.

5 The training opportunity matrix

We now have a wide and structured view of many things that can happen to, and happen in, a company which give rise to training needs, and to consequent training action, should the need be recognised in good time. We have called those situations, decisions and events which cause changes in company operations and systems the 'opportunity generators'. The word opportunity itself we have reserved for the places or occasions in which the person finds himself faced with a need to learn and a need to be trained. It must be pointed out that we refer to these as 'opportunities' quite deliberately for, although in a theoretical sense we are referring to occasions where there is a learning and training need, they remain to be specifically identified and acted on. The opportunity remains to be taken.

However, no matter how illuminating the range of headings and the descriptions which we have offered may be, they are little more than a very general aid to analysis and decision-making, in the form in which they rest at the present. From some points of view this plethora of things which need looking at, in order to make sure that every possible training requirement is given reasonable consideration, is bewildering rather than helpful, so we need to give all of the above ideas a bit more shape, and turn them into an instrument of potential usefulness to management.

We shall do this by presenting the headings of training opportunities in a tabular form, at the same time listing the variouis groups of people to whom these opportunities generally apply. The first illustration, we must emphasise, is purely to show the type of matrix which results; it is not offered as the matrix that will suit the requirements of any and every company. The construction of a suitable matrix, for use in a particular company, department or function, will be discussed in the next few pages. First, then, the training opportunity matrix for our hypothetical 'general purpose' company is shown in Figure 5.1.

We can see that, given the range of typical training opportunities shown on the left hand side, and assuming that all or most of these opportunities are relevant to each category of employee shown in the headings of the columns, each square of the matrix represents a more closely defined opportunity than we have so far considered. For example, we have the square representing the training associated

	Directors	Managers	Supervisors	Assistants	Clerks	Operators	Apprentices	
New recruits								
Transferees								
Promotees			A					
New plant/equipment						B		
New procedures								
New standards, rules and practices								
New relationships and authorities								
Maintenance of standards								
Maintenance of adaptability	C							

Figure 5.1 Training opportunity matrix

with the promotion of people into supervision (square A), a familiar training challenge; we have a square representing training for operators freshly provided with new and unfamiliar machinery (B), an often encountered work situation needing frequent training attention; and a square (C) which could represent middle-aged managers who have run their departments one way and one way only for the past ten years and who show resistance and inflexibility in the current changing demands on the enterprise.

All of the squares represents a realistic, potential, requirement. It would not be true to say that at any moment there were actual training requirements in every single square. But by presenting the opportunities in this way it is possible to visualise the entire company's potential requirement in a structured and related way. 'Structured', because that number of training opportunities – there are 56 squares – is very difficult to hold in one's head, to picture, and to think about with due thoroughness without the help of an aid of this type; to help, as it were, organise one's thinking. 'Related', because in considering any one area or single square of the matrix, one is virtually obliged to look at adjacent squares, or to examine, for example, the implications of 'New procedures' not merely for the clerks but for the whole range of employee categories.

We can say with confidence that the first thing that the training opportunity matrix provides is a useful *conceptual framework*. It enables those responsible for training to consider the various actual and possible requirements, and the many types of people to whom these requirements apply, with a greater clarity than otherwise.

It is not unreasonable to suggest that both training and line management in the larger and more complex concerns must, from time to time, look at all the types of people, all the courses and programmes, all the new propositions, and ask themselves the questions 'why do we have so many things going on; what is it all for?' The matrix is a first step in sorting out present activities, in producing a patterned picture of both what is done and what is not done. Thus it *contributes to an audit of training*. It is easy to see that every activity presently undertaken in a company can be marked in the appropriate square or squares, and that the sum total of all those things registered in the matrix shows where the activity is, and where it isn't. It is then possible to consider the propositions for new training and see if the resulting pattern is more satisfactory.

What the matrix does not do, in itself, is to indicate the actual need for training square by square, or whether the quality of the training indicated is satisfactory. These questions have to be asked and answered separately, as, indeed, separate questions have to be asked about the items of any inventory, balance sheet or portfolio. The actual need relating to any one square can only be gauged through knowledge of what is going on in the various parts of the company, and under the headings of opportunity generators. Obviously a close concentration on the pro forma, the blank sheets, of the opportunity matrix will not produce much information on what specific actions have to be taken; but an examination of the company's activities under each opportunity generator heading will bring one close to the information needed. Thus we see a further use for the matrix, as an *aid to systematic planning*.

The last use that may have wide application is as an *aid* to *management communication*. We have already briefly considered how the matrix enables, say, the training manager to visualise more clearly the total pattern of potential and actual requirement and activity. In discussions with colleagues and with departmental or corporate management the matrix can offer a similar facility, and assist understanding with others on the pattern of current and future activities, and the relationship between this pattern and the multiplicity of employee groups and their needs.

THE DESIGN OF THE MATRIX

So far we have referred to a general purpose matrix for both simplicity and ease of communication in this text. In practice the matrix will have to be constructed to suit local purposes and local organisation. It may be found that the advantages of the matrix approach, to the scanning, planning and control of training, are at a maximum when used simply as a conceptual framework, and of diminishing value as one tries to convert the idea into a software instrument. This is very likely to be the case if the matrix is inappropriate for the use to which it is being put. There are some simple design rules which should be observed.

1   The categories of employees should represent by name those actually present in the company. The headings shown in this chapter would clearly not be suitable for the members of ships' crews, or for the staff of a modern integrated oil refinery. In all cases the actual groups and levels of employees must be entered as the column headings.

2   The matrix must be of a manageable size. To try and represent a company with 50 categories of employees on one matrix is to present oneself not only with a prodigious task in draughtsmanship, but with frustration in attempting to read and scan such a large matrix. It is preferable to break the whole down into component work areas and associated employee groups. Such components as departments, functions, separate depots and branches suggest themselves, representing also areas of management authority. Hence in the company with 50 employee categories overall, there would be separate matrices for production, sales, transport, design, accounts and personnel, covering some 95 per cent of all people in the company. The remainder, i.e. the directors, advisors etc., would have to be dealt with separately. Each matrix is now meaningful to both line and training management, whereas the total matrix would have produced great problems in understanding had it been used as a basis for examining any one component area.

By producing component matrices it is now possible to use them as a means of making *interfunctional comparisons*, but only if the matrices carry a record of actual requirements and activities in each component area. The marking up of a matrix is a complex and sometimes unreliable step, whereas merely using the matrix as a conceptual framework, or as a reference for auditing, planning and progressing purposes is both powerful and non-misleading. In these latter uses the detail of training plans, progress etc. would be carried on other documents with the clarity and elaboration necessary; the role of the matrix would be to ensure that all significant opportunities receive attention, and that the total pattern of present and future requirement and action is perceived and then understood.

A BASIS FOR SYSTEMATIC TRAINING

Figure 5.1 shows as opportunities a number of examples which are characteristic of companies and other employing institutions the world over. If we examine these examples we shall see that they fall under two headings, namely 'notifiable' and 'non-notifiable'. By this we mean that within the communication systems in most companies, with particular reference to personnel systems, the first three headings, i.e. New recruits, Transferees and Promotees, describe people about whom a record is made in the files, and concerning whom notes are sent across the company indicating that, for example, 'John Roberts will join the tool-room as a gauge-maker on 7 March'. His number, age, rate of pay and other details are provided so that the pensions, rate-fixing, medical and some other sections all get the information they require for their own action. Similar notes will be sent about transferees; also about promotees although it is not often the case that significant changes into new levels of responsibility are indicated on the note, for no reference to this is normally regarded as necessary, important though such a change is.

The rest of the opportunities are not notified in the same way, although there will be in some instances some form of notification; but not of the 'John Roberts will...' type, not nailing the name of a *person* on to the announcement of an *actual* training opportunity. Let us look at this more closely. The non-notifiables are –

New plant/equipment, New procedures, New standards/rules/practices, New relationships/authorities, Maintenance of standards, and Maintenance of adaptability.

The new plant, which is, for the sake of illustration, new lifting gear for loading on to transport lorries, replaces very old and comparatively limited gear. The decision to introduce this change has been made 15 months before. It was the subject of much management debate at the time, notes and letter writing before the necessary directorial assent was given. The formal approval was then documented with action copies to the managers of stores, transport, materials and purchase, and accounts. But not to personnel nor to training, for there was no requisition put up at that time for new, replacement, or additional labour, as none was needed.

This is the sense in which we mean non-notifiable. One can see immediately, without further illustration, that the term applies equally to the headings New procedures, New standards/rules/practices, New relationships/authorities, although there will be companies which are exceptions to the rule. There will also be the same exceptions under the heading of New relationships/authorities, wherever such changes are announced by private note, circular or on the noticeboard or in the house magazine. But the notification is likely to stop at the identification of the principal person involved in the change. There will be no reference to the other people who are affected by the change and who will have to learn and adapt in their roles and relationships.

The Maintenance of standards is a requirement which is not produced normally by a single event or by a single management decision. There is unlikely to be anywhere in the company a file or a set of minuted meetings which lead deliberately and automatically into actions being taken for the declared purpose of standards maintenance. There are, of course, exceptions to this, the most notable being the frequent drills carried out by members of fire brigades, or those employees with fire-fighting responsibility in oil refineries and other equally sensitive plant. There are in addition the numerous *post hoc* training activities all over the world which are set up after a disaster of one type or another, such as spillage of dangerous chemicals, a mix up of customers' orders on a grand scale, or the death of foundrymen at work. These events, quickly followed by an enquiry into causes, are ascribed partly to malpractice, and part of the 'solution' is to introduce training, or retraining or refresher training, to ensure that proper practices are re-established, and that there is no departure from approved standards in the future. This training is the result of notification made for the purpose of bringing about that training, but occurs when things have already gone wrong. The maintenance of standards should not have to depend on a disaster happening before training action is thought of and agreed to.

The extent to which a company should invest in some form of continuous training is a question which we shall look at again. It clearly raises further questions of costs and of the value gained by undertaking such training, difficult points to deal with in brief, but of great importance in the ultimate analysis of the contribution of training to the well-being of the company as a whole.

The last non-notifiable on our list is the Maintenance of adaptability. This is even more elusive than the Maintenance of standards. The adaptability of employees, from the managing director down to the most junior assistant, is not something which is discussed regularly at meetings or put into memoranda, or even mentioned at all. Yet the company, to some extent, will depend on it. There will be periods of time when there are absolutely no problems arising from lack of adaptability, because where they are no changes there is no demand for adaptability. When changes come the company may be lucky to find that the changes are really very slight and are within everyone's compass, or that the major changes are borne by, say, a management and professional group who always relish a challenge. So every company has its own maintenance requirement. One would say: but what is it? What should company X be doing about it; how does it find out? Whatever the method adopted, it will not be dependent on regular notification designed for the purpose. This is discussed further in Chapters 21, 'Continuous development', and 23, 'Corporate change'.

6 Notifiable training

As we have discussed briefly, there are several reasons for paying close attention to the job training of new recruits, transferees and promotees. The first is to produce a standard output and rate of work to match 'production' requirements, whether of maintenance fitters, professional engineers or personnel officers. Normally it is not satisfactory that a person merely meets these requirements, but that he *knows* that they exist, and why lower standards are unacceptable. Thus skill and understanding go hand in hand. If the standards are unnecessarily, or ambitiously, high then, of course, the training will be unnecessarily rigorous.

The second reason is to produce an intelligent and collaborative response in the employee in all likely work situations, including upset conditions and emergencies. This demands not an exhortation to be interested and loyal, but knowledge and practice that will enable the employee correctly and quickly to interpret the regular and irregular situations as they arise. And those which demand further explanation will see him, ideally, turning for information to his supervisor in whom his confidence is rightly placed as a result of the effort made earlier by that supervisor to fully equip the employee to do a good day's work, with minimum problems and maximum satisfaction. The supervisor, fully accepting his responsibilities for communication and information giving, will respond to this – perhaps by seeking further information from colleagues in neighbouring functions to pass on to his subordinates.

How much more important this becomes if the person receiving the job training is an apprentice, or a first time employee straight from school, or a member of a particular development scheme in the company. For these people there will be needs in addition to those of others, such as more frequent progress reporting, emphasis on work flow methods for the management trainee, an introduction to other functions of the department for the apprentice, and so on. Without the foundation of good basic job training, however, none of these additions is likely to have the value, or to carry the conviction that the trainee often seeks.

In many companies there are unquestionably good job training standards and practices to be found in this department and that, but rarely to the same high standard across the whole company. Whatever is done to improve the overall standard of training, care has to be taken to preserve that which is already of a high quality. Before any moves are made to introduce new practices of job training a close understanding must be established with all managers and supervisors about the purpose of new systems of training and information, and what is to be kept and what is to go. The many years of job training within the experience of supervision and middle management, and the inventive genius of some in these positions, may have produced gems of training technique which may be discarded if an indiscriminate and general fiat is issued demanding that certain new systems and methods be adopted.

It is bad management to destroy useful assets. It is also bad management to decrease a feeling of collaboration amongst management, which one is likely to do if too blunt an approach is adopted. One has to hold firmly in mind that, as far as on-the-job training is concerned, not only is local supervision responsible for it, but that they actually do it or directly supervise it. In these circumstances new systems and methods are not likely to make best progress if they have been insensitively itnroduced.

The training manager with a genuine management responsibility has, as his objective, under the heading of job training, 'the acquisition of a defined level of skill and knowledge, by the employees under instruction'. To meet his objectives he certainly has to be concerned with methods of instruction whether on-the-job or off-the-job, whether for operating skills or for company information, but these methods and their actual application are not his principal concern as a manager. As such he is concerned with people, trainees, employees having acquired an agreed standard – through training. The training expertise which he displays is his professional skill. The setting of objectives, and reaching those objectives, is management skill. The information that he gathers to enable him to see if he is reaching his objectives is the information from which he will draw in order to satisfy his management that he is discharging his responsibilities adequately.

The training manager, then, does not focus exclusively on methods, but is ultimately concerned with end products. In consequence the data that he requires in order to see if the training of the groups we are presently concerned with is meeting objectives, is data on skill and job performance. The question about trainees which is most searching is 'Can they do their jobs?' It is not 'How is the training going?' although he has to deal with this too.

It is now a simple matter to establish what information is required for control and monitoring of the training of the 'notifiables'. The ease with which one can manage notifiable training will also be apparent; the ease and efficiency with which one can do the training is a distinct and different sort of problem, again the concern of the training officer and line management alike, and which needs careful handling if the ultimate objectives are to be met. As has often been observed, elaborate and sophisticated training practices do not in themselves guarantee satisfactory standards of job performance; nor does the absence of separate or even distinguishable training practices lead automatically to the lowering of performance standards, in every work situation.

For the monitoring of training against objectives, i.e. skill attainment, the following data needs to be provided:

1 The name of the employee
2 The employee's identification number
3 Special category not otherwise apparent, e.g. apprentice
4 Job title
5 Job location
6 Machine, equipment or procedure central to the job
7 Tasks comprising job
8 Starting date of training
9 Completion date of training
10 Performance check satisfactory/unsatisfactory
11 Signature of responsible supervisor

Of all the above information, items 1–8 are probably standard throughout the industrial world. They are necessary for other purposes, both local and legal; for copies of that data go to the manager of the employing department, to the foreman or section head, to the rate-fixer, pensions, the personnel officer, and to wages, and in the larger concern, to the medical department, and the sports and social club secretary as well. Notification *in excelcis*. Whether to that same sheet there should be added further headings to meet the requirements of training management is doubtful, for the further headings, from 9–11 are performance reports, and once completed constitute information which is confidential to management and the particular person concerned. Uncompleted or completed forms lying around in other departments for all and sundry to see, do not inspire confidence in employees.

This last point is, although important, a matter of detail. However the paperwork is administered, the information in items 9–11 has to be collected, collated with that from 1–10, and interpreted. Obviously any system that is complicated and laborious to operate will get little support from managers and supervisors, and a great deal of care must be given to simplicity and clarity. Putting these points on one side for the moment, we must go back to the role and responsibility of line management, for this control system is a test of the willingness of management openly to express and commit themselves in their training responsibility.

What they are asked to do is first to check in every important detail the competence of the person who has completed all, or a section of, his training whether it has been given on-the-job, in a separate training area, or in a classroom. It will be noted that the check will inevitably be by observing the employee doing the job itself, for there is no better way of ensuring that competence has been fully gained.

Whether the check is a formal occasion, or no more than a series of observations of sub-task performance without prior notification, is a matter for local judgement. Whatever checking method is used it must be sufficiently thorough and searching to produce worthwhile information. Otherwise there is on the one hand the risk of an otherwise good control system being abused and falling into disrepute, and, on the other hand, the risk that performance standards are not being adhered to in that area. Once supervision and their management undertake to operate a system, particularly one affecting employees, they must do it well. Not to do so is destructive not only of the system in which they participate, but also of the confidence of the employees for whom they are responsible.

Item 11 is the most critical one for, although a supervisor may be prepared to make a statement verbally, he may not be so willing to sign the same statement in writing. It is common experience that anyone in a position of responsibility in an organisation is likely to think twice before putting his own name against a statement of achievement of almost any kind if it relates to his authorised responsibilities and if he is not absolutely sure it is right and supportable. In this case, we must not forget that the satisfactory completion of training of, say, a new employee is not only a responsibility of line management and supervision; it is in their own best interests to see that the required performance standard is achieved, for the later smooth running of the work will depend on it.

Every right minded manager and supervisor will agree with this last point. But what they would be faced with by the introduction of this type of system would be more paper work, outside interference from a non-productive function, and the possibility of unwelcome correction and reprimand from their own superior management should the data reveal unwelcome facts about training progress. In consequence the establishment of a control system with the above features must be based on an understanding with line management that it is a service on their behalf, that the data and statistics then produced are for their own consideration, and that actions that need to be taken will be based on the conclusions and agreements arising from discussion with line management.

This type of monitoring, undertaken by specialist service function on behalf of the line manager, has many precedents. The accountant, and in particular the cost accountant, has much the same sort of relationship with the line manager. The manager is responsible in most organisations for the control of costs in his departments. It is he, with his manpower, machinery, floorspace, administration, materials and various other items, who costs the company money, and often he who actually spends it. Yet the accountant has access to information on the costs and expenditure in these departments, and has the right to examine more closely matters which seem to be heading for financial trouble. Even so the accountant does not instruct the manager on what he *must* do, although he is likely to advise him and his superiors on what they *ought* to do. The manager has come to see that the work done by the accountant is a service on his behalf, which helps him to meet his departmental objectives, a service which he himself can use to advantage once he understands what it has to offer. The training service stands in the same position relative to the line manager, but it is not always seen in this way.

ADMINISTRATION OF THE SYSTEMATIC TRAINING OF NOTIFIABLES

The system which we have described, to ensure the training to agreed performance standards of all who move into new jobs, has to be looked after both operationally and administratively if it is to avoid decline. Who is to do this administrative work, of seeing that the completed returns are made for each job learner? There are several possibilities.

The departmental manager or foreman might well wish to attend to every aspect of the whole administrative procedure, i.e. the notification to the appropriate section of the expected arrival date of the new person plus personal particulars; the issue of the appropriate job breakdown/analysis to the supervisor for training purposes; the initial check that the supervisor is fully prepared for action; the registration of the person's arrival on the training record; the completion of the training form, including performance check-out signature, preceded by any chasing that is needed if the training is not making good progress. Finally, in this piece of administration, the sending of a copy to the central training office of the company, and the filing of the original in the manager's own records. This is a simple set of tasks but, spread over a few days or weeks, could easily be overlooked by someone preoccupied with other more pressing responsibilities.

So the manager, or foreman, might give it to his secretary or clerk to do, if he has either, or to an assistant. These are not unreasonable alternatives, provided he instructs the person appointed to let him see regularly, say at two-weekly intervals, all forms completed during the past two weeks plus information on all overdue returns. He will also want to see how the total picture of training is building up as the year progresses, and this can be done by the same person once a method of presentation has been agreed on.

This brings us to the next two possibilities for undertaking this administrative task, the personnel officer and the training officer. In most companies of more than 500 people there will be personnel officers in addition to the personnel manager himself in proportion to the number of employees in the company. It is not unusual to find that the whole of one site is divided into areas and a personnel officer allocated to each area. In this way the personnel officer gets to know the managers, supervisors, employees, and their work and requirements with much greater intimacy and understanding than he would if he shared the whole site with other personnel officers. It is reasonable to suppose that the specific administrative tasks which we have described above might be undertaken by him, for, after all, he will in normal circumstances be the person in the personnel function who records the occurrence of the vacancy, processes the recruitment indent, briefs and in part inducts the new arrival, and conducts some sort of employment follow-up after some days or weeks to make sure that from the point of view of both employer and employee a square peg is in a square hole.

The personnel officer, constantly visiting the actual work area, familiar with the work and manpower situation, should be able to administer the production and collection of this training data with little extra effort. We must remember that, having referred to this type of training as notifiable, it is the personnel officer who is the principal agent of notification. It would be important, however, to make sure that no misunderstanding arose as a result of using the personnel officer in this role. The person who does the paperwork or the administrative work is sometimes mistaken for the person responsible for the whole activity. In this case the personnel officer, with his involvement in the whole cycle of replacement, recruitment and training, might assume responsibilities which are rightly those of the line manager and his supervisory team. The personnel officer should be acting in fact as an agent of line management, making sure that the systems for which they carry responsibility are functioning correctly. He would not be running the training and would not be in a position to alter any methods or administration without management agreement. This is a very important matter, for what goes on inside a department must be under the control of the management of that department, particularly when it concerns, as does job training, the job performance of employees in the department.

Of course the training officer or training manager himself could undertake this administrative work. He is most likely to be the person who receives all paper returns of this type from the various parts of the company, in order to analyse, compare and ultimately advise on progress and developments. Whether or not it would be economic to employ a member of the training function to do the administrative work in the company's departments would depend on a number of factors, such as the physical size of the company site, the number of trainees per week to be registered, the total size and commitment of the training staff.

Given that there are other ways of collecting this data, the training officer should not spend time on this sort of work, apart from the examination and interpretation of the data once assembled, and involvement in any ensuing action. There are much more profitable things for him to attend to. We have been looking closely at the handling of training of notifiables. We have seen how systems can be set up, how the day-to-day running of those systems can readily be placed in the hands of line management and the personnel officers, each contributing in accordance with his basic responsibilities. There need not even be a training officer on site if the system is well designed and administered.

This last point is in no sense in conflict with ideas on the effective management of training, which involves seeing that the right things are done and to the right standard. Who actually does these things will depend on such points as the acceptance of responsibility of line managers for training their own employees, and the most economic way of doing it. This takes us a long way from the point of view that the training function has to be visibly and physically involved in every training activity. That is neither possible nor necessary.

What the training officer and training management need to devote their time to is the other heading, 'non-notifiables', under which we have grouped the remainder of the training opportunities. To this heading we shall now turn our attention.

7 Non-notifiable training

I DEVELOPMENTS

It is tempting to give this chapter the title 'Ad Hockery' for it is the *ad hoc* treatment of the new that now concerns use. The training opportunity matrix (Figure 5.1) identified a very wide field of such situations which may occur in a company and which demand training attention of some sort. The opportunity generators, presented on page 37 are the root cause of these demands, and it must be clear that if one can only get at these root causes in good time, then one is in a position to deal with the training requirements before being overtaken by events. A simple concept, no doubt, but not normally so simple in practice.

First we shall look at an example, in an ideal company, of what happens if all goes well. The company makes roller bearings. The final assembly of the bearing is done by hand and the work study engineers have undertaken research into time and motion to such an extent that they have been able to produce a totally new design for the benches, the equipment and the inspection arrangement. The measured saving on assembly and inspection time in the laboratory, where there is a full scale prototype bench and equipment, is 35 per cent. The cost of change-over to the new system from the old, would be met by the savings in labour over a period of some six months. The labour thus saved and hence made redundant would be transferred to a new section elsewhere. The trade union has been consulted and sees advantages all round, with certain provisos, and has agreed the change-over.

No one now remembers who suggested it, but it was agreed readily by the work study manager, the manager of assembly, and by the works manager, that there should be a full scale effort to provide all the training that was needed to make the new system successful. This was worked out to include a wide range of items. The most elaborate was a course in work study for the foremen and charge-hands of assembly and inspection, focusing on the efficiency of manual work at the bench, given by the method study engineers, designed in such a way that mutual under-standing between the foremen and the engineers could flourish. The least elaborate was the short briefing sessions for the progress chasers, and midway came the new on-the-job training for the operators. The union representatives were provided with a separate short course on the new method, the savings and the effect on earnings of all concerned.

That the new system was launched successfully will be of no surprise. The issue we have to look into is why and how the training should happen at all. For, at another time in the same company, the introduction of a new personnel appraisal system saw no training beyond a few minutes of briefing, and the ultimate rejection of the system by line management.

The training manager could say, correctly but somewhat defensively, that when he was asked to provide a service he did so, successfully. When he was not asked he could not be expected to take action. He would make it look like a simple case of failure in communication. This however is an over simplification.

The first requirement is that both the training manager and the line and other managers must fully realise that the training opportunities and generators are as real and significant in their demand for action as are the more commonplace apprentice training or new recruit requirements. The fact that they may be some-what obscure in the first instance means that extra effort must be made to identify them in time for useful action to be planned and carried out. If the training manager fails to see this readily himself, or fails to respond convincingly, then perhaps that company has got the wrong training manager. A convincing response means a response in action, and not merely in words, based on an insight into company situations and the courage necessary to take suitable action in face of a corporate management which may not like having its mind changed or its attitudes challenged.

A management which spontaneously recognises the training implications of decisions at the opportunity generator level, one would call genuinely 'training minded', and the training manager would be grateful for such a state of affairs. Managements, though, are made up of managers, and each one would be, in his own way, interested or not interested, mindful or forgetful, co-operative or non-co-operative, and there cannot be a uniformly high level of spontaneous initiative right across a large management group subject to the pressures of production and the hundred and one things that lose them sleep at night. What is the answer? It is a key problem for the training manager, and he must seek a solution. The following are steps which can be taken to improve both communication and commitment.

1 Training representation at the planning level

In most organisations changes which are under consideration involving capital expenditure, or a reshaping of the company's pattern of operations or the reallo-cation of major responsibilities, are not the result of any one manager's whims, but the product of a great deal of work by the line and service functions. Within this work, particularly at the management level, there will be occasional or regular meetings to consider and approve proposals, as well as to study progress reports. If the training manager sits on the committee concerned with the planning of developments across the whole enterprise, he is in an ideal position to learn for himself about the majority of training opportunities in good time. He is also well placed to contribute to the planning of any development project in as far as it is sensible to ensure that the timetables of development work and of a preliminary training should be matched. This matching in major new plant developments can alter the date of arrival of both the commissioning teams of experts, who would be expected to contribute to the training effort, and of the trainees, as compared with the dates envisaged in terms of straight commissioning. And dates of arrival on site in turn will alter recruitment dates and release dates from elsewhere in the company.

However, such committee representation is rare, and there are reasons why this is so despite the acceptance of the idea in principle in many organisations. The main objection to direct representation, on a regular basis, is that in the majority of meetings the training manager might well be wasting his own time, for the endless discussion of the minutiae of the business in hand, whilst perhaps of interest to him, is not something to which he can make any real contribution. A further objection is frequently that within the management hierarchy the training manager is not of sufficient seniority to merit a place at the table. This is a poor reason; but it is the one that sees him displaced as it were by his own superior, who may or may not be able to represent this type of training interest.

2 Indirect representation at planning level

If the training function is represented on the planning committee by the head of personnel or of administration, assuming that the training function lies in these areas, we are faced with a new problem, should the identification of training opportunity generators not be the habit of many personnel or administration managers. This should not rule out the possibility of indirect representation, for the logic is not difficult to convey to whoever carries the torch on the training manager's behalf. The indirect represenation may of course be undertaken by the chairman of the committee, or the secretary, or by another nominated person. Whichever way it is played it is essential that that person is fully instructed on what constitutes a training opportunity and generator. The representative who says to the training manager, after the meeting, that 'there was nothing new tabled; but we did begin to discuss the idea that all of our stores records might go on to the computer' is helpful to the training man who has some vision. The representative who says that 'there was nothing of interest to you today; we didn't get round to talking about training', is probably the wrong man for the task.

3 Sight of the minutes

The recognised right to read the minutes, his own, or those lent for the purpose, is a great asset. Although it does not provide the same opportunity to join in the dialogue as does actual attendance at the planning meeting, it does provide the essential information which the training manager needs. It is an advantage if the minutes are openly copied to him, so that there is little or no problem of confidentiality when he decides to talk with the particular members of the committee concerned.

4   On call

If, in addition to receiving the minutes, he is invited at a member's suggestion, or at his own suggestion, to attend those parts of committee meetings which are of interest to him, he is in a strong position to pursue the opportunities as they arise. It is also more demanding on his capability and effectiveness, for comments and promises made at management meetings will be taken seriously, probably minuted, and he will have to live up to his promises.

The means described above of getting early warning about developments, are based on tapping into company information systems. The planning committee is part of the management information and decision-making system. There will be other comparable committees in a company, at varying levels, such as the product development committee, the research committee and so on. It is not a question of course of getting on to every single committee in the company, but of identifying those which are the nodal points of development decision-making, and, as a practical matter, establishing the minimum necessary working relationship with them and not the maximum possible.

In addition to these existing resources there is a further one which may be set up strictly for training purposes. It is usually called

5   The training committee

The most typical function for this committee is to provide an opportunity for line management periodically to discuss the conduct and progress of training schemes with the training manager and his staff, or with his superordinates, such as the personnel manager or the administration manager. Meetings may be held monthly or quarterly, or on an *ad hoc* basis according to requirement. They may include, if the circumstances of the company make it worth while, representatives from employee groups, although meetings between management and representatives are likely to be in addition to the sort of meeting now being described.

Training committee meetings do provide an opportunity to examine the anticipated developments in the company which provide training opportunities of the non-notifiable type. The membership would be asked to consider in advance those changes in systems organisation, machinery etc. which they at present have on their drawing boards, or those developments in objectives or strategy which are under consideration at top management level and which are likely, as opportunity generators, to produce an impact on the company when the implementation phase is reached. Such early warning of future events would enable the training manager to discuss, both in and out of the meetings, the training implications of the developments and reach agreement on what provision for training must be made. The provision would depend on the problem and the resources needed to deal with it beyond those immediately available. In some cases there may be no need for anything to be done, beyond the continuation of good articulate supervision in the places affected. In some cases there may be a need for the supervisors and managers to undergo some familiarisation with the new processes before commissioning, and to prepare by means of job analysis and the new operating manuals the materials to be used in the job instruction. And in further cases there may be a

45

requirement for re-education of management, supervision and operators alike, both on and off-the-job, as would be the case when a computer plus mathematical model is introduced for day to day decision-making.

The training committee provides an exceptional opportunity to go well beyond the initial step of identifying the anticipated training requirement. Later meetings of the committee can discuss progress and final achievement with a thoroughness that would be difficult to achieve elsewhere, even in the planning committee. By keeping a picture of the start-to-finish events, and of the end result, in front of line management, one is bringing about that education of management which is the basis of 'training mindedness' to which we referred earlier. Training mindedness developed in this way is much more likely to be realistic and practical than that which has been nurtured solely on courses and magazine articles.

We have now returned to one of our starting points – the need for managers to have an attitude towards training that enables them to perceive spontaneously the present and future learning requirements of their employees, and then to turn their minds towards doing something about it. There is a problem, though, that often impedes the progress of both training and line managers. It is the problem arising from the various meanings of the word training, and the differing views of the responsibilities of the training manager, as held by himself and other managers. An example will illustrate this.

The training officer visits the public relations manager in order, as he has already indicated, to discuss training in that function. It is their first serious discussion on the subject of training, or indeed on anything, for the PR manager joined the company from a consultancy only a few months before and asked to be allowed to settle in before turning his mind to things like training. Now the training officer is worried, because as far as he can see there is no training in that function. There is nothing on the record to show that any company apprentices have ever worked there, or that any member of PR has been on a course since the record system was established three years ago, or that any discussions on training have been held with PR at any time. But the training officer, aware of the very wide scope of training opportunity matrix for that sizeable function, is determined to begin what he regards as a promising dialogue. He finds himself confronted with a man of considerable worldliness who gives the impression of 'knowing all the answers'. In fact it is the PR man who, after a few pleasantries, says that he has given a lot of thought to the matter since they talked on the telephone and has come to the conclusion that there is really nothing that needs to be done in his function; certainly not by the training officer, and very little by himself. 'After all', he says 'we are not like the rest of management. There is no reason to send a PR man to Harvard – except of course as a well earned holiday – because we are not in that sort of management. A good PR man is born and not made, and we just have to hope that we get the right sort of people in the first place and then chuck 'em in at the deep end.' And so the discussion, or monologue, continues. He shows that for him the word training summons up the picture of certain set pieces; and that none of these set pieces is relevant to him and his function.

The training officer is in a difficult position. He wishes he had never mentioned the word training, for it so often produces this reaction. So he changes the direction of the conversation, quite deliberately, in order to show that training opportunities are much more frequent than some people realise. The PR manager has no difficulty in understanding what he now hears, but he raises further objections: he has never taken special steps in the past to train his people as the training officer seems to suggest he should, and if he were to decide to at some time in the future he would not turn to the training function for help. 'After all, what do you know about Public Relations, a highly specialist function. Your job in training is to look after the apprentices and the company induction courses. You do a good job. Stick to it. I'll stick to mine.'

The training officer is in an even more difficult position now, unless he has exceptional ambassadorial talent, for the discussion has led to a rejection of the points which he wished to establish. He has asked for trouble and he has got it. He has expected the orthodox questions about training which he asked earlier on the telephone to be given imaginative and unorthodox answers. He also tried to argue the case for the general need to give attention to the training opportunity matrix; from the general to the particular. Ideally one deals successfully with a *particular* problem of the client, and then, with a willing ear turned in one's direction, one points to the possibility of a number of similar situations benefiting from suitable attention. The client may welcome with a genuine interest the chance to discuss the full breadth and depth of the total opportunity matrix.

It is here that the virtue of a well run training committee, or something similar, which gives frequent and regular opportunity for management discussion of training questions, becomes apparent. In the meetings of this committee, the PR manager would learn things from his management colleagues that he would not accept from the training manager. He may then realise that the full scope of the training manager's responsibilities is wider than, and different from, his initial assumption; and that this was not because of a mere job description but because this was how the other managers wanted it to be. He would find, from the evidence of current and future business that training of personnel in what we call non-notifiable situations is taken more seriously and dealt with more thoroughly than has been his habit in the past. To his question 'is all this necessary?' the answer from the other managers would be a blunt 'do you think we would do it if we thought it wasn't? – if you're going to train someone, do it properly', and so on, the line managers present making it quite clear that they only did as much as was necessary – but they didn't do any less. They would also talk with him outside the meeting, and take him to see the set-up in their own departments, so that he would realise that they weren't shooting a line. One or two are, in fact, proud of their achievements, and are somewhat piqued at the suggestion that their efforts were not really necessary. Their comments would be chosen to remind the new manager that there was no reason at all to assume that his department was perfect, or that his way of running it could not be improved. These are comments which the training officer himself was tempted to make but could not, for the sake of good relations.

II MAINTENANCE

The remaining training opportunities with which we have to deal are also non-notifiables, but we shall see that they are of a completely different nature from those already discussed, and require a different form of management. They are the maintenance of standards and the maintenance of adaptability.

Previous non-notifiables considered in this chapter are all the result of the same class of opportunity generator, i.e. a particular event and decision leading to the introduction of some sort of development in the work of the company. Whatever the difficulty for the training manager in finding out about these impending changes, there is nothing particularly elusive about them. They are the normal consequence of management decision-making, and he has to develop a means of access to them. However, the two headings which we now have to discuss are not associated normally with specific and recorded events in the company; there is little that can be readily referred to in the way of communications to indicate exactly what steps to take.

We shall look at each maintenance item in turn, but before we do so it is as well to remind ourselves of the potential value of including these items in the training policy statement for the organisation as a whole. In the chapter on policies there is quoted a sample of the form which these two headings could take in a policy statement. It is not at all uncommon to find that corporate management will accept the inclusion of suitably worded paragraphs, such as these, because they know them to be right, before there is much done in the company in pursuit of the policies laid down. After all it is eminently good sense to maintain the standard of operations and of employee performance on which those operations depend. It is also good sense to provide the training that is essential for the maintenance of that performance. No modern manager would object to this so far; he would agree readily to the inclusion of this idea in any statement of company training policy.

What he would debate is the question of what training is needed to maintain standards, what form it should take, and how much he should be prepared to spend on it.

It also makes good sense to managers that an employee is a greater asset if he is able to maintain his adaptability, his ability to learn new tasks, theories, systems, in view of the fact that companies never stand still, and that employees have to change with the times as much as do the companies in which they work. It makes sense, too, in view of the need of the company to appoint employees from the operator level to become supervisors, clerks to become section heads, and junior managers to become middle managers. Not many managers would dispute the advantages of such adaptability, or the relationship that education and training bear to it. A lot of managers have reached their present levels in professional work as a direct result of the intellectual power that they gained through studies which they undertook at their own initiative; others have advanced as the result of their company investing in long and expensive courses for them. They cannot dispute the principle, and would probably accept the policy.

What they would dispute is the question of exactly what practices the company should adopt. At whom should the company aim any provision? What form should it take? Who pays? What is a reasonable cost and budget? And, of course, the question that everyone asks and few can answer, 'how do you measure your return on the money you spend?'

Hence these two maintenance headings are likely to be ones under which the company managers will express sympathy and some interest in the very beginning. If in fact they are included in a company policy statement, their sympathy is strengthened by the obligation to observe that policy. But beyond this there is little for the training manager to rely on, and if he is to make progress he has a lot more than conventional training analysis and practice to deal with. We shall begin with:

The maintenance of standards

To understand this we need to couple the need for training with the economics involved, for these two go hand in hand. There is a more thorough discussion in Chapter 12 on cost/benefit analysis, but here we shall concentrate on the economics of retraining. The reader will know of very many jobs in which the employees have never received any retraining, and as far as they can see, no one is any the worse for it. On the other hand there are many examples in and out of companies of the people who seem to be undergoing constant retraining for the one job which, to all intents and purposes, they can already do. Soldiers, firemen, chemical plant operators and airline pilots come into this category. And thank goodness for that, we all say, for the consequences of any lapse in skill would be disaster and human misery.

In these two extremes we can see the rationale behind decisions which have to be made about training for the maintenance of standards. We can state this best in the form of a series of questions:

1 If the operator does something wrong, what goes wrong in the machine or system or in the environment as a result?
2 What is the cost of something going wrong in the machine or system or environment?
3 How likely is the operator to do that wrong thing?
4 How does his performance decline in time, over a period of weeks, months or years?
5 What is the training needed to refresh the operator and to maintain or restore standards?
6 What does the training cost to do?

Questions 1 and 2 are relatively easy to answer in most work. For example, if a process operator in an oil refinery misunderstands the instructions for the setting of a crude oil distillation unit, or is negligent, the unit might run at the incorrect setting for hours producing the wrong product mix. The cost of this to the company in terms of lost sale opportunities, could be calculated at several score thousands of pounds.

Question 3 in this same example might receive the answer, 'It is very unlikely indeed that any of our operators would make that mistake. It has not happened for the last four years and then we put it right before it got very far'.

Question 4 in this example might then receive the answer, 'Yes there are signs of decline, particularly after a long period on nights. It shows in the little things; but not in plant operating; we wouldn't stand for that in any case'.

Questions 5 and 6 have many inexpensive answers, and a search for the most economical forms of training used in this type of situation shows that to put all the shift controllers and operators through some refresher training on plant operations would cost less than 1 per cent of the payroll for that plant for one year.

To conclude this oil example, although the works manager was not actively worried about that form of operating mistake, as it hardly ever happened, he knew it could happen. And if and when it did, the cost to the company would be high in cash terms, and perhaps with a loss of confidence from the point of view of the customers. Against this, the cost of retraining and the inconvenience of organising it, would be at most one-tenth of the estimated sales loss. His decision was to go ahead with the training. His argument was that, although the past history of mistakes on that unit was very favourable, a future error was far from impossible; the cost of retraining every year would be more than covered by the reduction in error frequency from once in four years to once in six years. He confessed that the figures of frequency were his own invention, but they seemed reasonable, and there were no others to go on.

The basic equation that he was wrestling with is simply, in words:

> If retraining can reduce the cost to the company of lowered performance standards and mistakes, then retrain IF the saving to the company is significantly greater than the cost of the retraining.

That is a commonsense statement. It stops being a simple commonsense matter when it is realised that the actual sums are very difficult to work out, that the factors involved are sometimes non-quantifiable, and that the events one is dealing with are of a probablistic nature, sometimes without the data needed to provide a reliable probability coefficient. Where there is no experience of retraining in company then the training manager must seek information on effectiveness outside, from companies or research institutions which have practical experience of situations comparable to those in his own company. He must also run any such training in his company on an experimental basis. Each venture will add to the knowledge of not merely training methods, but the changes in performance levels, the frequencies of incidents, and the occurrence of side effects, both observed and measured. In this way he will establish a surer foundation on which future situations can be approached, and be in a better position to advise his management on the likely effectiveness of alternative training methods in the full range of opportunities in the company.

The cost of the incident

Incidents vary considerably in their basic nature. The scrapping of work done on an automatic lathe, due to faulty tool-setting, would normally not be given such a title but it comes into this category for the purposes of this discussion, as would any high scrap rate of work done by clerks and operators, whether in offices or in workshops. Naturally, the occurrence of scrap at lower and acceptable rates is also of concern when the rate is significantly higher that produces unplanned-for costs. These, operator by operator, or clerk by clerk, may not be great, but collectively, and in terms of the hold-ups further down the production line, may have a high cumulative cost to the company.

If the incident endangers the plant itself, or human safety or human life, or the integrity of the environment, then the need for, and value of, retraining for the maintenance of work standards becomes unquestionable and high. The acceptable error rate in handling dangerous chemicals, in servicing aircraft, in discharging ballast must be zero. Frequent retraining in itself may not be enough to avoid actual errors occurring. The quality of supervisors and operators, the tedium of the job, the inherent safety of the plants its control and warning system need as much attention.

The maintenance of adaptability

Adaptability is the ability to deal successfully with changes in the environment in which you live, and in which you work. This ability is inherent in all living things, within limits, and therefore we do not have to be so much concerned with creating it as with making sure that the circumstances in which people live and work are favourable to its exercise and development. We also need to have some understanding about the limits within which individual members of homo sapiens can be expected to adapt.

By this definition adaptation occurs whenever reorganisation takes place, whenever procedural, technical or physical changes are introduced: when people are trained and retrained, transferred and promoted. Adaptation embraces changes in skills and knowledge, hours of work, work rate, physical effort, colleagues and supervisors. What happens at work may have an impact on domestic and social life. The limits to adaptation, which vary from person to person, will depend on that person's own constitution, physical, emotional and intellectual, and on personal background and expectations.

Fortunately, many of these factors have become more clearly recognised in recent years, and have influenced the trends of modern personnel practices. Recruitment and selection, transfer and promotion, job and workplace design, all consider, or should consider, the adaptability of specific individuals or of people in general to learn and work in new situations. The objective is to keep the stress of change down to a level that the individual can deal with. A little stress, we are told, is good for one. Too much can be harmful to health and to confidence. Moreover the sheer efficiency of the work effort will drop if these points are not given proper attention.

Clearly the many factors involved in a study of adaptability, plus the consideration of individual differences, make it a complex subject. But three factors which are of exceptional importance are experience, learning and confidence. Those who work in constant circumstances, without changes or challenges, become less able (although not necessarily unable) to deal with change, when the demand is made of them. An active private life may easily compensate for unchanging routines at work. The experience of change, and of adaptation, make it easier next time.

Within the changed circumstances there can be demanding new things to be learned, either physical or intellectual. Learning these can be difficult, and can be believed to be impossible, if no comparable learning has taken place for some years. There is much evidence that the ability to learn will continue well into middle age, often beyond, although the requirements of the learner himself have changed from his school days, and the teaching and learning methods have to be made suitable. If they are not suitable the adult may fail: the adult seeks to understand his study, and not merely to commit it to memory. The pace and dialogue in the lesson must take account of this.

If it does not, then failure to understand and make progress will produce, or

51

confirm, lack of confidence. And lack of confidence will inhibit learning: the familiar downward spiral has started. Lack of confidence, however, does not start only in a lesson or training session. It can have its origins in generally pessimistic self perception; or in job insecurity, or in mistrust of management's intentions; or in poor relationships between employee and supervisor. Even the self-motivated professional is likely to slow up if he loses confidence in his management. But whereas he may be able to take initiative to put things right through interviews and discussion, perhaps by leaving the company, many people are not in a position to take such steps, particularly the older employee stuck in mid- and late career.

Given the importance of confidence it becomes clear that it requires serious attention. It is not produced simply by changing peoples' jobs, providing practice in adaptation, nor by sending people on courses which stretch them intellectually, although these two can produce increased self confidence. For most efficient adaptation the employee needs sufficient confidence in his management to make him willing to make the change. This type of confidence cannot be produced overnight by announcements and pledges of trust, if little existed before. It takes time and experience to create. The employees' day to day dealings with their supervisors, the discussions in in-company courses, seminars and meetings, the policies and actions of top management, all contribute to it. The training manager who can objectively see what is happening in this field in his company is in a position to bring about improvements to both company and individual advantage. He has under his control ways of improving mutual understanding and confidence and, ultimately, the capability of individuals to adapt. He can also help management to neither overestimate nor underestimate employee adaptability.

How can one set about putting this into action? Where can one look in the company, or on the training opportunity matrix? First, in general terms, it is reasonable to suppose that no-one should spend a year in a company without some mind-stretching and confidence-giving experience. At school bits of new information are presented to the student 20 or more times a day. In middle age, in a routine job, this may become 10 times a year, or less. A few days in a year learning, re thinking and enjoying, new and old ideas, closing the gap with management, is valuable. The exercise must have understandable and acceptable purpose, as must job rotation if that is introduced into the office or workshop, otherwise it may produce uncertainty as to mangement's intentions. The whole company, office by office, group by group, in time can be examind to see what state employment has reached. In many areas nothing has to be done: in others, something needs attention and actions can be devised.

There are other possibilities. Promotions and promotion routes sometimes bypass pockets of employees, who become virtually stagnant. These can be searched for, and the possibility of future vacancies inducing a sequence of moves in such pockets can be explored. Extra training and greater patience may be called for to get things moving. Care must be taken not to close career development routes reserved for special purpose. Every company has its blackspots, e.g. the group of office employees who were transferred away from computer work when the computer was installed, because they were the least suitable. Now everything is even more sophisticated, and their chances of transfer and promotion are virtually zero. When computerisation is made 100%, then these people will have great difficulty in adapting – no recent intellectual stretching, no career prospects, no self confidence. Such black spots, or potential black spots, should be searched for and dealt with, or, if possible, anticipated and avoided.

Promotions, of all job changes, require adaptability for success, particularly when someone goes into an entirely new level of responsibility. The changes of work environment, reporting and co-operative relationships, and decision-making, can be dramatic. Some will take it in their stride; others will find it a continuing strain. A periodic review of impending promotions and of the management and supervisory development schemes and memberships, are start points for action to improve adaptation, where such help is needed.

Promotions, of course, are notifiables, and the planning information available on promotions makes it possible to make progress in an area that is otherwise non-notifiable. Whether or not the individuals require help with adaptation needs then to be explored.

The organisation itself also has to be able to reorganise its functions, structures and the tasks and responsibilities of those who work in it. It has to adapt to changing trading, social and political circumstances, and to new initiatives taken by the directors of the company. How such adaptation may be in conflict or in harmony with the interests of the employees, and the need for reconciliation between corporate and individual interest may be approached, is touched on in Chapters 19 and 21 of this book, and dealt with extensively in other literature.

One other means of organisational adaptation is dealt with in Chapters 16 and 23 in the discussion of manpower development. At one time in recent industrial history, it was not unknown to adapt by fire-and-hire. When, for example, an aircraft company changed from welded tube construction to sheet metal mono-coque construction, the head of the design department said that the staff who could work in the new technology would stay, and those who could not would leave, and soon. The gaps would be made up by recruitment, and thus the design organisation would adapt to the new requirements. This is a somewhat Darwinian approach to adaptation. Today training and re-training would enter prominently into the plans to meet major corporate changes and the training function finds itself at the interface of individual and corporate interests, often dealing with anxious individuals and groups whose confidence has become fragile and needs to be strengthened.

8   An agent of change

It has become popular to refer to training as an agent of change, and our attention has been given already in this book to those situations which arise because of change. The training opportunity matrix shows the dependence of training on situations of change; and, conversely, the dependence of future efficiency on training in these situations.

We must not forget however that training does not serve only the purpose of change, for it is also the means of maintaining standards and of ensuring that those who are introduced for the first time to existing work and practices, are able to maintain those standards. In these instances of training for maintenance of standards, of new recruits, of transferees, one could not claim, with reference to the company, that training was the agent of change. Even so, with reference to the new recruit, for example, that particular person is experiencing a personal change process, and it would not be an empty claim that training can be seen as an agent of change for that person. Indeed, many people seek training of one sort or another in order to bring about change in their skills, their capability and their personal circumstances. It is the promise offered by training, to each and every individual, of change and improvement in career and fortune, which acts often as a stimulus to employees at all levels in an organisation and gives the human momentum to the plans on the training officer's drawing board. It is also responsible for many side effects amongst employees, again at all levels, to which we referred in the earlier chapter on Intentions and Objectives. Such is its potency. We shall refer to this human aspect of change from time to time, but now we return to the question of change in the organisation.

Training is associated with change in the organisation in certain distinct ways and we shall look briefly at each. The training manager, as well as line management, needs to understand how the *role* of training differs from one change situation to the next, and, accordingly, what to expect from the training service available. We have, in the training opportunity matrix (Figure 5.1), a number of headings in the left hand column indicating the sorts of things that can change, such as plant, procedures, relationships. We know that these actual changes are generated by mangement decisions, which in turn have been reached in view of the need to bring about growth or development of the enterprise, or to maintain equilibrium with the outside social and political world.

What we have not considered yet is the relationship between training and change, with training contributing to the inspiration for change and not merely to the implementation of change. On the one hand members of a company can learn new things from courses, reading, or television, which they then want to introduce into their company; this is inspiration. On the other hand, once the decision has been taken to introduce any particular change, then people require some form of retraining in order to make the change work; this is implementation. Inspiration and implementation as quoted here are an oversimplification of the real situations in day to day life. There are many other factors to be taken into account if one wishes to summarise both inspiration and implementation. For example, inspiration, related here to training, arises also from observation and thinking, from argument in meetings, from following another company's example. We are concerned with what arises in training circumstances, but without forgetting the wide range of origins of new ideas.

Nor must we forget that the study of new ideas – at the inspiration phase – can go hand in hand with the study of implementation, and that the result may be that the inspiration is modified by recognition of the needs of the system and the people involved in putting the new ideas to work. If the people involved are brought into the discussion at an early date, i.e. before any final decisions have been made, and if they express, with encouragement from their management, their views on processes and organisation, then we have some of the ingredients of organisational development. In this book we shall not deal with this subject, but it is worthwhile recognising where it lies relative to our own discussion on training. We shall, of course, cross into organisational development territory from time to time in this and following chapters. It cannot be regarded as a totally separate discipline from training. Many training managers and their staffs are as dedicated to organisational development as they are to 'classical' training, and it is right that they should be. But the skills of organisational development demand their own study and separate reading is recommended.

We shall look at the different forms of inspiration-through-training by means of examples and discuss some of the problems of implementation as appropriate, for some of these are the direct consequence of the mismanagement of inspiration and of creativity.

EXAMPLE 1

A company, employing some 2,000 people of whom 200 are in the executive and management classification, is doing reasonably well. Its trading is secure for at least five years, profit margins are improving, and the small amount of capital needed beyond that retained from profits presents no problem. At the most recent executive committee meeting it was agreed that the lack of organised training amongst executives was not to be ignored. Whilst there were no particular problems to be approached through the avenue of training, and consequently no identifiable training objectives to be referred to, it was thought that in these modern times there must be real virtue in making oneself familiar with up-to-date management and business techniques. Besides, 'we have an up-and-coming gene-ration of younger management to prepare for future responsibilities, some already on this committee, and they should be given every opportunity to learn'. In addition, 'Jones and Company, our strongest competitors, have apparently been sending people to business school regularly for three years now, as have the State bank'.

With nothing more than a feeling of uncertainty, confident nevertheless that no harm can come of the move, and that the cost can be comfortably met in these profitable times, the company decides on a programme of business course attend-ance for its middle executives. This is a case of keeping up with the Jones's, and is one example of training without explicit objective. There are implicit objectives, based on the notion that if a man is sent to a course which improves his manage-ment knowledge, then the company must benefit from this after his return. Nothing, as history has sometimes shown, need be further from the truth.

The story of what happens after return, or 're-entry', is now familiar to most managers and students of management, but it holds a few lessons for us to note. The returning manager, absent from the company for ten long weeks, comes back a changed man. This is the intention of the course organisers; they do not see any point in having course members shrug off the lessons learnt in classes and case studies. If this is going to happen, why bother to go on the course at all? The executive has therefore acquired not merely new knowledge, but, much more important, new outlook and attitude, as well as some ambition to implement the ideas which he has developed.

The company to which he returns, however, has not changed at all, and the evangelical fire which he shows is not at all appreciated. Nor is his language fully understood. He becomes indignant, disappointed, and sometimes deeply frus-trated. But he does not put his ideas to one side. Nor does he reconcile himself to the indifference shown by his colleagues and his seniors; he sees this as an indication of the ineptness of the company management, and not of their better judgement. So he leaves the company. Of the six men sent in two years to long courses, two left within a year of their return. The reason given was that they could not now see a future in the company. Of the other four, all of whom stayed in the company more or less indefinitely, the two most aggressive had to be bribed by accelerated promotion, the other two being reasonably content with their lot, despite disappointment which they express at the lack of recognition of their having attended such prestigious courses.

Certainly one can say that in this case training was an agent of change, but not a change to the advantage of that company. The whole question of inspiration, and the digestion of new ideas was, and often is, ignored. There were to be no problems of implementation in this case; the process did not get that far. But change there was, as there always will be if management plays with the catalytic power of training. It is worth noting that as far as middle management were concerned, these events did not in any way subtract from the growing popularity of external management and business courses. On the contrary, there developed a clamour in the company, many middle managers insisting that it was their turn to go. And this was understandable, for they saw the ten weeks' absence as a sort of holiday, and they had seen two of the returning students leave to go to better paid jobs elsewhere, and two more gain quick promotion. What better recommendation could there be?

It must be said that the company, like many others in a similar position after a false start, did rethink what it was doing, and then recast its strategy to build in much more explicit objectives, and arrangements for dealing with the returning men in order to reach these objectives. These are covered by the examples which follow.

EXAMPLE 2

This company, of similar size and structure, has a management which includes a few adventurous spirits who genuinely believe that, despite the success of the company to date, it is not satisfactory nowadays to depend solely on home-grown ideas of management and business methods. They can see no obvious weakness in the company's performance, technology or management, but they recognise that the world of business competition is changing fast, and that the company's ability to deal with these changes has not, as yet, been severely tested. 'The day will come' they say, 'when we shall wish that we were a bit better able to deal with changes, and that we knew rather more than merely what we do from day to day.' They decide to re-educate about 15 middle managers in key jobs, and in a range of functions. The object of this is to familiarise the men with modern management and supervisory thinking; to learn from them which ideas are worth pursuing in the company; and, after proper consideration by management, develop those which will bring benefit. Clearly this company is using training as an agent of change in an imaginative way. Unfortunately, it finds that the actual experiences it has to face are by no means easy to contend with, nor as beneficial as hoped, for despite some real progress. Let us see what happened.

The management decision was that, instead of sending one or two men at a time to business school, which would mean a total programme of about four years, they would invite a competent teaching consultancy to put on two crash courses, each of two weeks' duration, for seven and eight managers respectively, in a quiet hotel in the country. This approach was well thought out. To send one or two men at a time would mean that these men would have no one to talk confidently and constructively to on return, in the first instances. By the time the last men had been the first would have become disillusioned. In any case, they all work in different parts of the company, and it would not be reasonable to expect a natural and spontaneous rapport to be built up between them. The alternative of dealing with them collectively, forming a sort of club of newly educated men, was very attractive. It would generate team spirit and confidence, and no company can have too much of that.

In the event all of these things came to pass. The 'drenching' of middle management, i.e. training a significant number instead of merely one or two, produced the hoped-for team spirit. But the fact that the drenching was at the same time and place, meant that during the course they were able to examine many of the company's systems, standards and practices, in critical detail. This was, of course, planned openly into the programme, but the depth of conviction that changes should be made in the company, and the number of changes thought necessary, were way beyond the level expected. Moreover, the most significant changes asked for were not in the activities managed by those sent on the courses, but at a higher level of management.

Another innocent mistake made by the company's top managers was to regard the all important inspiration and implementation phases as being mainly the responsibility of the training officer. He was asked to collect the ideas from the course members in special follow-up meetings which he organised. This he did, and laid them on the desk of the assistant general manager, where they lay for two months. He complained about lack of action from time to time, but was then reminded that this was 'really a line management matter and not for the training officer to concern himself with'. The momentum was nearly lost. However, good thinking won in the end and it was decided that the consideration of new ideas at this level should be with *full* management involvement and responsibility right from the start, with the following guidelines:

1   Don't send a group of executives into re-education without first obtaining a sound understanding amongst senior management that it is their responsibility to deal with, to elicit and encourage, the new ideas that arise from the re-education.
2   Management must deal with this as an operational and developmental matter and not as a training matter. They should use normal communication channels as far as possible.
3   The training officer will be professionally interested in the outcome of the inspiration and implementation phases, for these are the management intentions beyond the actual training objectives, and he cannot evalute the training unless he has some information on both of these phases.

EXAMPLE 3

In the third company the management are aware of existing and potential weaknesses and requirements on which information and understanding could be gained by the appropriate executives through attending courses which deal with the relevant subjects. The company knows that the analysis of marketing data, the speed and quality of sales decision-making, and the development of new product lines, is not as satisfactory as it could be. They have been advised on this by a consultant. He is right; and he has offered to put in new systems, with hardware and software, and train everyone to undertake their new tasks and responsibilties.

Management are very cautious. They know that probably something like this has to be done, but they recognise that the changes are fundamental, that they will affect several functions and the relationships between them, and that they are in the hands of one man. They might approach a second consultant; and then be dependent on another man. They want to be their own masters, but they have not the knowledge, skill or experience to make fully confident decisions, and face the problems of change which the future will bring.

They decide to do a number of things to familiarise themselves in much greater depth with the steps which they may have to take, and with the possible consequences of those steps. All of this familiarisation is, of course, training action. They are setting out to learn and to understand things which they have to do as part of their managerial responsibility. Amongst the actions taken are, with distinct training significance:

Visiting other friendly companies with similar systems to discuss their effectiveness
Attending outside conferences and meetings in which this form of data processing is a main topic for discussion
Reading articles in technical and management journals
Sending the more senior executives of the marketing, production and computer departments to senior executive courses in well established business schools where they will learn about this type of package, and its impact on the enterprise as a whole. There they will be able to talk at great length with other course members about the experiences in their companies at the time of the installation of such new systems.

Thus the ability of management to improve its decisions about future change is enhanced by training.

In the above examples we can see certain factors, which must be taken into account, in the consideration of training as an agent in the inspiration of change. The most important are:

1   The degree of specificity in the objective

In example 1 we saw that there was no specific training objective that bore any relationship to company objectives. In such a situation neither trainee nor management can have much idea of what to expect or what to do to derive any real benefit from the training, unless they have been in this situation several times before and have developed means of minimising the frustration, which they have come to recognise and anticipate. In Example 3 we see that there is a very specific objective, and that the use of training can be purposeful and cohesive in the building up of ideas and decisions, well before any decisions of actual implementation are made. In Example 2 we see that despite there being a clear objective in terms of the need to explore new methods and provide for the future, there was an almost complete lack of specificity in the decision by senior management as to what subject matter should be studied.

2   The size and distribution of the training group

In Example 1, one man constitutes the group, and he is virtually lost when he returns to the company from his course. He is followed by another man, but not only is he lost, he makes no contact with the first man. One can envisage a company in which a number of people have undergone re-education but, because of the size of the organisation, and the blocks in the internal communications, they are not likely to talk with one another unless special provision is made for their meeting.

In the second example the group numbered 15, living together for two weeks at a time, and continuing to feel this closeness even after their return to work. The result is very highly energising.

Example 3 also had a lot of people in the group but, as far as the actual training experiences were concerned, the people were not together. But they were together when it came to their sitting round a table from time to time in the company to discuss views and conclusions on future possibilities and decisions. Again, in this example of selective drenching, the whole of the multifunctional group, on a selective basis, were exposed to the new education in some form or another, and the group size is such as to produce greater energy through the rapport and confidence so created.

As a general rule then, when considering the role of training in the inspiration phase of change, one would take these two factors into account in the following way:

> The more specific the objective of the re-education, given that it relates to the company's interests, the more chance there is of the identification of something which would be of use in the enterprise from which the person comes.
>
> The more people with common interests that there are in the group undergoing education, the greater the conviction and energy displayed afterwards, given that there is easy communication between them.

One man sent on a course with no significant briefing, and finding that the subject matter did not closely relate to his interests, is hardly likely to return in a creative frame of mind. A tightly knit working group given simultaneous re-education on topics relating to the development of their own work responsibilities are likely to develop an intensity in their arguments and ideas about what might be done to change and improve their own situation.

EXPOSURE TO DIVERSITY

This is not to say that new thinking only comes in accordance with the above trends. Ideas come to people in the most unpredictable situations and circumstances, although there is probably always an element of personal interest and of association, conscious or unconscious, as the new idea surfaces. There are methods, to be studied elsewhere, for generating free and imaginative thinking amongst members of organisations, such as brainstorming sessions. Strictly speaking these are not training activities, although in some organisations the training manager may find himself involved in their use or their administration. They do depend, on the whole, on the effect of the group on each and every member of the group, and vice versa, and this is no contradiction with the above. It would not be true to say that the objective is non-specific, for people are often briefed carefully on objective and role. The subject matter may jump around quite a lot, but it is likely to be kept by agreement within a certain area of importance and interest.

One knows, too, of individuals who have gone on their own, or who have been sent to courses without briefing or clear understanding as to the objective or content, and have come back inspired and able to bring about changes in a manner that was not contemplated at the time of their departure. These cases are relatively rare, and they are normally people who already carry responsibility, and have sufficient sense of purpose and initiative, to influence the company in which they work. For such people the exposure to the diversity of teaching and people is both stimulating and creative, and of value to the individual and the company in the subsequent inspiration of change.

But who are they? If they can be confidently identified, should the opportunity for broad and open-ended management education be confined to them alone? The answer may be yes when considering long and expensive courses for high flyers. It is no, in fact, when considering external courses in general; for no matter how carefully specified and selected a course may be it will contain a great deal of diversity in subject matter and people which can never be suppressed. Lectures and discussions, case studies and seminars, always display the imaginative, lateral, thinking to which we are all prone. To all of this, any course member is exposed. What he does with it may distinguish him from most of his fellows.

WHAT ABOUT THE REST!

This chapter has focused on the way in which training, when well managed, can be of advantage to the company, and to the advantage of the individual manager and executive. The illustrations are of managers and executives, being given special attention, placed in 'learning situations', and being listened to when they have a new idea. What about the rest of the company who don't go on special courses, who get on with their work and are not expected to have useful ideas? Have they nothing to offer?

Many readers will know of occasions on which a junior has had an idea about his work, or somebody else's work, which has been used by his managers. Is this sort of thing to be encouraged? Is it reasonable to see employees as contributors to new thinking? How does this affect their relationships with their supervisor and managers? What skills and styles are appropriate for management if they are to help to establish and sustain creative employee thinking? This is discussed later in Chapter 21, 'Continuous development'.

9 Implementation and change

When we discuss the implementation of what has been learnt through training, we are discussing something which lies beyond the immediate responsibilities of the training function, and beyond the objectives of the training manager, according to our own view of responsibilities and objectives as expressed in an earlier chapter. The implementation and use of new ideas and capabilities, as well as the expression of new attitudes, is, and must be, the concern and responsibility of the line manager whose employees are undergoing training. Nevertheless, the training function has a role to play at this point. The question of implementation is a very important one, and has to be given as much consideration as the training itself, particularly when training is one means of bringing about change in work, systems or organisation.

The training manager, we must remember, is providing a service to line and other functional management. Their requirement for the problems of maintenance or development of capability in their departments is the root of the work ultimately undertaken by the training function. The training function therefore, in a manner of speaking, takes from a department that human material, and that problem situation, on which it has to work. The work done by the training function takes the form of examination and analysis, of proposals for training action, and then assistance in actually setting up and running the training which has been agreed as necessary. The training function has already intervened in the work area which it is servicing. Any objection to further intervention after the completion of training cannot be based on the notion that what goes on inside a department is not the concern of the training manager; he has already demonstrated that it is, and acceptably so.

The intervention during the implementation phase is, of course, of a different nature from what was necessary before and during the actual training. The period of implementation is one in which employees are back at work and getting on with their jobs once more, subject now to no more than the normal supervision typical of their department. As they are no longer under training, what place has the training function beyond asking questions about the success and acceptability of the training now completed?

The actual decision in any organisation on what role the training function has in the implementation phase is a matter of local choice. There are distinct problems that may arise during implementation, particularly in change situations, and someone has to be competent in anticipating and advising on them. This person can be, and sometimes is, the training manager. Even if it is not, he needs to understand the principles and be in a position to adjust his training propositions and methods in order to ease the problems of implementation, and to give assistance on an informed basis to whoever is assuming responsibility.

The implementation of training in existing practices, and to existing standards, presents no social problems, and we shall not devote much time to it here. But it must be emphasised that it is a critical phase in the maintenance of efficiency, and in the development of the individual. The principal source of trouble in implementation arises in cases where the place of training is not the place of work, and when the instructors are not the actual supervisors. There are indeed other problems which arise at the time of implementation, but in many cases what is being experienced is the exposure of some skill which has not been properly attended to during the earlier training. A few examples will clarify these points.

If a newly appointed supervisor is trained in a thorough and systematic way by his own manager, and if this manager is accurate in his understanding of company rules and regulations, then that supervisor, trained on the job, will do each and every part of his newly learnt work in such a way as to produce only the minimum of problems and friction. Similarly, a machine operator, trained by his fully competent supervisor on the same machine as the one on which he is to work, implements what he learns, as he learns, to the correct standards, and all under the control and influence of that same supervisor for whom he is still to work when fully competent. There is very little room for misunderstanding in these cases. If the supervisors do not understand their plant operations properly, or are slack and inattentive in their instruction, there will be problems during implementation, i.e. undue scrap and wastage, and dissatisfaction expressed by the new recruit or the supervisor, but this is not because of implementation itself but bad training.

If on the other hand the machine operator or the supervisor is sent to a separate training workshop, and to outside courses, the chance of their being taught exactly what is practised in the company is lessened, and the reception which they get from their supervisors will perhaps be tinged with mistrust. This leads to problems of implementation of what has been learnt, as well as problems in relationships. One of the frequent characteristics of supervisors and managers is their inclination to mistrust, and perhaps to reject, what is taught their employees about their jobs by other people. Any expression of this mistrust produces a variety of problems at the implementation phase, even if what has been learnt is perfectly correct. This problem is largely removed if the managers and supervisors become familiar with the people who are giving the instruction, and can exert their proper authority on them when it comes to questions of what is taught. In other words if it can be shown that the outside teachers and instructors are providing a service of scope and to standards laid down by the managers and supervisors themselves. Training ventures can be weakened because of lack of understanding of this need for retention of power or involvement by management, and can be quickly strengthened when adjustments in relationships are made.

Implementation of things learnt through training which produce, or are the result of, changes to present practices, constitutes a challenge of a far greater size and complexity, and we shall examine the situations and problems in some detail. We shall see that the central problem of implementation arises from what we shall call Organisational Incompatibility (OI). We shall also see that, although much future OI can be anticipated, it must be regarded as impossible to anticipate *all* that will actually arise, and that a dynamic approach to change must be adopted, never assuming that the latest decision is the final and correct one, and being continuously on the alert for signs that the new system, process or organisation is not working properly. Moreover, it is important to recognise that this is a satisfactory and positive method for approaching and handling change; that the subsequent adjustments to be made to the original plan are not a sign of weakness, but of strength.

It may be imagined that once a decision is made to introduce a new practice, or a new organisation, or a new style of working, then the specialists and designers, the managers and the organisation experts, will sit down at their drawing boards and, armed with all the information they require, work out everything that needs to be done to have the company running efficiently in the shortest possible time. Indeed this attention will be given, and everything that looks as though it needs to be modified, developed, or scrapped, will be worked on. But a large organisation, with complex and fragmented departments, operating internally through a myriad of personal and impersonal interfaces, cannot be fully 'seen' by any one individual, or by any group of expert analysts and designers. If the management are lucky, what has been overlooked does not give rise to trouble; and management congratulates itself on getting it right and on its understanding of the company. It may well be wrong on both counts.

The training function may find itself committed to this sort of change situation. Sometimes the original inspiration has arisen as a result of the training and education of one or more executives; as a result the training manager may find himself regarded as one of the people who started the activity, and who from now on carries a continuing responsibility to help bring the new proposals to fruition. At other times the decision for change started, and perhaps finished, with discussions at the executive committee meetings, as a result of the purchase of a competitor. In this case the training manager may have to 'impose' himself on a management who believe that, with the new organisation and roles and responsibilities about to be circulated to the key persons concerned, there is nothing more to be done. 'It is all absolutely clear', says the Managing Director. 'If it doesn't go well, we shall see . . . and sort it out,' What he sees he is clear about; but there may be a lot or a little that he does not see. Other people, from the top to the bottom of the company, are not clear and it is they who have to make the new arrangements work, not just the managing director.

As we have said, the training function has no single specific relationship to change, either from company to company, or from development to development within the one company. So, although the training manager may assume an ongoing responsibility for providing a service during change processes, the opportunities will present themselves in a wide diversity of forms, and a variety of reactions from management when he expresses his interest. His acceptance into the inner thinking of management will be based, not on the so-called right of the training manager to be consulted, but on the practical common sense and value of what he has to say and offer.

The implementation of training, in change situations, may be on a variety of scales ranging from the individuals who are trained in order to improve their present effectiveness, to the wholesale introduction of new practices and standards. In the following cases we shall be able to examine the forms that OI can take, before drawing conclusions on what action might be taken to resolve incompatibilities.

The works manager of a company producing footwear was unhappy about the failure to produce significant cost savings in any of the 16 departments of the main factory. He was convinced that savings were there to be made, and that the foremen were the people to achieve them in terms of shop efficiency, scrap control, power consumption, and so on. Some 18 months before, he had introduced a cost-saving bonus scheme for foremen; if their shop costs were reduced by certain percentages, then they obtained a small but worthwhile bonus for themselves on an individual basis. He also had the cost accountant produce monthly summary sheets, shop by shop, showing the breakdown of costs and their variation in time.

After about eight months of the bonus scheme, he realised that there was no real improvement, and decided that his foremen needed a course to teach them more about costs, cost-structures and ways of reducing costs. So he selected two to go to a three-day residential course. They returned full of praise for the course, convinced that it would prove to be useful, i.e. that the implementation of what they had learnt must be advantageous. Others were sent over the remaining months. The total achievement in cost savings was virtually zero; in fact it was negative, if one takes into account the cost of course fees and expenses.

No wonder the works manager was unhappy; he had introduced two changes:

1   A new standard of cost reduction for the foremen
2   A new data presentation for their use; and he had provided the training he regarded as necessary for the foremen to reach the new performance levels.

What could have gone wrong? The solution came from the foremen themselves, who previously had not been consulted, but who now were asked for their views on the problem. They disclosed that:

1   The courses were indeed good. The practical steps suggested to course members, for reviewing costs in company departments, were simple and logical, *provided the foremen were given the data*. But
2   'The foremen in our company are not given the data', they said. They may go to the cost office and look at their own sheets, but they may not take them away or even take written notes, for fear of trade union members finding the data in the foreman's office during the lightly supervised nightshift. Therefore they could not undertake any serious cost reviews and comparisons of their own; most stopped going to the cost office altogether, as a result of frustration and a degree of humiliation which they suffered in the hands of the cost accountant, whom they didn't like.
3   The bonuses for cost reductions are on a scale of diminishing returns, and

those who were able to effect some early savings have now lost interest as they can get no more bonus.

4   The service departments, i.e. the toolroom, the millwrights and others, incur costs as the result of production departments calling for their help. It seemed patently unfair that the foremen of the service departments should be personally penalised when they responded to appeals for help from the company's production line.

Items 2—4 are all organisational constraints on the implementation of skills which the training had helped to provide.

So, on both major and minor counts, the implementation of the skills learnt ran up against organisational incompatibility. There were in existence systems and practices which actually placed a constraint on the foremen doing what was expected of them. It is correct to say that the incompatibilities and constraints existed irrespective of the training. This is not in any way a contradiction of our thesis; training only helps to equip or perfect a person or persons in those tasks which he has otherwise been instructed to do. The foremen were faced with these constraints before they went for more thorough training. Happily, it was the new knowledge which they gained which helped them to express the seriousness of the constraints which already existed.

In our second example we shall examine what happens when the organisational incompatibilities exist in roles, responsibilities and relationships, and not in procedures.

A company well established in the design, manufacture and marketing of medical equipment to a limited number of very large clients, suddenly found itself facing outside competition in products in which it had previously dominated the market. This, coupled with rising costs and smaller profit margins, caused the directors to reappraise their position and then search for steps which would keep the company's trading secure. They knew that this was no time for either massive capital investment in new production lines, or for the rapid development of interests in technical and commercial areas which, although perhaps profitable, were beyond the technological and marketing capability of their company. They had to find a way of doing better and more profitably those things at which they were already very skilled, and in which they had a wealth of experience.

The sales director had to agree with the technical director that the pattern of marketing, particularly the selling effort, was not suitable for the present purposes, i.e. the identification of new opportunities and the taking hold of these opportunities and turning them into hard cash. 'All our Sales management are able to do', it was said, 'is go round to our existing customers and confirm the repeat orders. New customers have always come to us, and we have told them whether or not we can supply, and when. All that is finished. We have got to go out and get business. And as there isn't enough business to satisfy all of the companies who make these products, we had better think fast about getting business in something else that we can supply . . . like technical know-how.'

In the discussion which raged for some hours it became recognised that, whatever was going to be sold, something would have to be done about the sales force. They were not aggressive enough; they were not really the right type. 'What we need', finally said the technical director, 'is more entrepreneurs.' A lot of heads nodded in agreement at that, for everyone is presumed to know, probably does know, that the entrepreneur is a person good at sniffing out commercial opportunities, losing no time in buying his way in, running them at a considerable profit, and not being dismayed at the prospect of losing money if his judgememt is bad. Nor, indeed, is he unduly upset as and when he does lose money: he will get it back next time. It was all summed up in the descriptive phrase 'an eye for the main chance, highly motivated, and willing to take risks'.

Within a few days the training manager was instructed to explore the possibilities of setting up training to improve the entrepreneurial qualities of the sales force, but to leave out those whom the sales manager regarded as being past it. The personnel manager was told to collaborate with the sales manager to ensure that all those recruited into the sales force from outside or inside the company were of entrepreneurial type. The stage was set.

Six months later the word 'entrepreneur' was dead in that company. Those who had been given training in negotiation and selling as entrepreneurs were very quick to point out that, unless the whole company were to change, their training could not be put into practice. When they explained to the sales director the basis of their concern he could only agree that the matter was much more complicated than had appeared at first sight, and that the whole question would have to be re-examined. Their explanation was as follows.

If they were expected to work from the sales branch offices as entrepreneurs, they would in the course of time see an opportunity for business which appealed to them strongly. After reasonable enquiry into the viability of the opportunity, they would then make a bid for the business. 'Whose money are we going to offer?' they asked the sales director. 'If it is company money,' they continued, 'as it would have to be, then we don't see you putting up capital without our planning department first of all thoroughly studying the prospects.' 'Nor do I', said the sales director. 'In which case, our entrepreneurial judgement is no more than a start point for normal business analysis. Even if you then agree, you aren't going to let us run the business. And we can't see you giving us a large share of the profit it makes. So, our judgement is second to yours. There is no risk for us, no quick financial gain, and no motivation.

Their judgement about the company was, of course, accurate; the incompatibility of roles and responsibilities was considerable. The directors were not prepared to surrender the decision-making on business developments to men in the field. The whole exercise was stopped; the term entrepreneur became a slight joke for a short time. But lessons had been learnt by all involved about the necessity of examining the organisational implications of even the most promising development proposition, before getting deeply involved; that organisational incompatibility can arise in the area of role and responsibility just as readily as in practices and procedures.

What can be done to ensure maximum possible success in implementation? There are a few principles, which will have become apparent from the preceding examples.

First   Any change which is under consideration by management for possible later implementation must be regarded as an event which needs managing, and not merely causing to happen.

Second   All changes which at first sight appear to be restricted to one location or system, have an impact to some extent on the surrounding organisation, systems and roles and relationships.

Third   Whilst many of these impacts may be without serious consequence, some will be important, and some even be revealed in the form of constraints on the change which the company is trying to make.

Fourth   Although close study and analysis of the whole enterprise may be made, management cannot presume to know all the consequences of the change they wish to introduce, particularly in the area of roles, responsibilities and relationships.

Fifth   Nor does the workforce know what the full consequence of future changes is going to be, whatever the extent of consultation before and during the introduction of the change.

The above five points having the appearance of little more than a series of warnings, we can now suggest some more positive steps that can be taken, and which should lie within the capability of the training function.

It is obvious that one has to search for more information on the details of systems and working relationships, as they are at the present and as they might become if the changes envisaged were implemented. One is also searching for knowledge of how people will react to the changes, and how their reaction will affect their motivation and collaboration. If their unique knowledge of their own work areas, and relationships, can be drawn on in order to improve the design of, say, a new administrative system, then there will be a technical advantage. If they themselves are in some authentic way involved in the examination of the proposals, then they can give their knowledge, have it acknowledged, see it embodied, take some pride in the result, and become so motivated as to want the new system to work. Assuming, of course, that they have no profound objection to it.

A simple formula for the introduction of changes therefore is as follows.

1   Information should be given to and dialogue exchanged with those who are directly and indirectly affected by the change, before the final plans are laid. This dialogue might be a simple conversation with several toolsetters to advise them that a new type of grindwheel is to be introduced next month for toolgrinding. A simple enough piece of information; but they suggest that the grinding machine might as well be moved to this end of the shop, and save them a long walk every time.

Or the dialogue may be in the form of educational seminars for various layers of management, supervision and technical specialists, on the work being done to integrate production planning and market forecasting into the one mathematical model, which, with the aid of the computer, will produce optimum production and sales targets. Everyone has a lot to learn before they can sensibly examine that aspect of the project with which they are most familiar; this learning requirement is looked after by the teaching elements in the seminars, on mathematics, economics and company models. Then they are able to argue with each other and with their managements so much the more effectively, and take in their stride anticipated problems of role and relationship. The designers, and senior management, will have probably learnt more from the seminar members than will the members themselves; and it is useful knowledge, to be embodied in the design of the systems and procedures which have to be provided, as well as indicating areas of sensitivity under the heading of organisation and relationships.

Such seminars, conducted in the atmosphere of creative learning typical of much good training, may be continued and modified as required to ensure a sufficient depth of understanding and rapport, both technical and human, as is required to ensure good total design.

2   All those who are directly or indirectly involved in the change to be either retrained in or informed about the new systems, tasks etc. once they have been finalised, when they are introduced. This is a straightforward piece of job training, but it must not be forgotten that not only has the content of each person's job changed, but also his relationships with surrounding functions, and this needs close attention. At this point it will be found that those under retraining, or being given information on the new arrangements, will have quite a lot to say, even if they have already been in the seminars in item 1 above. They should be listened to, both to help build up their sense of commitment and also to learn if there are any things in the new system that look wrong.

3   Those who are involved in operating the new system should be asked their views on whether it is working well; and if not, why not. This is simple to do with our toolsetters, in the workshop itself, alongside the machine. But for the complex group of executives involved in the use of the new computer programmes, it would be necessary to get them together in order to get a satisfactory examination of attitudes and relationships, as well as to take many points of view into account should modifications be proposed. Clearly the meeting cannot be regarded as a mere training exercise, for it is an examination of operational efficiency; but the same free atmosphere of criticism and suggestion, without fear of reprimand, as was generated in the earlier seminars, is of great value, and the co-operation of the training manager might properly be sought in companies without a strong tradition for this type of meeting.

The methods provided by organisation development specialists are, by and large, a refinement of the steps described above, using often a closer view of the organisation than has been suggested here to determine at what points precisely employee involvement should be invoked and by what method. The end object is the same in that by drawing on the knowledge of the actual situation, which employees (at any level) possess, and testing out ideas of change with them before final decisions are made, the quality of the decision is improved and the motivation of all concerned can be enhanced.

In a later chapter, 'Corporate change', we shall extend the use of this simple formula to the introduction of company-wide changes which are based on existing practices and principles, and changes which require new ways of thinking, new attitudes, new values.

10 The evaluation of training

There are a number of expressions used to describe steps taken by management and by training officers at the conclusion of training, and during the days or weeks afterwards. These expressions include validation; evaluation; follow-up and implementation, as well as cost benefit, which has appeared in more recent years. We are interested in all of these and have already tackled one of them, implementation, and we start by giving our definitions in order to establish a clearer picture of what each is, and how they relate to each other.

Validation is establishing that what you set out to do, you have actually done. Thus the validation that is concerned with training means that, when the training is finished, someone inspects the evidence available to see whether the right things have been taught, in the agreed manner and to agreed standards, and that the trainees have learnt to an expected level of proficiency. This is a normal management procedure relating, as one can quickly see, to a variety of services undertaken on behalf of a client or customer, as well as to the control of the activities and expenditure of any function inside a company. Generally speaking, if you undertake to deliver a certain product by a certain date, you check to see that it has been done. We shall not devote more time to this aspect of management, as it produces no undue problems, provided a system *is* established to check and validate.

Evaluation of training, or, indeed, of anything, consists simply of putting a value to it. The person who undertakes to validate is not immediately concerned with saying whether he likes the thing he is validating, or whether any benefit arises from it, or whether it was the right thing to have done. He is concerned simply with saying whether or not it happened. But to evaluate training means undertaking a search for the effect that it has had on the people and the situations which it influences, and then trying to measure or estimate whether this is advantageous or disadvantageous. We shall devote this chapter to examining how evaluation of training can be approached. One of the values that one can attach to training and to its effect is money value, and in the chapter on Cost benefit analysis we shall discuss the ways in which the costs of training and the financial benefits which follow from training can be assessed.

Follow-up is an expression which has acquired a variety of meanings, but as some of these have now been allocated to the expressions defined above we can give to follow-up a definition which is used already by some and is of particular pertinence to training. It is an action of a further training nature, taken in order to reinforce learning. If someone attends a course on finance, and then, on return to home or the office, undertakes further reading, or programmed instruction, or visits his accounts department for discussion on points which he met in his course, this constitutes follow-up. The importance of follow-up in all learning has been stressed by educational psychologists during the last 25 years: learning to any level of proficiency is dependent on the repetition of what has to be mastered. The first lesson is rarely enough, although our educational systems appear to assume that it is.

Follow-up, and the consequent reinforcement, sometimes occurs naturally or spontaneously; and sometimes it has to be organised. An employee taught to fill in the ledgers will be slow, even though reasonably accurate, after initial training. There is no need to arrange further special training to increase speed and accuracy, for the work itself will provide this. On the other hand, an engineer who is taught discounted cash flow techniques, which he might use in the calculations of return on capital invested in new projects, has no such natural opportunity to reinforce his skill. He does this type of calculation rarely, and when the next opportunity occurs he has lost touch, lost interest perhaps, in applying the skill which he had developed to a low level whilst on the course some months before.

The role of the training function with respect to follow-up is to assess the extent to which the new ideas, skills, motivations, will get a natural opportunity for exercise and reinforcement; and, having done this, to recommend steps which have to be specially organised to make good any serious lack in natural opportunity. This tends to be one of the overlooked responsibilities of the training manager. He, himself, together with his training officers, may omit to conduct even the briefest examination of the follow-up/reinforcement requirements of the training in hand, and may regard the completion of a course or programme as the end of his obligation, apart from conducting some form of evaluation. This attitude indicates perhaps an insufficient understanding of learning processes, and one has to be thankful that the natural interest and energy of motivated trainees will often see them taking personal reinforcement actions without waiting for initiative to be shown by others.

With the above distinctions in mind let us now look at the question of how to evaluate training. In the chapter on intentions and objectives we saw how the activity of training, i.e. the organisation and conduct of the teaching/learning processes, can be regarded as a point on a longer chain of intentions. It is this chain that justifies carrying out the actual training, for training is not self-justifying, and it is therefore into the chain of intentions that we have to look when we are seeking a full evaluation. This, of course, will not be simply an evaluation of the training process, but will be an evaluation of the whole process of maintenance or change or development within which training has a part to play. We shall see that at the level of pure training there is an evaluation to be made, but that the principal evaluations are at a higher level in the chain. We shall start with an example.

Some years ago one of the largest of marketing companies decided to look carefully at the practice of windscreen cleaning on the filling station forecourt, at that time popular amongst the oil companies. It was believed to be desirable, and ultimately profitable, for forecourt attendants to wash and wipe the windscreens of cars drawn up at the pumps waiting for service. The atmosphere of inter-company competition had forced management to seek every way of attracting and holding custom, and this was reckoned to be one way of doing it. However, in this company a doubt existed about the pay-off from windscreen wiping and led to an examination of its real value. The company had several thousand filling stations and of these some 200, known to be co-operative and competent, were selected to try out this new practice. The forecourt attendants were given appropriate training in how to approach the customer and in a quick and effective method of cleaning the windscreen. The filling station managers were also given some training in the supervision of the forecourt attendants, and what to do on a forecourt when cleaning windscreens holds up the progress of queues of impatient motorists.

The stage was set, and the new practice was launched. Some months later it was possible to compare the sales of gasoline of these filling stations with those of other comparable stations at which no windscreen cleaning had been introduced. The evidence was that the selected 200 stations were no better and no worse than the rest. The practice was abandoned, and the management was pleased to know that it had avoided unnecessary expense and disillusionment at a later date.

This perhaps untypical sequence of events provides us with a useful illustration within which we can identify certain principal features. First the chain of intentions is clear at the outset:

1 The forecourt attendants were to receive training to a defined level of competence.
2 They were then to apply their new capability correctly during the service which they gave to motorists.
3 The motorists would respond to this with a reaction of pleasure; and would tend to use that particular station rather more, thus increasing the amount of gasoline sold.
4 The increased sales, and negligible increased costs, would improve the revenue and the profits.

Second, the validation, which can best be seen against the steps above:

1 The attendants did receive their training and it was to the performance level required.
2 The attendants did clean the windscreens according to the standards laid down.

So far so good.

3 The motorists *may* have responded with pleasure; but no serious appraisal of response was undertaken. They did not, on the whole, buy more petrol at those stations.

4   Sales did not improve, nor did revenue.

The last two intentions have not been achieved, have not been validated, or, in common sense language, it is not a valid assumption that windscreen washing will increase sales.

Note that the 'failure' of the total exercise does not mean that the training itself was a failure. In fact, the training manager completely met *his* objectives, in producing, at the end of the training, competent attendants. If one wishes to evaluate the training, one has to take the data used to validate the assumption about sales increases and see whether it justifies the training. So one expects to find that data used for validation at a particular point in the hierarchy is used for evaluation at a point lower down the hierarchy. This might possibly lead to confusion on whether one was concerned with validation or evaluation, but it is a somewhat academic issue.

It must be clear that the major and important evaluation in this example is one relating to the achievement of raised sales figures. But what is one evaluating in this case? It would be foolish to suggest that it is an evaluation of mere training, for what was being tested was the practice of washing windscreens. The training was no more than a means of enabling the attendants to do the washing correctly. If the scheme had worked, no one would have said, 'Our profits have gone up because of training'. That would be missing the real point. What they would have said was, 'Our profits have gone up because of windscreen washing'.

The washing is the new technology, and the training is the means, or one means, of introducing it. Sometimes organised training may not be necessary. It is virtually impossible to separate the training from the technology if one is attempting to allocate attributes. The major evaluation, of the type described above, should not be regarded as an evaluation of training, but as an evaluation of the new technology. This has to be done, and often the training function finds itself involved. It must be careful not to lose sight of the real nature of such an evaluation.

In this case, and in other comparable cases in which organised training is used to assist with the introduction of a new technology, the contribution the training uniquely offers, in measurable terms, is to be seen by envisaging what would happen if the technology were to be introduced *without* organised training. Maybe it is calculable that only half the benefit would then accrue. Or, to take an example, this could mean that by introducing new organised training in existing methods for routing clerks in transport depots we save an *extra* £20,000 a year. Training might be assumed to be therefore worth £20,000 p.a., but this is not the full statement. It should read, 'training in this particular transport technology saves £20,000 a year'. This confirms the indivisibility of training from the technology being taught; it is particularly important in cost/benefit studies and we shall return to this point in the next chapter.

SOME PRACTICAL CONSIDERATIONS

The training manager may read the above and ask himself the question 'Why should I be concerned with the range of evaluations implied by the paragraphs above? Is it not sufficient to confine my attention to course content and the maintenance of standards of training?' The answer must be that, given that training serves some client's objective, at least the training function must examine the whole process of implementation through to the end in order to ensure the full relevance of the training to the ultimate requirement. This is only one step from a major evaluation. However, it is a step which is often difficult to take. What are the difficulties?

In the forecourt example, in which management displayed a rare scientific flair, the whole situation, with another management, might have been different. We might have seen the sales manager deciding right at the start that this new forecourt practice was unquestionably beneficial, and moving straight into large scale programmes of training and implementation. We might have then seen, some months later, anxiety when sales had not appreciably improved, followed by an instruction to adjust and improve the training. We would have seen, in fact, sales management and training management playing their hunches endlessly without stepping back to ask the question 'Is it worth it?' – the question which underlies most major evaluations.

Some managers and executives in industry and commerce are allowed, others are even expected, to play their hunches. Entrepreneurs are admired for it to some extent, and others, recruiters, advertisers and planners, do it because their activities include an ingredient of vision and of acts of faith. Frequently training officers operate in this way. They have licence to design and run programmes because it is believed that they will be beneficial. Surprisingly, the success or failure of the training is not often systematically examined and evaluated, despite the dogma which one encounters in most organisations emphasising the import-ance of the firm establishment of needs and objectives. It is important to under-stand why this is so often the case.

First, why studies are often difficult to conduct. The difficulties may be concep-tual, in that it seems impossible even to define the factors and relationships which should be measured or assessed; or they may be practical, in that although one can say what it is that needs to be measured, the sheer collection or analysis of the data is too forbidding. In the forecourt case above the essential factors are almost self-evident, and the measurements and analysis necessary for evaluation are easy and almost routine. There is also, conceptually, a direct relationship between skills, performance, throughput and profit. On a continuous process plant no such simple direct relationship exists, and it is much more difficult to see *how to analyse* the data on throughput and costs which is usually readily available. Thus we have a conceptual problem.

Second, people are generally reluctant to question their own convictions. It is characteristic of the average man that on reaching a conclusion about future actions, whether by flash of intuition, or after some careful thought, he will take that action with little or no consideration of how he can systematically test his earlier decision or the actual success of the action. In everyday life the man in the street has quite a lot of feedback in his minute-to-minute or day-to-day personal activities, and he is able to adjust his actions if things appear to be going wrong. Hence, with luck, he avoids injury or disaster. But, if the decisions he makes are in connection with a much longer term and more complex set of actions, many of which may not be actually within his own field of vision, he is not naturally well equipped to inform and adapt himself.

Hence in business we have to develop management information and control systems, to enable us to know whether we are still going in the direction we set out in, and whether that direction remains profitable. Testing, questioning and evaluating one's own convictions is, therefore, a rare characteristic in man, although, it must be added, doubting *other* people's convictions is not.

Third, a profound obstacle to systematic examination and evaluation lies in the inhibiting effect of authority. In the army a man follows the instructions of his superior officer. In modern industry, no matter how democratised it may have become, there are strong hierarchical influences which persuade most people, including training officers, not to overdo their arguments with their superiors, and not to devise an examination of results which could show those superiors, who asked for the actions to be taken, to be wrong.

These three factors compound to maintain in most companies the atmosphere and tradition in which a somewhat non-critical and non-analytical approach to the consequences of training is normal.

11 Costs and benefits

All costing and accounting involves problems and arbitrariness, whether it is in connection with training or any other activity in the company. So one must not hope for formulae which will resolve all difficulties when it comes to ascribing costs to training activities and putting numbers against the benefits. What one must do in each case that requires analysis is get a thorough understanding of everything that is going on in the training, in the technology, and the improvements that are brought about by both, as well as of the cost and financial elements which have to enter into the calculations. We must remember, for example, that although terms such as marginal cost, incremental cost, fixed cost, and so on, all have generally accepted definitions, what constitutes a marginal cost in one calculation for one particular purpose, may be regarded correctly as a fixed cost in another calculation for a totally different purpose. How you compute and regard the costs and the various cost elements depends very much on what you are trying to achieve. So the questions might always be asked, as examples, 'What is this marginal cost marginal to?' or 'Relative to what is this cost fixed?'

The main rule must be that one understands the physical and organisational processes and activities. One cannot deal with numbers alone, nor can one simply ask the accountant for *the* fixed cost or for *the* opportunity cost. Fortunately our approach to processes and organisation through the chain of intentions enables us to build up just the sort of process/organisation/cost picture that is needed, as well as an understanding of where the benefits are intended to arise. We must also be on the look-out for the occurrence of side effects, for they, too, must be included in the total equation.

All of this is no more than good but conventional accountancy practice with which the reader will already be familiar. In our examination of several cases later we shall be able to illustrate some of the more typical situations and approaches to their analysis. There is, however, a further matter with which we have to deal, other than the mere sorting out of process and organisational complexities and the allocation of costs to this or that, with which the accountant is familiar already. It is the question of human behaviour and human values.

One could say that training and cost/benefit studies fall into one of two distinct classes. The first is where the implementation is no more and no less than putting industrial process into action, as a system or a machine. The benefit of training the lathe operator to work fast and accurately is to be measured in terms of machine output; the benefit of training the maintenance fitter is savings in lost machine hours; the benefit of training the systems analyst is quick and profitable management decisions. Although there are people in these situations, working the machines and operating the systems, it is machine and system output that is measured and evaluated. The man is, ultimately, subordinate to the machine, and his identity is lost in the numbers.

The second class is where human experience and reaction is the object of the exercise, and in which the impact of this on performance back on the job is secondary to the contribution the training helps to make to the quality of industrial life. This is a contentious area; some managers would say, no doubt, that all training and education provided by the company should be so designed as to enable people's work and motivation to improve. However, whilst this is undoubtedly a proper company objective, the question of quality of life is important and demands attention for its own sake. That is to say, the company runs not only a financial balance sheet and accounts, but also a human account in which things are done for the benefit of the employee simply because people matter as much as money.

This is an extreme viewpoint to which many company managements would give some lip service, but would do little more than they were forced to do by law or by employee pressure. But the fact is there are often measurable benefits to be gained, in output and financial terms if one attends to the question of quality of industrial life. So we find managements backing training in this sector because of the material outcome.

Even more confusing is the fact that between these two classes, of machine output and human values, is a great area of mixture of the two. They cannot be separated, no matter what the objective of any training, in full company terms. The lathe operator, referred to above, has his own human experience and reaction during and after his training. If these are unpleasant he may not work so well; he may leave. If he does not like his rate of pay he may go slow. So preventive measures have to be taken to avoid displeasure in the trainee; and positive steps taken to build up incentive and motivation. The quality factors are there, given deliberate attention by organisers of both the training and the work, and often much appreciated by the employees.

The cultivation of interest, knowledge, motivation, creativity and, last but not least, loyalty, has become one of the preoccupations of management, and training functions often find themselves carrying a considerable responsibility for giving assistance in this cultivation.

THE COSTS

How do costs arise in the first place? We shall approach this generally to start with, and list the principal cost elements.

Three main headings under which, for initial convenience, costs may be seen to fall are:

1   Establishment costs
2   Marginal expenditure
3   Interference costs

and we define them as follows.

1   Establishment costs

These are the costs of the training organisation within the company and, typically, comprise such elements as

(a) the salaries, insurance, pension contributions and all other benefits given by the company to the members of that unit

(b) the cost of the space occupied and services used by the organisation, in terms of rent, rates, power, maintenance, cleaning, furniture and equipment etc.
These costs may include elements arising from the expenditure of cash by other functions in the company, e.g. the office services function may actually pay and supervise the cleaners, but will charge or allocate to each client function a reasonable proportion of its own costs – as will the canteen and the medical functions.

(c) the support costs allocated to the training function (as to other functions) – the cost of 'supporting' other functions which are declared as 'non-earning' although essential. For example, the board of directors, with its secretariat, has to be paid for. It does not produce goods and services in the normal commercial sense and it *may* be the decision of the management that its costs are to be distributed between the various 'earning' functions of the company and passed on to their clients or customers in turn.

The training function will report to someone: say, to the administration manager who has a personal assistant, a secretary and two clerks. These all have to be accounted for, and a part of their cost, it may be decided, is to be allocated to the training function, as well as to recruitment, industrial relations and others under the control of the administration manager.

Finally, who constitutes the training establishment? They are all the people who are employed to work under the training manager on a regular basis, and who come on his budget, i.e. the training officers, instructors, the secretarial staff and the clerical staff.

In a small company there may be only one training officer (perhaps doubling up as recruitment officer), sharing a secretary with other executives; and in the large company there may be, for example, a training manager, three training officers, a full time secretary and a full time clerk, plus two other people allocated full time to act as instructors to apprentices and induction courses. In this, and larger training units, the training manager himself may be regarded as presenting a 'support cost', an overhead to be carried by his training officers and instructors, partially or totally, depending on how much he 'earns' as a training specialist.

The 'space and service' costs to be carried by the above will relate to their offices, lecture rooms, training workshops and any other places in the company allocated permanently to the training unit.

2 Marginal expenditure

By this we mean the additional money which has to be spent, in addition to establishment costs, in order to carry out any one training activity. Although these monies may be lumped in with establishment costs for annual budgeting purposes, they need to be separated for cost/benefit purposes. The more typical instances are:

(a) External course fees, for those who are to attend courses outside the company. These fees not only vary widely from one course to the next, but may provide a significant, large element in, for example, programmes for management training.

(b) Outside lecturers' fees and expenses. These are demanded by university staff, consultants etc., hired to make a presentation to an internally organised company course. They can vary a great deal, from the zero charge made by the director of a friendly company to many hundreds of pounds asked for by a consultant of world-wide reputation for a single appearance.

(c) Books, materials, equipment hire. Most courses require support beyond mere chalk and talk: the provision of appropriate specialist reading, of specially constructed models, of computer terminals and attendant technicians, or of a packaged computerised management game, constitute an expenditure which is often specific to that particular training activity.

(d) External accommodation costs. Frequently, today, companies run courses which demand an atmosphere removed from the hurly-burly of the office, and accommodation in the form of lecture rooms, and sometimes bedrooms and meals round the clock are sought from hotels or independent training centres. The cost, in total and per head, can be a significant element in the total account for any training activity.

(e) Personal expenditure. A person going on a course or training visit away from home, requires money to meet travel costs, accommodation, food, refreshment and entertainment, domestic disturbance and contingencies. Every company has to produce its rules, to contain and control the expenses arising from the above. They can be very high. An executive from Boston or from Kuwait on a course in Geneva needs to be financed well beyond the level of the mere course fee; a long absence from home may cause domestic expense which the company is prepared to pay for. Most course members, at any level, find themselves obliged to treat other course members, sometimes faculty members, to refreshments or a meal, and money has to be available for this.

Contingencies do occur, although they will be minimised by careful course planning and experience. To find that all members of your own course are expected, by tradition, to buy gifts for all other members, may be a shock for the course member as well as for the management who sent him there. As is the discovery that the cost of travel from, say, Paris to Lyons, to enable course members to study the industrial developments there, has to be met from the course member's pocket. Something extra has to be provided to meet unexpected expenses.

3   Interference costs

When anyone gives time and effort to training, and thus ceases to be occupied in his main task – which is other than training – there is an interference with the output with which he is primarily concerned. This interference with output or with normal work obviously has an associated cost. We must give close attention to this point, for it lends itself to a range of interpretations and to a great deal of misunderstanding. It can also be one of the larger elements to be included in some cost/benefit studies. To assist in our definitions we shall consider first several examples of interference.

Trevor Jones is employed as a glass blower, making highly priced table ware. The company decides that its representatives and salesmen should be given a two-day updating course, enabling them to understand better, amongst other things, the manufacture of current and future items of glassware, its economics and technical problems, and the pattern of optimum output from the works. Jones is to demonstrate manufacturing methods to the course and be available during the afternoon to enter into the classroom discussion concerning manufacturing economics and methods.

'But', says the work superintendent, 'what about output? We are in the middle of a production run that is selling well and a full day's loss is a lot of money down the drain. We can't make it up at any time either; we are all on overtime already.'

The interference cost is one man day's output reduced to terms of net profit lost. This is calculable and non-ambiguous.

In example two, in the same works, six months later, the same course is repeated for a different group of representatives. But this time it is decided that Trevor Jones should be replaced by the works superintendent who is still sufficiently skilled to demonstrate glass blowing, and better able to deal with discussion in the classroom. 'This time', says the sales manager, 'there will be no bleat about lost production, because the superintendent does not produce anything. His supervisory role can be interrupted for a day because he is available for any emergency that arises, and there are no administrative tasks which cannot be put off for a few hours.' There is no interference cost in this case, although there could be one if he were missing from his post more than that short time, and something went wrong that he was not able to deal with.

Our two examples have drawn a distinction between product output and supervisory output and we should add to these service output and design output as well as management output. The questions that have to be asked are:

1   When the man is missing, does the output stop, slow down or deteriorate – whether it is in goods, services, supervision or design?
2   If it does, can it be made up quickly by some acceptable arrangement?
3   What is the resulting loss and cost of the above?

We can see immediately that the arithmetic of product output calculations is much less troublesome than that of the others. A supervisor, manager, designer or director leaving his place of work for an hour, a half-day, a day, perhaps a week, to contribute to a training activity will certainly be hard put to give a money value to the loss of effort so arising, and on the ultimate impact on product output further down the line.

Moreover, there are some jobs, the senior designer's for example, which do not depend on the person's presence at his desk for their execution or inspiration. Many senior executives do, in fact, work round the clock, and do not begin their work simply as they arrive in the office. It is a continuous conscious and sub-conscious process. Going to, talking to, courses, may be as creatively fruitful as going to the office, over a limited time.

The assessment of interference costs is based on the principle of marginal costing. We are concerned with looking for the net change in output resulting from removing a person from his work for the period demanded by training. We must, of course, look beyond his immediate workplace – at potential loss of sales, at the interference with other intermediary functions in the organisation.

By the same token we can see that the interference cost is not that person's wage or salary over the time of involvement in training. Generally, the wage or salary is to be regarded as a fixed cost, whether the employee is at his workplace or giving instruction elsewhere for the afternoon to apprentices. The net value of the loss of output will have taken account of the continued payment of wage or salary during his absence from work. It is not uncommon, however, for the wage or salary to be entered into costings, and there are occasions when this is a reason-able procedure. We shall come on to this point in the next section.

Costing

Having now grouped the wide range of cost elements associated with a training activity, we must consider how the costing is to be done, how the total cost is to be computed. We must remember that the computation will take the form demanded by the objective of the computation. Computation may be for the purpose of producing a scale of charges for training people outside the company for commer-cial gain; or for determining inter-functional training charges inside the company; or for a radical cost/benefit analysis. All will differ in their composition. We are here concerned with the question of cost/benefit analysis and will restrict our costing discussion to that required for this one purpose. But as the computation of the benefits of the training may influence the costing process it is worthwhile delaying the consideration of final cost computation until we have covered the question of benefits, and then deal with the computation of both at the same time.

THE BENEFITS

In order to understand the complexities of estimating the value of benefits arising from training we refer once again to the chain of intentions which presents the picture of the interrelationship between the objectives of those functions involved in training, and in its implementation. We need to consider side effects of training action at the same time. The evaluation of the *benefit* of training cannot be

81

undertaken by restricting the study purely to those things within the limits of the functional responsibility of the training manager. The evaluation must extend throughout the chain of intentions as far as is considered necessary. That is to say that the analysis would stop at a point beyond which there is confidence that there would be no significant change in the result.

The analysis is an interfunctional one, and although it may be undertaken by the training manager, or by an accountant, it has to be based on data and viewpoints provided by the functions along that particular chain. We must remember, too, that the evaluation of the benefit of training is bound up with the evaluation of technology which forms the substance of the training, and we shall need to make some distinction between the two.

Some obstacles to analysis

There are a number of obstacles which the analyst has to deal with in the evaluation process, and which are sometimes difficult enough to put a stop to further cost/benefit study. The principal ones are:

(a) Uncertainty

When the outcome of training cannot be predicted in a satisfactorily deterministic manner, and there is uncertainty about the time and quantity of the benefit, there is a problem for the analyst to overcome. This uncertainty can exist even though those responsible for the technology and the training are psychologically confident of a favourable outcome. Clearly this is a problem for the analyst attempting to estimate benefits beforehand in order to justify *future* training. It can remain a problem *after* the training is done if the benefits are expected, but with uncertainty, over a considerable length of time.

There are techniques for coping with this type of statistical and probabilistic problem which lie outside the scope of this book; there are also methods of a rough and ready nature which will produce approximate answers indicating the 'order' of the benefit, which when compared with the cost, indicate the net value of the training-technology exercise.

(b) Data cost

To collect the data necessary for computation of benefit may sometimes be possible but, in practice, a lengthy and costly exercise. An evaluation will come to a halt when the analyst realises the cost and impracticability of collecting the actual full range of data needed. He may resort to sampling techniques or the analysis of opinions.

(c) Attributability

When training is followed by improvement in performance it is easy to attribute the improvement to the training itself and to the technological substance of the training. In some cases this may be so obvious as to be unquestionable. But the

82

classic Hawthorne case* must make everyone aware of the virtue of questioning the unquestionable, when human interest and motivation play a large part in performance. In some cases it may be openly recognised that training is not the only change factor operating on the people undergoing training, and that the resulting change of performance has a number of possible origins, all of which must be taken into account in the analysis.

Again, the statistician has techniques for dealing with this, but the cost of data collection and the probabilistic nature of some results of analysis may not satisfy management. The training manager needs to be fully aware of the question of attributability, and, even though unable sometimes to achieve an actual analysis, be in a position to consider and discuss the other possible causal factors, and the weight which should be given to them.

(d) Measurements before and after training

Obviously training which is undertaken in order to bring about an improvement in performance, be it of man, machine, unit, function, or company – or all of them – can only be fully evaluated, in terms of benefit, by comparing the 'after training' performance (human, mechanical or financial) with the 'before training' performance. Frequently, although this point is obvious, the realisation of the need for 'before training' data only occurs when the training is actually happening or is completed. The training manager with foresight will, of course, build his 'before training' data collection into his total training plan when this is necessary.

Now there are, broadly speaking, two types of data, of totally different nature and reliability. One type is of a mechanical/quantitative nature, and the other of a qualitative/human nature. The mechanical/quantitative data will include all financial information, production and consumption figures, materials, purchase, scrap rates and so on. Moreover, in most companies of more than the smallest size this data is on record. So, when the cost/benefit analyst says that he would like to see the scrap rates, or labour wastage rates, of the past two years, he may be able to lay his hands on them. Thus he has 'before training' data, useful in his analysis.

Unfortunately, this is not the case with qualitative/human data. It is often true that a departmental manager does not know how often, and how effectively, his subordinate manager counselled his employees during the past 12 months. He may *think* he knows, but there is no evidence, generally speaking, that this type of observation is ever made by departmental managers of their middle managers on a systematic basis. There is frequent evidence that they say that they know, but

---

*In 1926 a Harvard group started research in the Western Electric Company at Hawthorne, near Chicago, based on the hypothesis that 'given the proper economic incentives, productive efficiency is a direct and simple function of the relationship between objective working conditions (lighting, room temperature, humidity, length of working day, etc) and certain other objective factors in the constitution of the individual worker (health, physical stamina, blood pressure, etc).' In the first studies, increased lighting for the test group (all female) led to increased output for the test group *and* the control group. When the lighting was decreased for the test group, output again went up for both groups. In further studies, over five years, no matter when environmental changes were made in the test group room, production went up. Elaborate statistical analyses of output and so-called objective factors, such as fatigue, hours of work, and many more, showed not one significant correlation; nor did the girls themselves have any sensation of working faster. It seemed to be the case, however, that the interest that management was taking in them produced increasing friendliness and confidence, and this relieved the inhibiting nervous tensions under which they previously and typically worked.

that they are probably wrong. Such lack of real data, replaced by guesswork which can be totally wrong, produces a very great problem in the before–after comparison of human performance in areas of interviewing, counselling, collaborating, supervising, indeed in all aspects of individual and group performance. This is particularly important, whether the benefit analysis is rigorous or not, for, unfortunately, it is too often believed by employer and employee alike that, following training in some interesting and appealing aspect of human behaviour, there has been an effective adoption of the new concepts, at the work place. Each instance of behaviour which appears to derive from that concept is noted and regarded on its own as evidence of success. Similar instances may have occurred before the training, and were not noticed, but they are now prominent as a result of both manager and employee having become sensitised to that sort of behaviour.

12 Cost/benefit analysis

We shall now consider some cases of training activity and consequent *benefits* which illustrate the points so far raised. We shall also consider the *costs* of training, and attempt a cost/benefit comparison in each case. The way of entering the various cost elements will become clear as we work through the cases, as will be the identification of legitimate benefits.

CASE 1 – NEW PLANT COMMISSIONING

The Valley Group own and operate chemical and oil plant, and have an expansion and development programme which will lead to new plant commissionings on five sites during the next few years. At this moment attention is focused on the completion of plant construction and the manning and commissioning of the new plant at the Lowland site. This is a new location for the company, in the industrial area of a small but developing town from which it is intended that most of the new employees should come.

The Valley Group intend to provide management, supervisory and senior technical staff from its other centres, to be employed on the main process work, maintenance, services and accounting. Below senior operator level on process work, and below supervisory levels on maintenance work, local people will be recruited. It is very unlikely that more than a few locals will have had industrial experience of this type before, and, therefore, it is agreed a considerable amount of training will have to be provided for them.

During the period of commissioning of the plant the manpower referred to above will be reinforced by specialists from the contractors responsible for plant design and construction, and specialist technicians from the instrument and equipment companies. These will depart shortly after start-up of the plant, and the proving of the units for which they are responsible. The manpower will also be reinforced by 21 men from elsewhere in the Valley Group, experts in operations and commissioning, who will remain on site as long as thought necessary to get the whole plant processes and services running smoothly for the purpose of day-to-day operations.

Although no one in management has asked for a training cost/benefit study of the process and service operator training to be done, there is some dispute about this part of the total training; and the dispute is basically of a cost/benefit nature. The refinery manager wants to see the locally recruited process and service personnel brought into the company up to three months before starting of the plant; the process superintendent considers that about ten days before start up will be enough.

The refinery manager wins the day, partly by his seniority, and partly by his conviction that 'Although it will cost us more in the first instance to pay and train these new men, we will save far more than that in the long run. It is well worth the extra expense'.

How much more will they save in the long run? This is the question to which an answer has to be found, even if only an approximate answer. Let us first look at the cost, not of the total training, but of that additional training period of the newly recruited operators, of whom there are 52.

The additional period will be devoted to gaining a sound understanding of the processes, services and organisation of the total site: the physics and chemistry of the processes on which the operators are to be engaged; the specific plant and control systems which are to be operated; special dangers and emergency procedures; and the behaviour of the plant once it is operating. The refinery manager holds the opinion that this knowledge, essential for good operators, can only be given to them before commissioning. Any attempt to give such extensive theoretical instruction during or after commissioning will be frustrated by the continuing demands on the supervisors – who are to be the instructors – of the various problems of operations as they arise from day to day.

The analysis will, in its main components, look like this:

(i)	Cost of *additional* operator wages/insurance 52 men for an average of say 2 months	£120,000
(ii)	Cost of short familiarisation visits to comparable plant and to manufacturers, for the 15 most senior recruits	£4,000
(iii)	Cost of training equipment, models, materials	£4,500
(iv)	Cost of modifications/extension of additional rooms for training groups	£40,000
(v)	Cost of group training officer, and secretary, on site for additional 6 months	£15,000
	Total additional cost	£183,500

It is assumed that no other additional costs are incurred by increasing the length of time in training; for example, advancing the recruitment date of the operators does not materially increase the cost of recruitment.

(vi)	Benefit to process	
	Group profit on finished product from 24 hours (1 day) of output from Lowland site is	£70,000
	Number of days of shutdown estimated to be saved through reduced operator error in first 18 months, is 5 days	

	Hence net profit is 5 × £70,000	£350,000
(vii)	Benefit to plant	
	Reduction in plant repair/replacement costs in first 18 months, due to reduced human errors	£110,000
(viii)	Reduction in commissioning team costs through earlier withdrawal averaging 3 months (100 days) per man	
	Disturbance living and out-of-pocket costs per man average £50 per day for 21 men	
	Hence total cost is approximately 21 × 50 × 100	£105,000
	Total of the above benefits	£565,000

In the above it is clear that the costs can be listed in a relatively straightforward way; more details than the above can be added but without significantly altering the total cost figure. However, the estimate of benefit is far from being either simple or accurate. No one can accept the above benefit figures as being right or even reasonable in the form in which they are presented, without further explanation.

The items (vi) Benefit to process and (vii) Benefit to plant are based on the 'reasonable' assumption that a group of operators brought in for many weeks of mixed classroom and plant instruction, well thought out and well presented, with frequent checks on understanding and progress, will acquire operating skill more surely and more rapidly than those who are brought in at, or shortly after, the time of commissioning, and given instruction only when supervision and management have time to spare from the problems and occasional upsets of new plant. Training given in the pre-commissioning weeks enables operator and supervisor to establish rapport and working relationships of benefit to later organisation and work situations, for during this sort of training time is available.

Although the above may be agreed the questions remain – what then will be the *reduction* in human error and failing? What sort of upset and emergency situations are likely to be handled better? What plant and equipment are likely to be saved? And how many days of output do we save as a net result? The most convincing answer would come from a detailed study of a number of plant commissionings, in comparable local cultures, some with a long pre-commissioning training, and some with little or no pre-commissioning training. A comparison would be made of the difference in frequency of incident due to human failure, and the nature and cost of these incidents. From this analysis it would be possible to infer the *probabilities* of failure in the next commissioning with long or brief training, and assess the *likely* savings.

Such an analysis is unusual: and it is not our concern to persuade the reader that it should be done. What should be done is to determine the cost of shutdown, per day, per week, of any unit or group of units if they are integrated or interdependent. It is also important to know to what extent human error can produce a shutdown or human proficiency can help avoid a disaster should a process start to get out of hand.

This information will then be a basis of weighing the 'benefit' of process and plant against the 'cost' of extra training. In our example, given that the profit loss per day from a stoppage in total process output is correct at £70,000 per day, we have to pay attention to questions of technical detail – as will the refinery manager and process superintendent – on the minimum length of a shutdown. Some plant can totally stop and start within hours: some may take many days. The refinery manager is not likely to be over-concerned with the figure produced by the statistical analyst. He will be more concerned with ensuring that certain highly sensitive parts of the process and plant are kept running, knowing that a major failure of the furnaces, or the main compressor, might put the whole plant out of action for several weeks. The total cost of that would be half a million pounds. If a bit more money spent on well directed training can help diminish this risk, it is worth it.

Item (viii) Reduction in commissioning team costs means that the better trained operators, benefiting from the knowledge, rapport and more developed sense of responsibility acquired in the earlier training, are able to acquit themselves in this work better and sooner. This encourages the resident management and supervising groups towards taking over the reins themselves rather earlier from the specialist commissioners. Also through the actual greater capability of the whole employee force, there are perhaps fewer mechanical and process problems to be dealt with. The new recruits will have *proved* themselves to be a help rather than the burden that they would otherwise surely have been. The commissioning team can therefore leave earlier.

The question will be asked why not keep the commissioning team, perhaps in reduced numbers, permanently on the Lowland site? One could then reduce the number of local recruits, perhaps to zero; and problems of human capability and the cost of failure would be overcome. There are several answers which may apply in this sort of situation. First, the commissioners may be required for other work, for other commissionings, elsewhere. If they are left in Lowland they could not move on to the new Estuary site in the near future.

Second, there may be pressure from local government to maximise the employment of local people in all local factories. Companies such as Valley Group may be expected to minimise the importation of external skills, and to make every effort to train local people as fast as possible. This demands the presence of imported skill to provide instruction, and the removal of this skill when the local employees are equipped to take responsibility.

There are other reasons such as the lack of interest of the members of a commissioning team in living in Lowland, indefinitely away from home; and a further cost consideration is that an imported expert often (but not always) costs much more than a home grown local employee.

In summary, we can say that all aspects of cost assessment are, *conceptually,* within the grasp of management and analyst. They will know the cost elements that demand consideration, and the areas in which benefits lie, together with the associated financial figures. The computation of benefits, however, as either 'estimates' for the future, or 'actuals' of the past and present, is much more elusive. Data for estimating purposes is to be treated probabilistically and may be very hard to get in the first place; and, because no manager can say what particular losses his well trained staff have avoided, the computation of actual benefits also has to be treated probabilistically.

As a result one resorts to the comparison of the 'orders' of costs and benefits, and to assumptions as to whether it is 'reasonable' to expect losses to be avoided (i.e. benefits to occur) by the raising of personal capability. Thus conclusions of some validity and conviction may be reached by cost/benefit analysis, in situations of uncertainty, without incurring high data collection and analysis costs.

CASE 2 – FUEL ECONOMY

The National Power Company runs electricity generating stations all over the country. They are fuelled by oil or by gas, depending on their location. The central technical department have come to the conclusion that over the past five years there has been a decline in furnace efficiency that is not the result of faulty equipment, but a deterioration in the operating practices of furnace men and supervisors, which has become accepted by local power station managements. Operations department management agree with this without hesitation, and it is decided to look at alternative ways of quickly altering operating practices, in accordance with the long standing technical note TN 35 issued by the technical department to the operations department 12 years before and still, with recent amendments, totally relevant.

The simplest ways are discussed first: none seems to be satisfactory. To send a note to each power station manager would see the piece of paper put indefinitely into the pending tray in many cases: to visit each station might be more effective but it would take a very long time to complete the large number of visits and normal visits have little impact in any case. There might be an item on the agenda of the next quarterly meeting of power station managers, normally run by the operations department manager and attended by the technical department manager: the opportunity would be taken to discuss fuel economy and good operating practices. But that was done only 18 months before with little or no effect: there is obviously more than a little regional and personal stubbornness to be overcome whenever central management attempt to correct established practices in the power stations in the regions.

It is decided, nevertheless, to repeat the message on fuel economy and operating practices to the power station managers at this next meeting, and to issue a revised version of TN 35. There will also be an extended discussion of the economics of fuel utilisation; and there will be a full discussion of the retraining courses to be staged in the near future, and to be located at one of the power stations.

It is recognised that, although the power station managers may agree to the need to get fuel consumption down, a lasting change of practice in the furnaces cannot be expected without special action. During the past five years furnaceman labour wastage and replacement have led to about 40 per cent of all existing operators having been trained, by their supervisors and colleagues, in some malpractices. More than a brief re-instruction is needed to change this widespread pattern of inefficiency, and the new central courses, it is hoped, will provide interest and incentive as well as knowledge and skill.

In the course of the next meeting the discussion on fuel economy with the power station managers takes place and it is accepted by them that the courses should be held and should be attended by the senior furnacemen who carry supervisory responsibility. The managers themselves will advise their own superintendents of the plans and make sure that there is acceptance and understanding at this level of senior supervision in the power station. In order to make sure that the furnacemen, at junior level, understand the instructions and the reasons for them, the power station managers will each organise short courses of instruction and discussion for the furnacemen in their own power station: and if assistance is needed in giving technical information the central technical department will provide material, or send someone to contribute to the discussion. Following this retraining effort a report will be issued to the power station managers, detailing the actual progress made in fuel economy.

Within the following three months the whole exercise is completed and considerable economies achieved and, later, maintained. At first the reduction in fuel consumption was not as much as expected, for some of the equipment in the older power stations was faulty and needed attention. There was no question in anyone's mind of the favourable nature of the cost/benefit balance of the whole exercise, but it is worth while examining the main features, particularly because of the close integration of the training effort and the technology, and of the cost of training and the costs of the technologists.

The costs to be considered

1 The training officer's time

There is a full time central training manager and permanent staff of training officers, secretaries and clerks. One training officer has devoted the equivalent of six months' full time work to this exercise, with support from his colleagues, secretaries etc. as required. Hence Training officer cost, with full overheads as described in earlier sections, is £19,000.

Note that this is not a marginal cost, i.e. not the *extra* money to be paid for training services. It is based on *pro rata* allocation of the cost of running a central training department (for purposes such as this) in proportion to the time spent on this particular work. The marginal cost is zero.

2 Management and technologists' time

In the design of the central courses, and in instructing on them and in preparing their personal contributions, five managers and technologists were involved to varying extents, their time adding up to approximately 4 man months' total. The cost of this time, with full overhead, is £15,000.

Note that this is not a marginal cost – it is not extra money spent by the company, but an allocation of time and the corresponding salary and overheads to this particular exercise. The marginal cost is zero.

3 Interfererence costs

(a) There is no interference with the output of the power stations or with the cost of maintaining that output. Hence power station output interference cost is zero.

(b) There is interference with the output of both managers and technologists who might (in 'opportunity cost' terms) use that time more profitably on other work. However, both groups suggested that in view of the priority of this particular economy problem it was unnecessary to consider an alternative use of their time.

Hence, management/technologists interference cost is assumed zero.

4   Marginal expenditure

The extra cash needed to run these courses is as follows:

(a) Fuel consumed by stand-by furnaces used solely for the purpose of instruc-
tion/demonstration/practice   £9000

(b) Out of pocket, travel and accommodation expenses
of training officer, managers, technologists and trainees   £2000

(c) Printing of programmes, handouts, hire of films and other
equipment for instruction   £800

To compute the total cost we can include either
(i)   Only the marginal cost, as in Section 4, producing a figure of   £11,800
or
(ii) Add the marginal costs, the other allocated costs and interference costs, thus,

Total marginal cost	£11,800
Training officer allocation	£19,000
	£30,800
Management and technologists allocation	£15,000
	£45,800
Interference cost	zero
Grand total cost	£45,800

Which is the correct figure? In terms of the extra cash needed, it is the marginal cost
of £11,800. If one regards the annual costs of central training as having to be
justified by exercises such as this, then the allocation of the training officer service
costs is a reasonable addition, making £30,800.

Whether or not management and technologists' time given to this training exercise should be included in the training cost is not important. It does not represent
extra money spent: it is a measure of the time given to the courses. But, we must
remember, the time given to the courses is only a fraction of the total time given by
the management and the technologists to the question of fuel economies – in
meetings, writing technical notes, visits, investigation design work and so on. The
time put into the training exercise is given in order to make more effective the
impact of decisions reached in the rest of this time. From management's point of
view the two types of effort are indivisible. What is important is not so much to know
a so-called 'correct' total figure for the cost, but to know the elements, how they are
arrived at, and hence the meaning of the various totals that may be produced.

The benefits

These are, for the technologist, easy to estimate. If the furnaces run on correct fuel/
air ratios, and if the approved start up, shutdown and other procedures are
observed, then the consumption of each furnace is closely predictable. This may be
compared with present consumption figures, which are known and the difference is
the benefit in fuel oil saved, from which the annual cash saving may be worked out.
In addition, there will be some saving in furnace equipment maintenance and
replacement costs, more difficult to estimate and left out of our present totals:

Hence, estimated saving in fuel oils per annum   £450,000

This is, according to the technologists, a low but realistic figure, which could rise to £600,000 p.a. if high standards were rigorously and continuously observed in all the stations.

The cost/benefit equation

In this case we can see that after 'spending' between £11,800 and £30,800 on training, £450,000 per annum is to be saved. The training manager is delighted at the figures, for they seem overwhelmingly to justify the training exercise and the existence of the central training department. But is the benefit a *training* benefit? Is the analysis a cost/benefit analysis of training?

It is not exclusively either of these. The benefit is that of using the best technology – you need the technology in the first place, and you have to use it in the second place. Training helps in ensuring that it is used.

However, the size of the financial benefit has little to do with the training effort itself. The same training effort might be put into making sure that employees made proper use of the new cycle and car parking facilities – with a totally different, and financially much lower, benefit. The size and value of the benefit relates to the commercial and human nature of the objective, not to the quality of the training.

An astute training manager will, of course, be watching out for those opportunities for bringing training to bear on activities in the company which are commercially and financially most significant, and of most human value, in order to produce the greatest benefit. That is good training management, as distinct from good training.

CASE 3 – MANAGEMENT TRAINING

Continental Coast is a shipping company which boasts that it carries and delivers anything anywhere. With its head office, its sub-offices and agents world-wide, its wholly owned and chartered ships, it is a very considerable concern, although not amongst the largest in the country. Some directors and senior managers are worried that methods, organisation and ideas in the company seem to be unchanging over the years. There is little improvement to be seen in the quality of management decision. External circumstances force the company into difficulties from time to time, from which they are rescued by a more favourable turn in those circumstances. Is this good management or good luck?

Two schools of thought have developed. One comprises those who think that the company has a perfectly sound management, able to steer by experience and feel. The other comprises those who think that the company has moved into an era in which yesterday's management methods are no longer sufficient: should trading circumstances become less favourable the company will not be able to deal with its business, and, in any case, it will become steadily less effective and less competitive.

It is, nevertheless, agreed by the managing directors that action is to be taken to improve management capability, and, as a result, the quality of the systems, organisation and work of the company. Knowing that modern business courses and management courses contain a great deal of subject matter of relevance to the problems of all companies, and that it is possible to attend courses in which the teachers and the other course members, of comparable seniority and experience, provide continuous opportunity for comparing notes and learning about management problems and practical solutions, it is decided to invest in a large programme of management education.

This programme is to have the following short term objectives:

1   To enable managers to understand better current approaches to commercial, organisational and management problems.
2   To encourage managers to identify better those areas within Continental Coast which appear to lend themselves to improvement.

Following agreement between managers and directors on which areas of company are to be improved the next objective to be met by the training programme is

3   To enable managers to bring about in an efficient way those changes regarded as necessary.

At the moment of reaching the above decisions there is no clear idea of exactly what is ultimately going to be effected as the consequence of this hoped-for wave of new thinking. Each person has his own ideas on the possible outcome but, because of the interdependence of the functions of the company, no one idea, now or in the future, can be implemented without testing its effect on the working and economics of other surrounding functions. There will need to be a high degree of co-ordination and integration. It is agreed that such co-ordination and integration will be so much the less effective if only a small proportion of management understand the concepts, objectives and language arising from the new training programmes. The programmes have, therefore, to extend across the management and supervisory structure of the company *as far* as possible – not as little as possible.

At this point the questions of cost and benefit arise. The training manager has informed the recently formed steering committee that the course fees alone for a major business course of about ten weeks' length can be £5,000 – £6,000. Add to that the travel accommodation, and disturbance allowances, and the cost per head is then, say, typically £8,000 for the more prestigious courses. The plan emerging from the steering committee discussion is to send, over the next two to three years, a very senior manager from each function. This would mean sending some 30 men at a cost, in terms of cash expenditure (a marginal cost), of between £210,000 and £240,000. There also would have to be other in-house shorter programmes of teaching and seminars, yet to be discussed, but their cost would be negligible.

How can such a large expenditure be justified? One managing director has the answer. He says,

(a) Given that any system and organisation, subject to normal neglect over a period of years, will lend itself to improvement, we can therefore anticipate improvements in our own company provided we tackle the question seriously and with knowledge and energy.
(b) Some consultants consider that a company such as our own could save up to

93

20 per cent on costs and investments as a result of improved management decisions.

(c) We spend £150,000,000 a year on salaries, purchases, capital investment, repair and maintenance and equipment. If we save, not 20 but 1 per cent of this, through improved management decision, we shall save £1,500,000 per annum.

(d) To spend £105,000 – £120,000 per annum in order to help ensure that we can save £1,500,000 is a good use of our money. We have the cash and we should go ahead.

(e) We must make sure that the programmes of management training are drawn up and agreed in good time: that there is no undue interference with important work: that course attendance is maintained according to programme: *and that the ideas arising from all of this are exploited to the maximum* benefit of the company and the employees.

In this case, again, the *cost* of training is seen to be the easier of the two figures to estimate. We have not included the salaries of managers attending courses as these are not marginal costs. Nor have we allowed for interference costs resulting from their absence from work – there is to be sufficient temporary re-organisation to enable work to proceed smoothly, and no one will go away on a course if he is absolutely essential to the progress of some expensive project or negotiation at that moment.

The interesting feature of the benefit estimate is that it is not known exactly what changes and improvements will be achieved. It might be important to consider, in some comparable company situations, more detail of areas in which savings are to be brought about, for example, in chartering versus ownership of ships, frequency of overhauls, future bulk transport, supervision of construction, assessment of risk, and so on. But generally speaking in cases of management training where it is hoped the improvement will result in a new level for inspiration, collaboration and implementation, it is probably sufficient to estimate probable benefits on a percentage basis, as above. The future has a probabilistic, not a deterministic nature in such a case, and a study of frequencies and size of improvement against the size of training investment, would provide a quantitative basis for decision of a statistical nature. But no relevant data, beyond a few rough assertions and occasional business school papers, exist.

The feeling of taking a chance on this sort of training investment must be reduced by the decision to exploit the results of training, i.e. to take positive steps to enable and oblige managers to implement the improvements considered suitable for the company, in an integrated way. As in all cases, without implementation the benefit of the lessons and skills learnt in training may be zero; with implementation, organised in this case at a high level, the benefits can be great.

Finally, the question again of whether the benefit is a training benefit. The benefit arises from the application of a range of management technology to company problems and requirements. Training given through attendance at courses enables the managers to understand better this technology. The very large size of the benefit is because of the fact that these managers are responsible for *all* the money that the company sends, and *all* the money that the company receives. Hence the technology, and the application of that technology to rewarding areas, produce the benefit, with training as an agent in this process.

CASE 4 – THE LOST LEGION

For five years the Iqbal Trading Company has undergone a self-imposed reorganisation and management, executive and supervisory development. The results are encouraging from the point of view of those who have engineered the changes and those whose careers have advanced as a result of the changes. The trading position and the balance sheet also are witnesses to a 'better' company having been created.

One of the department heads, however, is not so happy. He approves of what *has* been done: but he is worried about what has *not* been done. There are 900 people in the main offices and operations: of these 180 are in management and supervision, and another 310 are in professional, technical and key posts. This 490 have received training, moves, counselling, as a result of the recent developments; many have benefited and a lot more can envisage benefits arising as a result of normal or accelerated career progression. That leaves 410 people in the company in middle and junior clerical, labour, and other unskilled occupations. None of these has derived any marked benefit from the recent developments.

This inequity, as the department head calls it, is made much less acceptable by the fact that the half of the company chosen for moves and development are regarded by the other half as privileged and earmarked for promotion. The under-privileged half are not only less likely to progress than before, they *know* they are less likely to progress.

There are, therefore, two issues demanding attention. Is is right to create an underprivileged group in this way? This is a moral or ethical question, and the answer varies from person to person, and culture to culture.

Second, what is the cost to the company of any frustrations and disaffection or incompetence in the underprivileged? This is a totally different question, not to be confused with the first, and a great deal of attention was given to it by training and personnel management, as well as by departmental management in Iqbal.

The observations made were that

(a) The population of 410 was made up of people of generally markedly lower educational and qualificational level than the rest of the company; without education and/or qualification employees were not considered for progress beyond certain low levels and grades of occupation.

(b) Of the total of 410, 170 were below the age of 40, the rest being up to 65 years of age. Those below 40 years of age were likely to be most ambitious.

(c) Amongst the 170, and also amongst the older men, there were known to be some particularly bright people as far as their work enabled them to demonstrate their brightness.

(d) There had been no significant increase in industrial disputes or in labour wastage, in this group during the past five years. The employment conditions and the pay were good, and on the whole people employed by the company were regarded as fortunate by outsiders.

(e) The elaborate methods of performance appraisal and succession planning etc. used for the management, executive and professional groups were not used for this population of employees.

The conclusions finally reached were that

1 It was not right, not acceptable to management, to make this sort of distinction between two populations of employees.
2 Although there was no cost (apparently) to the company at present, the differentiation now being made could not be regarded as the best foundation for the future of individual relations, motivation, and employee upgrading.
3 Steps must be taken to
    (a) Improve lower grade employees' educational levels and qualifications
    (b) Appraise employees' performance standards and potentials
    (c) Upgrade, promote or move employees to their, and the company's, advantage, where practical.

We shall examine these in turn with a view, first, to estimating the cost of actions to be taken.

Improving employee education

There could be no question of sending everyone to classes – most people would not accept in any case. It was decided to confirm and develop the existing further education scheme, which enabled any employee to receive advice, financial support and possible time-off for studies; and to arrange for all employees under the age of 40 to be interviewed for education counselling, unless they refused. Anyone over 40 years of age would also be counselled, on his own initiative. There was no compulsion to be counselled or educated, and all information would be in strict personal confidence.

The cost of this was feared initially to be high. The successful counselling of at least 100 people, perhaps as many as 200, with up to three interviews per person and some other enquiries also to be made about locating education opportunities, could not be taken on by the training or personnel departments without an increase in staff and facilities. The payment for, and administration of, the resulting education, attendance and study progress would demand a continuation of this extra effort.

Employee appraisal

For the 410 employees, the existing very simple annual reporting on work performance – demanding no more than a satisfactory/not satisfactory response from the foreman – has to be replaced by more elaborate appraisal paperwork and interviews on the shop floor, and recording and analysis in the personnel department. There need be no increase in strength at the foreman and supervisor level, for there are sufficient of them to take care of this work increase without too much difficulty. There will be no interference cost on the shop floor, for the small interruptions in work will be made up without cost.

In the personnel department, small in size, an extra half person will be needed at professional level during the first year of operation, when the teething troubles will be highest, and it is decided to increase the strength by one person with a view to reduction/reoganisation in 12 or 18 months, the rest of that person's effort going into administering upgrades and moves, as below.

Employee upgrades and moves

It is reckoned that something substantial must happen under this heading, if the scheme is to avoid disrepute. There will be a reluctance on the part of managers and supervisors to receive employees from the previously unfavoured grades of employees, and a certain amount of 'strong-arm' management backing must be brought to bear until the moves, in the course of time, prove themselves to be successful.

The total marginal cost is, therefore, estimated to be, during the first two years of the scheme, including only relevant overheads in the salaries for counselling:

	Per annum
1 training officer	£20,000
1 secretary/clerk	£9,500
Materials, phones etc.	£700
For course fees for, say 50 persons ‖ £70 per head	£3,505
For books, travel for 50 persons ‖ £70 per head	£3,500
For employee appraisal and movement: 1 personnel officer	£20,000
Materials, storage	£1,000
Total cost	£58,200

Estimate of benefit
1. Removal of inequity, addition to the quality of industrial life – no financial estimate.
2. Reduction of risk of industrial relations problems at some moment in the future – no financial estimate made, although an interruption through industrial action with 'through-put' amounting to a minimum of £3m per month, is a figure to bear in mind.
3. Reduction in labour wastage in the future. At present it stands at 11 per cent per annum in this employee group. It could rise to about the national average of 18 per cent per annum – an increase of 7 per cent per annum. It is calculated that recruitment and training costs, and cost of inefficiencies due to loss of labour and slowness of new labour, amount to no more than £400 per head. The maximum saving, in cash terms, is likely to be about £12,000 per annum of marginal cost.

We see, therefore, that the benefit estimate is a very untidy set of terms. One has to do with the quality of industrial life; the other two are probabilistic and are based on future events which may be considered no more than unduly pessimistic speculation.

Confronted with the cost figure of £58,200 p.a., the general manager approved the scheme and commented that the cost of improving the quality of industrial life of the 410 employees was rather less than the cost of providing motor cars for a much smaller group of top management. This was not spoken in jest. It is not an unusual way of obtaining a view of the cost of an activity, comparing it with the costs of other already accepted activities of the same nature and the same general purpose.

COST/BENEFIT – SOME CONCLUSION

We can now conclude with a few points which may be of help in approaching cost/benefit problems, and in deciding what should be included in the analyses.

1 Estimates versus actuals

It is not unusual to take estimating more seriously than the measurement of actual cost and actual benefit. If data collection is difficult, either because of the cost of collection or because of uncertainty as to the origin of benefits, i.e. to what extent they can be attributed to training, then it is understandable that post-training assessment of benefit may also have to remain in the form of an estimate, although with more substance that pre-training estimates.

It is nevertheless important to pursue the measurement of actuals particularly where benefits are concerned. The training manager should not find himself on his own in this for he shares the interest in benefit measurement with line management – on whose behalf the training is staged. But, as often as not, it is necessary before the training takes place to point to the need for the measurement of actuals, whilst interest and enthusiasm are high; and to set up simple systems for collecting both pre- and post-training data, if this is possible. Once the training has been completed busy line management and busy training management are inclined to shift their attentions to other work which is more pressing.

2 Short, medium and long term benefits

It is convenient at times to speak of a training action as providing short term, medium term or long term benefits, reflecting the length of time that one will have to wait in order to achieve implementation of new skills, knowledge and attitudes, and for consequent benefit to arise. In our examples in the preceding pages we see that the power station fuel economy training will produce benefits within a few days of the training taking place, and hence arise in the short term. The benefits, if they continue indefinitely, will then extend into the medium and long term.

In the new plant commissioning case the actual benefit of withdrawing the commissioning team early will not materialise until some months after the operator training and will extend over a period of several months more. The benefit arises in the medium term. The probabilistic benefit to process and plant will arise in the medium and the long term, i.e. indefinitely into the future.

In the management training case, the creation of a good working atmosphere and the development of new ideas and schemes will not be achieved in under two years and is, therefore, to be seen as a benefit arising in the medium term, and extending into the long term.

If we run an apprenticeship scheme of four years' programme length we may say that the 16–17 year old is 20–21 years old on graduation, but will not be really effective as a fully responsible skilled man until, say, the age of 26 or later. This is a ten-year wait; and the benefits, that is to say the principal benefits which correspond to the objectives of the scheme, arise in the long term.

Benefits, therefore, first arise in either the short, medium or long term: they may, and often do, continue for a further fixed or indefinite period into the future. This can have the effect of making the short term benefit look like a long term benefit. There is no need for misunderstanding, provided the terms are sufficiently well defined.

3   The hidden benefit

There is, however, another sense in which short, medium and long term training benefits are combined. If, for example, people are well trained with a view to benefits arising in the short term, rather more than these short term benefits may be achieved. The learning experience undergone produces some interest and personal satisfaction, which may remain with those people. It can provide a basis for future incentive, learning and responsibility in action. The training provided, in other words, does not merely produce a more efficient mechanical action: it also helps that person to grow and develop in knowledge and outlook and to become thereby better equipped to deal with such future new demands of learning and adaptation as may arise.

Whereas the planned short, medium and long term benefits lend themselves to some form of analysis and evaluation, the evaluation of a contribution to personal growth and development is much more difficult to undertake. One might approach the question in terms of orders of magnitude. One could say that if, for example the present throughput of a company, valued at £50,000,000 is to be increased, by virtue of product development, sales growth and associated reoganisations, by 25 per cent over the next five years, then this figure will be assured to some extent by having more educable and flexible management, executive and supervisory force. One could suppose that the result of the hidden benefit is to achieve the 25 per cent growth figure sooner or to reach 25 instead of 24 per cent. The latter difference of 1 per cent amounts to a benefit – a hidden benefit – of £500,000 throughput per annum. The figure is neither 'right' nor 'wrong', but on the assumption that throughput growth is sensitive to human capability and energy, it is a figure that gives some idea of the size of the benefit which may be obtainable.

The cost of getting this benefit is zero. We are speaking of the cost of producing growth and development continuously in employees by means of training actions. Each training action, a course, a seminar, is for some specific purpose – an openly declared purpose, such as fuel economy or plant commissioning – for which there is a separate cost/benefit account. Thus the cost of the training is already met and the hidden benefit is a sort of free bonus, but a very valuable one indeed.

4   Approximation methods

We have referrred several times to the questions of 'probability' (e.g. of a shutdown of new plant) and of 'order' (e.g. the value of annual throughput, and of a 1 per cent saving), and we suggest that there is considerable advantage in approaching some estimating of benefits in such a way as to make use of these concepts. This is particularly true when a thorough analytic approach is out of the question because of the cost of data or because of the difficulties of setting up the correct model of the actions and interactions which arise from training.

The training manager may be obliged to say, in such circumstances, 'Yes, it is impossible to estimate or monitor afterwards with conventional cost accounting techniques, exactly what the benefit is in financial terms; but it is possible to guess at the order of savings and benefits and at the probability of these occurring.' He must, of course, then get his information from the right source, from line management and from accounts management, and, as often as not, from other specialist services such as operational reserach, in order that the guesswork is informed.

5   The cost and benefit of the training function

It is sometimes the case that cost of the training function and of the time given by executives and supervisors in the line is looked at as a whole, with a view to determining, as far as possible, whether the company is spending about the right amount of money on training. It is also sometimes the case that attempts are made to produce inter-company comparisons of money spent on training. What should be the basis of such assessments?

Training costs should not be judged merely as a percentage of labour costs, or payroll, or administration costs but should be considered in the light of

1   The total value of processes and products.
2   The total value of plant, equipment etc. and
3   The extent to which the efficient management and handling of the above depends on human skill, knowledge and motivation.

Without taking the above into account, the training cost and intercompany cost comparisons may become meaningless. This does not mean that the bigger the values of 1 and 2 the bigger the training cost *must* be; it would mean that a higher training cost may be justifiable and can be regarded as essential expenditure, and not as extravagance – unless it is otherwise shown to be so.

The assessment of benefits must obviously contain training's contribution to the financial well-being of the company; it should also include the achievements in human development and in raising the quality of industrial life.

13 The use of objectives

TRAINING OBJECTIVES

It will be clear from the preceding chapters that objectives feature prominently in the management of training, and that objective setting and management by objectives must enter, implicitly or explicitly, into the calendar of activities of training managers.

The statement and agreement of training objectives can, and should, lead also to subsidiary statements necessary to successful later control and ultimate achievement of the objectives stated. Perhaps more than any other function training is a collaborative service: it does things for other functions, to suit the purpose of other functions, and does them with the other functions. Training which is not fully collaborative is likely to be sterile, ineffective: objectives which do not reflect active collaborative relationships are likely to be pipe-dreams.

So in drawing up training objectives there must be information on the following, either included or otherwise available.

1 The name of the responsible client and function
2 The present situation and need for training action
3 The training objectives
4 The training action proposed, with dates
5 The corporative objective, with dates for action
6 The estimated cost and benefits
7 Resources for training

We shall look briefly at these headings, taking a particular case as a means of providing illustrations. The case is that of fuel economy in Chapter 12. Reference to that chapter may be helpful for the reader, although it is hoped that the notes below will be sufficient in themselves for the present purpose.

1 Client and function

The manager, central operations department, and operations function. He agrees that the whole exercise of training in and implementation of good practices should be carried out and is asking for it to be done. He assumes the responsibility for it in terms of his power stations and the power station managers who report to him. (The manager of the central technical department might be considered as their client: he certainly is dedicated to fuel economy, but the managers of the power stations do not report to him.)

2 The present situation and need

The existence of inefficient practices in furnace operations now leads to a marked increase in fuel consumption at an unacceptable cost to the company. The need is to improve the understanding and application of proper practices amongst furnacemen, many of whom have habits of malpractice.

3 The training objective

To raise the understanding and practical skill of furnacemen at senior, middle and junior levels in all power stations to the standards defined or implied by technical note TN 35.

4 Training action

(a) Briefing of power station managers in the March monthly management meeting

(b) Run three two-day central courses for senior supervisory furnacemen during last week of March and April at West-Central Power Station

(c) Each power station to consolidate the teaching of the central courses by staging local courses for remaining furnacemen; to be completed by mid-May.

5 Corporate objectives and action

(a) Implement operating practice in all power stations according to TN 35. To be completed by end May.

(b) Achieve corresponding reduction in fuel consumption. Consumption returns to be examined by management meetings May–September.

(c) Achieve corresponding cost reduction. Cost saving to be presented to directors' quarterly meeting in September and December.

(d) Achieve savings in equipment maintenance and replacement costs. Chief engineer to advise directors' quarterly meetings during next 24 months.

6 Estimated costs and benefits

Cost	Marginal cash outlay	£11,800
	Interference cost	zero

Benefit   Minimum on fuel saving   £450,000 p.a.
             Maximum on fuel saving   £600,000 p.a.

7   Resources for training

(i)   (a)   Overall design and control: training officer A. Smith
      (b)   Contribution to central courses: managers/staff of technical and ope-
            rations departments
      (b)   Contribution to local courses: staff of technical and operations depart-
            ments, and local superintendents.
(ii) (a)   Cash for travel and out of pocket expenses: local budgets
      (b)   Cash for programmes, films: central training budget
      (c)   Fuel oil, and use of furnaces: manager, operations department.

Use of the objective statement

The statement of objective, plus the resource information shown in the above
example has a number of uses, mainly under the heading of management approval
and control. We can envisage, diagrammatically, the relations between the principal executives and managers involved, being as follows:

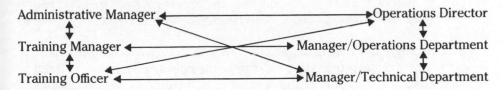

All of the people shown are concerned with the training and corporate objectives,
and it is important that there is a framework of common understanding between
them on the objectives, methods and resourcing of the whole exercise. The
objectives statement as suggested here can provide, in paper form, such a framework, and before any action is taken. We shall examine the advantages to each
member of this group using such a statement.

The training officer who is given the task of organising and progressing the
training along the lines indicated knows that he has little chance of success unless
there is full support from line management in operations and technical departments, and in the power stations themselves. Some training officers do try,
successfully, to gain understanding and support for themselves: some do depend
to some extent on their training manager, with his greater seniority in the organisation, to do this for them. The objectives statement provides the training officer
with a set of authorised and agreed targets which he cannot achieve on his own.
Each point can only be satisfactorily understood if it is seen as part of a total
pattern of actions to be taken, helping to achieve a clear objective.

The training officer may be the person who draws up the objective statement in
the first instance, for submission to his training manager. Alternatively, he may be
provided with the statement by his manager, following a higher level study and a
decision that he is the most suitable person to handle the exercise.

The training manager will not give approval for a new training activity to go

103

ahead until he is confident that all sections of the objective statement are completed, either totally, or to his satisfaction if not totally. The statement provides him with a basis for

(a) Approval for the actions to be taken by his training officer
(b) Confidence that it contributes to real and not hypothetical corporate objectives
(c) Confidence that line management are in a position to implement what is learnt from the training courses
(d) A basis for controlling, checking on, and helping, the work of his training officer during the next few months.

The administration manager to whom the training manager reports, may be required to give approval to any new training activity, particularly if it needs money beyond present limits. This approval will be based on confidence that costs and resources are satisfactory, and that objectives and collaboration are in the corporate interest. The objective statement provides him with the information required; he should be able to contact the operation director or manager and discuss, with confidence, the proposition and agreements in the statement. He also has a basis, as has the training manager, for monitoring the progress of the training, implementation, and fuel economy, during the following months, as far as he requires to do this.

The operations director, and the managers of the operations and technical departments will all be provided with a copy of the objectives statement, in full or reduced form. The managers of the operations and technical departments must agree with it if training is to proceed. They will, of course, already be fully aware of what it says, in views of the weeks of discussion with the training manager and one or more training officers, but the statement will enable misunderstandings to be identified before too late, and full collaboration to be confirmed.

They will have their own documents relating to estimated savings, and to the steps to be taken to monitor these, and it is reasonable to ask that the objectives in the training statement of objectives is consistent with their own view of implementation and savings, and their own objectives statement.

OVERALL OBJECTIVES STATEMENT

Whereas the training officer will be preoccupied with pursuing the objectives relating to certain specific training activities, the training manager, the administrative manager to whom he reports, and the director responsible for the training function, need statements which show the overall pattern of objectives. This is to be constructed by entering all the statements of objective for specific activities on to one set of sheets, and classifying and grouping them under headings appropriate to the company's organisation, interests and requirements for training.

Thus, one set of groupings might reflect the departmental or functional organisation of the company, grouping the activities under the headings: production, marketing, research, and administration; and another might reflect the current and future priorities for growth and training, e.g. industrial and employee relations, cost effectiveness, safety, and development.

Two sets of statements, in detail or outline, may be needed. One will provide an adequate picture, function by function of what is intended for the coming year or two, and for what purpose and benefit; the other shows how the main and most important growth and problem aspects of the company are being attended to by the training function, and by the collaborative line functions.

Examination of the overall objectives statement

The training manager – and his own manager and director – has therefore not merely to draw up the overall objectives statement. They have also to examine and test it. He then has to use it. We shall deal first with examining and testing: how is this to be done? There are several approaches to be considered.

1 Comparison with company objectives and other functional objectives

In studying the documents issued by other departments and by the chief executive it is possible to check whether any one item of objectives shown on their statements has a corresponding item on the training statements. Where it has, the training manager is, according to his judgement, able to assume that their training need is being looked after. A check with his training officer should confirm this. Where it has not, then, again after a check with his training officer, he may have to assume that a training need has perhaps been overlooked. This should be noted, and an enquiry made into the requirements of that specific item.

He may then enter the item on to his overall objectives sheet, by virtue of the high corporate benefit figure of the item and its need for training, but without, as yet, any detail of exactly what training action is to be taken. It is an item awaiting agreement and attention; it helps to complete the overall picture of need and objectives. In a large company this approach may involve an unacceptably high amount of paperwork. In a small one it should not.

2 Reference to the training opportunity matrix

By scanning the training opportunity matrix the need to rack one's mind in order to remember the possibilities for training is met more easily. A matrix which is in constant use for exploratory and planning purposes will provide more than a set of named areas of potential training need: it will provide additional information in note form of priorities, plans and activities.

3 Discussion with subordinates

These are of great value for the examination of specific objective entries and can offer opportunities for exchange of views, and for counselling, between manager and subordinate. They can also offer a further opportunity for the training officer to see and discuss his own work in the context of the total training effort and the total situation of the company and the contribution which training is making to the progress of the company and the people who work in it.

4 Discussion with managements of other functions

This is to be done in addition to the examination (see above, item 1) of other documents on functional and company objectives. It may be a necessity for the responsible director and the administration manager, as far as they feel that further information is needed at a top management level. It will be necessary for the training manager if he needs confirmation whether or not training is needed to support new developments; that these developments are likely to take place in the short or medium term future; the extent to which they may be resourced by the function concerned.

The use of the overall objective statement

Let us assume that the statement has been approved. What has been its use so far? What will its use be in the future? The uses may be considered under four headings.

1 Priorities

The question of priorities is also bound up with those of planning and resourcing: but for the moment we shall concentrate on three economic and personal factors which have to be taken into account. First, as a result of examining the total range of training propositions, and the estimated benefit associated with each, a comparison of the values of the propositions may be made. A scale of benefits from highest to lowest may be constructed, if necessary, to help clarify the problem associated with approving propositions for further training. It would be naive to assume that only those propositions which come high on the scale can qualify for approval. Not all benefits can be quantified, as we have seen, whilst others are quantifiable only if one talks in terms of probability and order. Even so, it is useful and realistic to see the relative values of future training before proceeding further.

The second factor is that each proposition for training will have a high priority from the point of view of the client, irrespective of its position on any scale of benefits covering the full range of propositions across all functions in the company. It will mean little to the sales manager that his requirement for training produces a likely net benefit ranking only fourth on the corporate list, behind those of production, computers and research. From his point of view – and this can be true of all line managers in all functions – the need for sales training is absolute. It must be done, by the end of the next quarter, in order to produce the employee capability needed for the new sales drive.

Thus we can see that although management at a more senior level, i.e. from the training manager upwards, will wish to see the whole pattern of benefits likely to arise from training during the short, medium and long term futures, the decision on priorities – and hence on resources – cannot be based simply on scales and ranking. It could be said that almost every proposition for training, properly worked out by line management and training officer, will have an associated net benefit which far outweighs its cost.

If objectives and benefits are established with the rigour which we have discussed in the preceding pages, then it is conceivable that all propositions, as they arise, would find ready acceptance by management, and a search for resources to meet agreed timetables of events would follow. Unfortunately, this rigour is hard to sustain. The details suggested for the presentation of overall objectives, plus a scale of benefits, provide senior management with the fullest information for the close examination of the claims made under the headings of objective, cost and benefit, and covering the company as a whole.

The third factor that has to be taken into account is the professional interest of the training officer himself. In the same way that the professional engineering designer is sometimes accused of pursuing designs and design details which interest him personally – irrespective of the interest of the company – so we observe from time to time specialist training officer interests dominating discussion on what training action is needed. This can become most noticeable as and when new practices or 'packages' in training become popular.

2 Planning and resourcing

Whatever doubts one may have about the ultimate usefulnes of overall objectives statements as a basis of establishing priorities, there is no doubt about its value in the examination and provision of resources, and in providing a framework for more detailed planning and co-ordination of training activities. Resources, in terms of money, people and facilities, will be provided in part by the training function, and in part by other functions. If the overall objective statement is to carry conviction there must be prior agreement on who provides the cash, the teachers and the rooms, and – this may be a matter of great concern in some companies – on whose budget these items are to appear.

The amount of money and time to be spent in, say, the next two years, may be far in excess of the existing approved training function budget. It may then be necessary, by virtue of a company rule, to summarise the extra, marginal, finance needed to carry through the proposition; and to summarise the way in which management, executive and supervisory time is to be drawn on, in order to get director approval for their release. Much of this information is available in a structured way on the overall statement of objectives.

The effective use of these resources depends largely on planning. Here the training manager has to ensure that the dates proposed for every item of the year meet the following requirements:

1 The timing of the training is right for the operations which it serves, e.g. the operator training is timed to produce competent operators by the time the commissioning team leaves the new plant.
2 The timing suits the availability of his own training officers and other members of the company, when all their other commitments are taken into account.

It is common experience that even though, in broad terms, the resources are available in the training function and in the company at large, there can be, and often are, problems in planning the use of these resources, i.e. company executives and training officers alike, so that everything can be done on time. Here the question of priorities and benefits arises. Those items which are already approved and planned for will take precedence from the point of view of the training manager over things which are new. He will be inclined to say that the new training request cannot be met; that these resources are fully stretched already and there is no possibility of starting anything new for many months.

But what if the new and unexpected training requirement has to meet an implementation date only weeks away, and well before the first gap in existing training plans? The answer cannot be 'no' for the training function is there to meet the needs of, and to bring benefit to, the company as a whole; it is not there merely to provide a limited, previously agreed, set of training activities.

Again we see the advantages of working against a backcloth of overall objectives. The training manager is able to see the new request in company perspective and weigh up its value, and its interference with other training activities, in a more realistic way than otherwise. Moreover, his ability to see training activities as contributing to company efficiency and human well-being, and not merely as providing more or less work for his training officers, will find him listening to new requests with interest, and questioning them in terms of implementation and corporate benefit, and pressing more effectively for increased effort or resources.

3   Progressing and monitoring

The training officers concerned, and the training manager himself, are likely to become preoccupied with the technical detail of their work, its planning and execution, even to the point of overlooking the final training objective and the other objectives which lie beyond the training objective. The full objectives statement provides the training manager with material with which he can progress the work of his training officers. He must ensure that the training programmes are such as to enable the trainees to attain the specified standards, and thus enhance the possibility of successful implementation.

It also provides a necessary reminder, particularly over a long period of time, of what that training is for. This may seem an unnecessary comment, but with the lapse of time, changes in line and training management, and of training officer, the original training objectives may become obscure. Changes may have been made to suit personal taste, and administrative convenience. But the beginnings of decline may pass unnoticed: only later will it be realised, perhaps after some waste and frustration, that the training effort has lost quality and reputation.

Management cannot progress and monitor any operation without adequate points of reference and appropriate data. The objectives statements are necessary for both.

4   Evaluation

Clearly, any action taken to provide an evaluation of the benefits of a particular training activity, must start with an examination of the training and the corporate objectives, the implementation, and the areas of anticipated benefit. This provides a fundamental evaluation role for the document. Any attempt at evaluation that is made without reference to it, is likely to be ill conceived and not to answer management's questions.

An additional virtue of having the evaluator refer to the basic document lies in the more precise identification of side effects, i.e. those events which, anticipated or not, do not constitute the main objectives of the training and subsequent implementation. Some side effects may be noted already, in anticipation, in the original document. Some will not be. Both will be examined by the evaluator. They may be just as significant in their impact on the company as are the main objectives.

14 Offering a service

Both line and training managements may be uncertain about exactly where the boundaries of authority lie, and the extensivenes of the service which the training function could offer. We shall do best to look at this problem in a hypothetical company and one of its departments.

The department is operations and is responsible for storage and transport of the company's products. It has a number of depots in the south-east region, and a transport fleet of road vehicles. It owns some rail cars and has storage and loading facilities at strategic points in the country. This is a familiar picture of such a function, as is the fact that it is always under pressure due to breakdowns, shortage of suitable labour and the sorting out of customers' complaints about delivery.

It is agreed between operations management and training management that more effective training, plus a tighter control of its progress, should be developed with particular reference to operators and drivers, whose errors have risen in recent months to an unacceptable level. It is considered that the heavy labour turnover of the past three years has, through a declining overall concern for standards, resulted in too many relative newcomers working at a sub-standard level. Action had already been taken with respect to the supervisors throughout operations; they have attended meetings at which the position has been made clear, and they have been instructed to allow no future decline from the mandatory standards as defined in the Operations Handbook. They have also been told that management have decided to invite the training department to help strengthen the training of all who join operations from now on, whether from outside the company or from other parts of the company.

From now on, who is responsible for what? And who does what? In outline, as one would expect, we have the following sequence of events. The italics indicate the different people involved in the service.

1 Agreements

The *training manager* and the *operations manager* discuss their relative responsibilities, agreeing that the final choice of practice will lie with the operations manager. They also define and agree

(a) on *the employees* at various levels who are affected, including *their supervisors*

(b) on the sort of job analysis that is to be done as a basis for future training

(c) that the future training will be largely on-the-job, given by the supervisors, with some training to be given off-the-job, also by supervisors or *managers* and *specialists from associated functions,* but that this will be determined after the job analysis

(d) that the analysis and more detailed job training recommendations will be made by a *training officer* working in conjunction with a named *senior supervisor* from operations

(e) that all of the above will be communicated to all other managers and supervisors in operations in order to avoid misunderstandings

2 Planning

On completion of the above the recommendations of the training officer are, with small modifications, accepted by the operations manager. They are that

(a) The remaining job analyses will be done by the same training officer, working now with the *supervisor of each section* in which the new training methods are to be introduced.

(b) The job analyses will be reviewed by a *senior operations engineer* and the *safety engineer* to ensure that the required standards are incorporated.

(c) The supervisors will undergo a short course on operations training. It will review the practices and standards necessary for the company's operations and the dependence on vigilant supervision. It will train the supervisors in the methods of instruction necessary in the future.

(d) The *other managers in operations,* to whom the supervisors report, will be briefed by the operations manager on the above, and will contribute to the course in 2(c) for their supervisors, by chairing and teaching during the course.

(e) The application of the new methods of instruction will be the direct responsibility of each supervisor, but each manager will be held accountable to the operations manager for making sure than the new rules are being followed.

(f) The *personnel officer* will send a copy to the training officer of all notifications of new recruits, transferees and promotions into operations with the normal four days' notice.

(g) The operations manager will arrange for a training/performance checkout sheet for each learner to be fully completed and signed on the completion of all or an agreed part of training and a copy (there are carbons in the book) sent to the training officer.

(h) Periodic reports on operations training will be submitted to the operations manager, by the training officer, based on the analysis of the check-outs and on follow-up discussions with supervisors and trainees.

3 Implementation

The above steps are taken. Inevitably, during the course of meetings and the supervisors' courses, questions are asked revealing the varied levels of understanding in both supervision and management, and answers have to be found. Closer rapport established across the levels of the hierarchy thus enabled the more profound doubts and scepticism about the company systems to be expressed, and appreciated by both operations and training managements.

The supervisors were able to point to weaknesses in the propositions and enable the management to modify not only the training content but also those aspects of their administration which militated against effective job training. For example, it was pointed out that new recruits going on shift from their very first day would run the risk of changing their supervisor at the end of the first week, before the completion of training to required standards. Or they might find themselves doing nights in one of the two depots where, from time to time, night work was under the control of a leading hand. Neither, they suggested, was very satisfactory; management should do something about it if they wanted their supervisors to sign for the completed training.

The course of time showed that despite all the good intentions of management and supervision, the implementation of the system left a lot to be desired. This was not, the operations manager himself pointed out, because of any weakness in the system, in the principle, or in the paperwork demands, but because of the failure of the supervisors to undertake the full scope of their on-the-job training responsibilities. In some instances the training was not being completed, in others the check-out tests were not being given, whilst in far too many instances the training was being passed over to another operator to do in the supervisor's absence. 'Clearly', said the operations manager, 'we have got to do something about this. We can't just let it go on like this.'

How did he know what was happening? Simply by reviewing the records as they accumulated. The ones that were fully completed gave him little to be concerned about, but the ones which were not he had to chase. These, in most cases, were not available in the expected time because the training or check-out had not been completed; he wanted to know why, and he then put it right. He was particularly stung by the observation, made by the training officer, that of all the notified training in the six months since the introduction of the new arrangements only 46 per cent appeared to have been handled completely satisfactorily.

4 Review

A further discussion with a selection of operations management, and with some of the supervisors, pointed to the root of the problems dogging effective training.

'How can I be expected to give attention to training the new man when my own manager tells me that the new trucks *must* be on the road next week?'

'What can I do if the learner doesn't seem to understand what I'm trying to get him to do?'

'I've been away sick quite a bit these last few weeks and there's no one standing in for me, because hospital visits are only half a day at a time.'

Thus problems of priorities, standards of recruitment, and stand-ins for temporary absence had to be tackled, and a better working arrangement reached.

5 Conclusion

We conclude this picture with a chat between the operations manager and the training manager.

TM: 'All this seems to have given you a lot of trouble.'

OM: 'The trouble was there all the time. All that has happened is that we can now see what it is, and we can't duck it.'

TM: 'Do you want us to carry on monitoring your job training?'

OM: 'Yes it's helpful; it's easy for us to lose sight of what's going on, or close our eyes to it.'

We make no apologies for the simple 'training officer makes good' example, for it is the simplest and most direct way of showing certain principles in action. The first is the application of training policy to the group of employees whom we have designated notifiables, and for whom systematic training and appropriate control systems can be set up with comparative ease thanks to the availability of initial data, and to the general uniformity of the training requirement and its implementation.

The second principle demonstrated by the example is that of the preservation of line management's authority whilst rendering a service which takes the specialist right into line management's territory. Of course, one can say, the specialist can work without paying so much attention to the preservation of line management's authority, by ignoring it or challenging it, or by going round it in some way. The ultimate answer to that could be that the service will probably not be accepted or, if accepted, not implemented properly.

The management of any service function, if it is to make a continuous and useful contribution to the organisation which it serves, pays close attention to the way it asserts itself in the departments which it is in a position to service. This has been found to be vital over the years during which so-called scientific management has developed, and during which sophisticated services have separated out within companies, under many different titles. The more well known include work study, method study, operations research, which are there to tell the manager how to run his operations more economically; personnel and industrial relations, who have expertise on handling the human situation; safety and security who know about avoiding accidents and losses. There are others which are functionally much closer to the minute-to-minute work of the line department, like inspection and quality control, and such specialisms as production control, materials and information technology.

The training service is to be seen normally, perhaps regretably, as a service at the beginning of that list: something of an outsider relative to the line function, not vital to operations, unless it proves itself to be so. This would not be said of, say, production control, which is such a vital service that it comes to be seen as virtually a line function, directly under the works manager, with responsibility for meeting the same deadlines as the manufacturing departments. The frequent meetings, the high degree of mutual dependence, the continuous flow of workaday data in both directions characterise the relationships between the services of production control and the production department. How different the relationships between other services and line departments are depends to a large extent on how necessary each service is to the line department, and how much and how often it is given.

It is also dependent, as pointed out above, on how the service function and its management conducts itself. This is of such great importance in a study of the Management of Training that some further points must be made. A successful service function must observe two principles of etiquette as follows.

First, it works in such a way as will sustain the authority of the management with which it is dealing. Service functions, that is to say the individual specialists and their assistants, have been known to erode or undermine the authority of their clients, by their attitude, or by announcing conclusions without full consultation and agreement. As one would expect, this does not normally lead to the downfall of the line manager; the reverse is more often the case. For the sense of outrage, or mistrust, so generated can lead the line manager into rejecting the propositions offered, and declining further offers of assistance. Alternatively, should the propositions now be in the phase of implementation, it is not too difficult for the line manager to demonstrate that the new arrangement is not very satisfactory. Sabotage is not much of a problem on your home territory, particularly if there is no material damage contemplated.

These may seem to be somewhat negative but the positive side is equally important; the authority of management has to be sustained, or even in some way enhanced if it is initially weak, if any new scheme is to be convincingly presented to the employees by that management, and properly supervised by that same management during its installation and subsequent operation. No outside specialist would wish to see his ideas, once accepted, founder because of weak management; it is therefore in his own interests to do everything he can, in the course of his working relationships, to strengthen that management and its capability to deal with the forthcoming changes.

Second, it must be fully prepared to teach all that is needed by management and supervision to enable them to understand the rationale of their approach and of their conclusions. The form which this teaching takes will vary from specialisation to specialisation and from management to management, sometimes very simple and spontaneous, and sometimes highly complex, organised and expensive to do.

Let us consider two totally different examples, in order to illustrate the full range of teaching possibilities.

Our first example is one we have already referred to concerning the introduction of systematic training to high standards for notifiable trainees (see Chapter 6). There is nothing in the training methods, or in the administration, or in the objectives, which is beyond the easy understanding of the managers, supervisors and the other employees, once all of these have been explained to them. But no one will understand with sufficient precision any proposition if full information has not been given to them. So, simple though the ideas are, they need to be taught. Once the line manager and the training manager have agreed on the basic training methods, records and administration, they must tell all managers, supervisors and others affected, what the new training plans are. There are various ways of doing this, i.e.

(a) To pass the information by word of mouth, using the management and supervisory chain down to the lowest employee level affected.
(b) To gain management understanding at the normal, or at specially enlarged, management meetings, set up to provide the opportunity for management/specialist dialogue during the project
(c) To put an announcement on the notice board for all to see
(d) To send an explanatory note to those affected
(e) To stage extraordinary meetings at which those affected will be given information, and will be able to ask questions and discuss their worries with managers.

One or more of the above steps must be taken, however simple the project. The experienced specialist and service adviser knows that there is many a slip 'twixt cup and lip' and that if satisfactory understanding is not established, the chance of something going wrong, in even the simplest of schemes, is considerable. In this first example, illustrating the teaching responsibility of the service function in the simplest of circumstances, it is not acceptable merely to hope that the project will proceed satisfactory because of the simple nature of the technology – in this case 'job training technology'. 'Training' is a convenient example of a technology with everyday language and concepts, and the line manager readily understands its talk, once he is put in the picture.

For our second example we shall see what happens if the service specialist uses a technology which is difficult and obscure, and the extent to which he has to be prepared to teach. We shall keep in mind all that was illustrated in the first example and look at the additional problem provided by a new esoteric technology and language. We must remind ourselves that this is not something confined to, say, the computer systems service; even the training officer well versed in the behavioural sciences, and the personnel officer specialising in the study of 'optimal steady-state manpower structures', can puzzle line management with language and concepts.

A computer department investigator, following up a recommendation from the marketing director, has to go and talk to the finished goods stores manager, the sales manager and the distribution manager about the possibiity, already mentioned to them by the marketing director, of improving the efficiency of the storage, depot and transport systems of the company, which take the products from the factories to the customers. Everyone agrees that something should be done, for the present arrangements have grown over a period of many years without satisfactory logic or control and inefficiency is evident today. The three senior managers principally involved all have their own personal solutions, and each in turn is able to argue clearly and forcefully what should be done, and why. The computer man does not know the answer; he only knows the approach, for the problem looks familiar to him. He is not looking for arguments, just information which he will build into his model. He is worried, fortunately, having realised that none of the managers is schooled in mathematical modelling or in the costing and economics which are essential to his analysis. He fears, moreover, that if he merely gets hold of the data which he requires and does his sums without giving a description of how he is tackling the problem, he will 'lose' the managers for good. This could be a disaster, for the solution might be an improbable looking one, and the initial rejection of it by the managers would then make further progress very difficult, perhaps impossible.

His choices are: should he spend time teaching the managers about the models, mathematics and economics before getting into the analysis; or wait until the analysis is done and the propositions available, and then fight it out? He chooses the former, for he sees that some early education will help the collection of data, enable him to discuss more thoroughly some moot points of objectives and costs, and make it easier for the managers to look objectively at the findings and conclusions of the study. He will then also get better backing from the wide range of other executives whom he has to approach during his research work, for they will sense the confidence felt by the three principal managers, once the latter have gained a satisfactory grasp of what the study will contain and how it will be done. He is aware, moreover, that he is not in any sense to try to brainwash the managers and others who need this education, and that the ultimate acceptance of the final proposition will be based on their estimate of the costs and benefits of the recommended system, and not on their acceptance of his esoteric mathematics, which they know they can ignore.

Readers will be familiar with the sort of course for senior managers which was then devised, in-company with some outside teachers, some papers read by internal management illustrating the need for accurate economic analysis, and on the importance of taking full account of employee interests. The objective was the development of understanding between the managers and the specialists, producing a greater mutual interest and trust, as well as a much franker awareness of each other's strengths and weaknesses. It is not always appreciated, however, that this educational effort is part of the necessary work of the service specialist. Such a course may be regarded by many as just another event on the company's training calendar, interesting and useful, no doubt, but not seen as functionally integrated into the progressive actions of specialist and line management. The training manager, of course is part of the inspiration of such training and education, on behalf of any service activity. It is a part of his own *raison d'être*; he keeps an eye on their activities and on their newest ideas throughout the year.

In between these two examples there is a full spectrum of instances of the ways in which the service specialist provides teaching for client departments and functions. The training function itself provides one of the technologically least complicated services. It nevertheless needs to work in the same way that it would expect other service functions to work and clarify even the simplest of ideas and propositions which might affect other people's work and responsibility. In other words, it has to explain itself.

15 Training officers

In this part of the book we have looked at many situations in companies which require some sort of training action, and we have considered a range of factors which help or hinder the application of training. Although we have referred from time to time to the training manager, or to the training officer, it has not been the intention to imply that the situation could only be handled satisfactorily if there actually was a training manager or officer available. We have left until now the discussion of the need for a training function in a company, and of how the training function itself is staffed and managed.

What is a training officer? What does he do? We are all familiar with various organisations in companies according to which training officers are allocated their responsibilities. One type of organisation divides the work of the function to correspond with the employee-hierarchical groups, i.e. management and supervisor training looked after by one training officer or training unit; operator training looked after by another training officer or unit; apprentice training looked after by another; and so on, covering such things as induction, retirement, further education and vacation training within the framework of the main divisions as far as possible.

This is an approach which has its strengths and its weaknesses. It is strong in that these employee groups are identified with particular training officers, and progress in each sector through unambiguous communication between the training function and line management can be easily maintained. That, at least, is the theory. The potential weakness lies in the fact that although, for example, management training actions may be separate from apprentice training actions, the same people are likely to be involved in both.

This is a very significant point. To elaborate – the objectives, facilities and methods, the numbers of apprentices and the quality of instruction given by on-line supervisors, are all matters of concern to the managers of the works, or the departments, or the service functions, concerned with apprentices. Discussions on future plans and on progress must be held with them or their deputies from time to time. The apprentice training specialist therefore is likely to become, on occasions, immersed in the problems and preoccupations of management and supervision.

On the other hand, the supervisor training specialist, examining and discussing the work of first-line supervisors and managers, can find himself immersed in the problems of relationships between supervisors and apprentices, and in 'the difficulties of motivating today's youth'. These are problems of prime importance to the apprentice training specialist: they are also management and supervisor problems.

Now there is nothing wrong in any one specialist finding himself exposed to issues which are the prime concern of other types of specialist, but it does call for co-ordination and communication between the specialist units and the individual specialists in the training function. This co-ordinating role is one of the responsibilities of the training manager.

The overlap in communication, in having different training specialists dealing with the same people – which is a general rule – points to the 'indivisibility of training'. This is a principle which has to be appreciated by all training officers. It requires that each training officer, in no matter which specialisation, must develop an awareness of the training needs, actual and potential, under other specialist headings; and must be sufficiently perceptive to see or to sense that he is, at times, confronted with new training needs which are the prime responsibility of other specialists. What action he takes, in such instances, depends on his understanding with his colleagues and on the traditions of the training function. It seems reasonable to suggest that, as a maxim, he should report back to his colleagues, or to his training manager, what he has encountered.

A second type of organisation is based on physical areas. That is to say, if the company is sufficiently large, in employee numbers and geographical spread, it may be divided into areas and each area allocated a training officer. For example, a company on a 100 hectare site, may have its office/administration block with 800 people as one area; the north side of the works with 'raw materials, machinery and heat treatment' employing 900 people as a second area; and the south side 'assembly, inspection and despatch' employing 1,200 people as the third area. The offices, the north side and the south side are, on this large site, a long way from each other. The types of work in each are, on the whole, different from area to area. Each area training officer gets to know the work of his area in some detail, gets to know the people well, and looks after the day-to-day training of transferees, of new recruits, new plant, with the efficiency that comes from knowing the area and its people and its work well, and not wasting time in walking unnecessary and great distances.

This arrangement, too, has its weaknesses. There can easily be, for example, uneven supervisory and management training from area to area if there is no central control and no single set of standards for all to follow. The apprentices and other trainees are moved from one area to another; should they report to different area training officers during their apprenticeship or traineeship, or would it be best to appoint a separate specialist training officer concerned only with the apprentices? These are questions with which companies have to grapple. The answers, and the resulting organisation, come from considering the circumstances of each particular company – the size, the amount of training activity, the quality of the training officers, and their relationships with each other and with management.

Whatever the organisation, the training manager has the task of co-ordinating and synthesising the work of the individual training officers. He is likely to find that there is no ideal organisation that remains fully valid for very long. The changes, over a few years, in the quality of the training officers, the demand from management for new training services, the size and organisation of the company, will all force him to revise his own organisation. He must be careful, at the same time, to avoid frequent changes in the training schemes or programmes themselves. Although company employees and managers may welcome the introduction of new training schemes they do not welcome the news that, for example, the supervisor development programme, which was established four years before, and which has been revised twice already, is to be revised yet again. Small changes in schemes, which bring about no disturbances to managers or trainees, and which obviously improve some weakness, may be applauded by the managers and trainees, but frequent major changes to such things as eligibility, length and pattern of contents, can weaken the confidence of the company in both the programme and the training function. Such changes can also be demoralising for the trainees themselves because of the feeling of uncertainty which arises in the face of frequent change.

Any change in the organisation of the training function which leads to a different training officer assuming responsibility for a particular scheme, can lead to pressure from that new training officer to alter the scheme. He may alter it to suit his administrative style and convenience, or because he genuinely believes that the changes will produce more cost-effective training. The changes may be inspired by laziness, or overactiveness, and can be much more an indication of the type of person in charge of the scheme than of the needs of the trainees and the schemes themselves. Knowing when to leave a scheme alone is as important a skill as knowing when to make a change in it.

Let us look further at the basic skills of the training officer – not at the skills of analysis, design and administration, important though they are, but at the more fundamental social and inter-personal characteristics which tend to separate training officers into two classes: those who voluntarily focus a lot of attention on the myriad complex situations which occur continuously in the company, and those who voluntarily focus a lot of attention on the training schemes run by, or in conjunction with the training function. The first we might call outward looking and the second inward looking. They are not mutually exclusive, and any one person will show himself to have some of each in the way he works and the interest which he demonstrates in outward and inward situations, actions and involvement. The different balance between the two produces different types of training officers, with different value and potential for the training function. If we take an example of a training situation in a company, and contrast the ways in which it may be handled, we can see these differences more clearly.

We are considering a company which undertakes civil engineering construction. It has a home head office with the managers and their staff of all the company functions. The head of the project accounting and control department is worried about the upward drift in project costs. Although some drift is due to more or less predictable material and labour costs, for which the contracts with clients include suitable protections, nevertheless there is some drift which arises from internal causes – unsatisfactory communication and organisation of resources, unsatisfactory understanding and co-operation between the various functions involved in any one of the many jobs which the company undertakes. What does the head do? What does the training function do? There are, hypothetically, several alternative actions which might be taken by each, and we now look at some of them. Each of the following three scenarios represents a different set of actions.

SCENARIO 1

(a) The head of project accounts becomes preoccupied with the possibility of introducing additional controls which will cover and co-ordinate all the processes and transactions from preliminary estimates through to completion. He discusses this possibility with his colleagues, and the design of the new controls is started.

(b) At the same time, independent of the above, a training officer, who is outward looking, has learnt of the problems of cost control from discussion with several contacts in the company and from reading internal reports to which he has access. He concludes that there is probably a gap in mutual understanding and communication, and that if there is, then some form of educational and training process could be helpful.

(c) The training officer asks to see the head of project accounts to discuss. They already know one another a little because the training officer makes a point of maintaining some formal and informal contact with senior managers. As a result of this discussion the head of project accounts readily agrees that the new controls need to be learned and understood, and not merely imposed; and that the rapport produced between functional representatives in a well designed seminar on the new controls could lead to improved co-ordination and communication, and a greater sense of resolve in those involved.

(d) A three-day seminar is then organised and run to the satisfaction of project accounts and training, and of the participants. The new controls are launched and operated with some efficiency, and the consequent communications are distinctly better than before. It is too soon to say what the actual cost savings are. The project accounts head wants another seminar within six months for those unable to attend the first, and one each year for the next three years for more junior executives.

Comment

The outward look of the training officer brought some success in this instance because he was disposed also to take action in the outward direction. He might have sat in his office shy, nervous or otherwise disinclined to face a senior member of another function. Instead, he got up and went. For the training officer, this is the critical moment of distinction between inward and outward effectiveness.

SCENARIO 2

(a) In this scenario the head of project accounts has decided for himself that the problems can be met by not only providing a new control system, but also by taking positive steps to educate, train and get support from the many executives involved. How to do this, he wonders? He asks for the training officer to come to his office.

(b) The training officer is pleased by the invitation, and quickly and intelligently understands the situation as described by the head of project accounts. The training officer has ideas about group learning and motivation, and about seminar organisation. Between the two of them they discuss the company problem, the information flow and decision-making, reach agreement on the general form and objectives of future seminars – which correspond very much to those of Scenario 1 above.

(c) The first seminars are held with success, to be followed by three further seminars at yearly intervals.

Comment

In this scenario the training officer did not show outward characteristics as far as initiative was concerned; it was the head of accounts who was outward, both in thinking about the solution of the interpersonal problems and in taking a first step towards the training officer. However, in this situation the training officer is put in a position of being able to use his professional training skills at a consultative, design and administrative level, and the net result is good.

SCENARIO 3

(a) In this instance the head of project accounts with his colleagues have thought out everything for themselves – they need additional control systems, plus seminars for which they have, with some ability, designed the programme.

(b) The head of accounts tells the training officer that the above has been decided; he would, of course, welcome comments and he would like to reserve rooms and facilities in the company training centre at appropriate dates. The training officer consults his schedule and the training centre staff and the dates and arrangements are entered into the diary of training activities.

(c) The seminars are run with the training officer undertaking an administrative role concerning programmes, handouts, visual aids and transport arrangements. They are successful and the training officer is thanked, with sincerity, by the head of project accounts for his help in making the seminars go well.

Comment

In this scenario the training officer, with no outward initiative or action, uses solely his ability in course administration. The initiatives are all taken by the head of project accounts, who obtains a limited, although very important, service from the training function.

DISCUSSION OF THE THREE SCENARIOS

The three scenarios show how good overall results are obtained with different levels of management and training initiative and, perhaps, capability. In each case someone had to have some initiative: either the line manager or the training officer. If neither had either the idea or the initiative, then that sort of training activity would not take place. Further hypothetical scenarios, with which we shall not tire the reader would show how an unsatisfactory result can be obtained if the sum total of line and specialist initiatives and capabilities are not as favourable as in the three scenarios we have presented.

Which scenario is best, one might ask? There is nothing to choose between them as far as one can see. The first scenario depicted shows the way in which the initiative taken by the training officer, and his outwardness, met the requirements of the situation, with success.

However, if the inward-looking head of project accounts worked in the same company as inward-looking training officers, there would be many missed opportunities. The opportunities described in Chapter 5 on the training opportunity matrix have to be actually taken. In a company with a very high level of management outwardness and training initiative, the function of the head of training might be predominantly to record that the opportunities have been taken. It is our view that his function is also to make sure that future opportunities are being identified, particularly the non-notifiable, and that action will be taken. It does not matter very much who starts that action, provided it is taken, and to a good standard.

In fact, most companies have a mixture of levels of initiative and outwardness in both line management and the training officers. The training manager needs to understand the qualities of his company's line managers and then to do what he can to make sure that the contribution made by his training officers matches and complements the requirements and capabilities of the line managers. How can a suitable team of training officers be acquired? Where do they come from?

THE ORIGINS OF TRAINING OFFICERS

Until recent years many, but by no means all, training officers were recruited from amongst instructors, fitters and operators. At a time when by far the greater part of organised industrial training was for engineering apprentices and operators there was some logic in choosing training officers with that type and level of experience. Unfortunately, it was not always recognised that, for example, the apprentice training officer does not only deal with apprentices. He deals with supervisors and managers also, and he must be concerned with the optimum understanding of many aspects of work and not solely the acquisition of certain skills. A training officer who has spent many earlier years confined to working in limited technical areas, developing thereby an inward look, and who has always been subordinate to foremen and superintendents, enters his new calling with potentially great handicaps. He may find it difficult, or impossible, to think and act with initiative in the company of men who have previously been his bosses. The traditions and feelings of us and them, of the superior and the subordinate, are hard to eradicate.

Nevertheless, extremely good training officers have come up this way, and have been able to deal with situations and problems far wider in scope than they have ever experienced before. Provided their education continues, and their experience is expansive enough to take them out of a preoccupation with previously acquired technical skills, their potential and value as training officers can be high. If, on the other hand, they are exploited by using them only in work with which they are already thoroughly familiar (as is the temptation), they cannot readily develop much further.

Unfortunately, with this group of men transferred into the training function from other work, have come some who have presented their managements with problems of career. The unsuccessful foreman, the convalescing ex-superintendent, the failed supervisor and many others have arrived in the training function not because they wanted to be training officers, or instructors, but because their management didn't know what to do with them. The fact that training for many years in many companies has been a Cinderella function, a helpful but not very important function, has enabled some managers to transfer men who, whilst of value, were nevertheless misfits, into the training function. In some cases, it has simply produced another misfit, which has become more and more evident as the training function itself has developed a more significant and recognisable role.

If these are unreliable sources of recruits into training, where should one turn? The recent years have seen changes which are encouraging. As a consequence of the greater emphasis on training today with statutory requirements in the countries of Europe, the growing reputation of business schools and the popularity of degrees and diplomas in business and administration, there has been a small but marked increase in the number of young professionals who have chosen to make a career as a training officer; or to work as a training officer as part of a career in personnel work. This is a valuable source, ensuring that it maintains some recruitment at a professional level and helps maintain its capability for dialogue with the other specialist functions in the company.

A second encouraging source has been from amongst students of what are broadly known as the behaviourial sciences. Many of these entrants, with a great deal of knowledge of human performance, and with techniques for examining and interpreting attitudes and relationships, bring with them an appetite for examining the human situation as well as for human engineering. But they, too, have their handicap. Although they may be equipped to deal with human situations, with the training and development needs of the company, these situations and needs are not self evident. The theory orientated ex-student needs to gain experience in perceiving what people do, how they relate to one another, how they learn their work and acquire their attitudes. To develop this outwardness, he needs to go out into the offices and workshops for sufficient time to perceive and digest the whole spectrum of working life, either as a workshop employee (like sandwich students), or by having his training officer job positioned right in the heart of operations. If such a job does not exist for him, then, as we shall discuss in Chapter 28, one may have to be created, even if only for a few months.

There is another source of training officers of the greatest value. They may be transferred from the other departments and functions of the company in mid career, on a temporary basis. These are not men for whom there is no future in their present work, men of indifferent capability. They are men of promise and skill, already proven as accountants or as engineers or as marketing executives, and to be found on the management succession charts. Is not this a waste? Is a transfer to such work acceptable to the man or to his management, one may ask?

The chairman or president of almost any company is liable to say, in his annual

124

statement, that the greatest asset of the company is its workforce, its operators, supervisors and managers. He, and other senior managers, will also confirm, and even defend, that the training of this valuable asset is the responsibility of management, of the managers and the supervisors. For them to discharge this responsibility they depend on their own intelligence and willingness, on the support given to them by the company's training function, and on the relatively small amount of teaching they receive about training methods. To this one must, of course, add their occasional conversations, reading, and observations of training and development practices throughout their careers.

Sometimes managers, supervisors and executives do, in addition, spend a few days, weeks or months on loan to the training function, usually because a change in technology, or an expansion of a function, has produced an exceptional load of training analysis, planning and administration. The function concerned does itself a good turn by asking one of its members to concentrate on training, and he does this either from his own office, or from a new desk in the training department. Sometimes, also, a function appoints one of its senior managers to act as the training liaison for the function and he becomes the focal point of contact for the company's training officers and helps them and guides them in their work with all parts of that function, lending his managerial authority whenever needed.

So there are precedents. Is any more needed? There can be no universal rule on a matter such as this, but there is a case for companies doing a lot more than at present, given that the human asset is so valuable (from every point of view) and it is management's responsibility to safeguard and to develop that human asset – or, to put it rather more acceptably, to enable that human asset to develop itself. What could be done? Well, take for example, an operations unit of, say, 350 people most of whom are likely to make their careers in the company. Of that number 80 are in operations management and senior supervision. Amongst the top 25 are several men in their middle thirties. To remove one of these is not going to harm operations, although there could be strong opposition. This one person, for two years, could work on the training and development needs and programmes of the operations department.

He would become a colleague in the training function, and would receive training himself in aspects of training, individual appraisal and development, and skills of counselling and group leadership – all required by the modern training officer and equally required by the modern manager. As a 'member' of the personnel function he would be exposed to, and would study and enter into, manpower forecasting and planning, with particular reference to his own parent function. During this time he would work on behalf of the training needs of the many individuals and groups in the operations function, and he would be seen to be so doing.

This would produce in him not merely a heightened skill in matters of the human asset, but also an ineradicable dedication. For anyone who has worked to help people to learn successfully, and enabled people to help themselves, knows of the satisfaction that comes from this profound human experience. The employees themselves are likely to feel closer to the man who, although a line manager, works expressly in the interests of their learning and their progress. A management–employee gap, of an unnecessary type, is likely to close.

Such a move needs to be a positive management policy, a part of positive career development and not a move to fill a hole in the training function, or to dispose of a middle executive of doubtful future. This must be made clear to the chosen man, and he must be told that not only will his technical career *not* suffer, but that it is likely to be enhanced.

With such a policy, at the end of ten years the operations function will find itself with up to six of its top management fully versed in training and development, able to take or guide manpower actions needed in operations, respected and liked by the employees, better organisers and better communicators. All this at virtually no cost. Where it has been tried and adopted, it has worked well. It requires management courage, and confidence on the part of the men transferred, if it is to be adopted.

HOW MANY TRAINING OFFICERS?

How many training officers does a company need? The number must, obviously, be dependent on the size of the company; it is also dependent on the state of the company, the quality of its management, on its attitudes and traditions, on the present capability of the workforce. In addition, it will be influenced by the education and training resources available and accessible outside the company.

The state of the company refers to its rate of change: its rate of growth, the rate at which new plant and processes are being introduced, and the rate at which people are leaving and joining the company, and are being transferred and promoted within the company. Let us take two companies doing the same work, each with 1,000 people in total. Company Alpha is in an almost static state. The annual loss and replacement of manpower is 7 per cent, i.e. 70 new people a year join. It has plans to develop some new plant and to grow in manpower by a modest 2 per cent per annum over the next three years, which means another 20 people a year will join. The internal promotions and transfers for all reasons will amount to 130 per annum. Hence in one year the total number of people faced with major new work is 220, who require job training whether as operators, clerks, supervisors or managers.

Company Beta of 1,000 people has an annual labour turnover of 20 per cent, i.e. 200 people per annum. It plans to develop new plant and process, in the existing departments as well as in a new department, and this will require an additional 12 per cent manpower per annum for three years, i.e. about 120 new people per annum. The effect of the internal changes in plant and jobs will call for the major retraining of people in 180 of the existing jobs. The additional internal promotions and transfers are estimated to be 150 per annum. Hence in one year the total number of people faced with new major work, requiring job training, is about 600. This is 50 less than the 650 which would be produced by simply adding the above numbers, for it is anticipated that some of the promotions and transfers will be into the newly created jobs, and double counting has to be avoided.

In terms of basic job training company Beta, with 600, has nearly three times the load of company Alpha, with 220. Company Beta has also distinctly more training to do amongst its managers and supervisors, of whom there are 210, in order to help their reorientation to reorganisation, new procedures, new products and some changes in standards. This is in addition to the ongoing supervisor and management training, in both companies, aimed at a steady improvement and updating of performance. Both companies, to complete the picture, run apprenticeship schemes of the same size to provide skilled and professional employees, in technical and commercial work, and each company has a total apprenticeship group of 60–70 young people including some new university graduates.

Company Alpha has one senior training officer and an assistant training officer. These two comfortably cope with the work at all levels. Alpha management and supervision are co-operative, perceptive and take initiative in running and developing training in their own work areas. The task of the senior training officer is mainly that of ensuring that the excellent momentum of line management and supervision is sustained in all areas of training, old and new. The task of the assistant training officer is mainly in providing assistance in the organisation of the induction and training of the new recruits and transferees and the planning and progressing of apprentice training and movements. Both men share the design and running of internal seminars and courses and of administration generally. At a pinch all the work could be done by one man, but this would leave no time at all to explore the possible new developments in training, and it could force the incumbent into becoming inward-looking. If there were only one man his absence on leave, or for sickness, could be embarrassing in view of the large number of day-to-day commitments which would have to be neglected until his return. Nor would it be satisfactory during the days and longer periods when, due to the inevitable coincidence of several activities, there is a peak of workload which demands a full continuous effort from both men. In that company, two good training officers do the work comfortably, and the small growth in manpower now planned will present no undue strain either on the training officers or on line management.

Company Beta is different. It, too, has two training officers of good quality, but irrespective of the plans for company growth, both are already full stretched. This is partly due to the very much greater load of promotions, transferees and new recruits. Whereas in company Alpha there are many co-operative managers with good initiative, in Company Beta this is not the case – at least not yet. The relative incompetence of the Beta managers and supervisors in job training, in analysing and teaching jobs and in organising all of this, throws much more administrative work on the training officers. The sheer size of the training load in some departments has produced a feeling of near despair amongst the supervisors who have developed an attitude of 'leave it to the Training Department'. Hence the load carried by the training officers is not merely that produced by the larger number of trainees, but that produced by supervisors, and their management, who are reluctant to become directly involved in systematic and planned training.

The planned expansion in Beta, which is to produce an increase in training load far greater than the mere increase in numbers, will require a considerable enlargement of training resources. In this company the present work and operating manuals are incomplete and contain errors due to failure to keep them up-to-date; the present training materials relating to jobs are complete for about only 35 per cent of these existing jobs which are due to be modified by future changes. There are as yet no work and operating manuals for the new plant, procedures and jobs. There are, of course, no training materials for the job training of people in those new jobs. The supervisors are reluctant, have never fully digested the principles and practices of training, and will, in their present anxious mood, be of little use in helping launch and run an extended training operation.

How many training officers does Beta need? Eventually two will be enough, as company Alpha has demonstrated. But in the next three or four years there will need to be more, to tackle the backlog and the new job training, to take the load off supervision in its present inefficient state, to bring about a change in management and supervisory thinking and participation.

To do all of these things requires impressive capability in the training officers. The additional training officers should be able to deal with management and supervision, to talk about costs, risks, and job performance, and persuasively deal with questions on supervisory responsibility. The present training officers are failing to do this. Their new assistants must be better than they are in this respect.

One source of recruitment would be from amongst the middle managers or professionals of the company, as discussed earlier in this chapter. Two of these would bring about a complete transformation. Unfortunately the general manager, in his wisdom, has suggested that a Number 1 operator, aged 53 with increasing problems from arthritis, should be transferred into training from his present job. The general manager intends that this should be done, even though six such men would not make much difference. Someone must put him right.

TRAINING OFFICER CAPABILITIES

Before moving on to Part II let us summarise the capabilities required of a training officer – or of the T & D function as a whole – in order to work according to the requirements of Part I, and of Part II.

The broad heading are as follows:

1. Understanding situations

This includes the ability to gain insight into such things as boss–subordinate relations, the needs of functions or departments, inter-functional relationships, management's use of power ... right across the spectrum to understanding the career and domestic frustration of individual employees. This all amounts to seeing and understanding the company as a complete living entity, and not as an organisation chart with some names on it.

2. Working with and through people

This means working, as the day-to-day situation requires, alongside people from the chairman to the doorman, from the youngest trainees to the principal of a cooperative business school.

3. Analysis and design

The analysis of current and future situations; the identification of training/learning needs; the proposal of methods to be adopted/encouraged; the design of pro-grammes: the selection of suitable external programmes.

4. Administration

This can be for a short, one-day, workshop: or, at the other extreme, of training and development programmes for individuals or groups, lasting months or years. Based on the design in (3) above, the administration ranges from the briefing of whoever is involved as teachers or as learners, to the mountain of detailed arrangements that have to be made, and checked, for room hire, food, transport, programme printing, expense accounts, membership lists, progress reports etc.

5. The management of learning

This is distinct from programme administration (4). It is concerned with making sure that the methods and content of teaching and learning, in workshops, seminars, courses, on-the-job instruction, coaching, tutoring or counselling, is what is needed.

There are many further sub-headings that fit under the five headings above, but these suffice to identify the diversity of capabilities necessary for the success of training officers and for the function as a whole.

Part II
THE MANAGEMENT OF MANPOWER DEVELOPMENT

16 Training and manpower development

In Part I we have seen the close and necessary relationship of the training function with the other functions of the company, and the consequent collaboration which is required between the training manager and the line manager. In Part II we shall see a further collaborative relationship: this time between the training function and the other parts of the personnel function concerned with ensuring that posts are correctly filled, both now and in the future. Entering into this picture, also, will be the line manager, who is the direct employer of the post holders, and the post holders themselves.

Our first task is to gain an understanding of the full process of manpower development. We can then identify what has to be done to produce a favourable development, and come to some conclusions about roles and relationships. Within this picture the place of the training function should become clear. It will not however be possible or meaningful to discuss training in isolation, any more than it was in Part I.

We shall start by examining in outline the general case of any company whose present situation is reasonably well understood by its management, and whose future is under close scrutiny by that management. One question which is being asked concerns future manpower: are the right steps being taken to make sure that the numbers and qualities of employees are correct and to the right level? This is a question often asked by directors. They must be given an answer that does not merely state that something is being done, but that the right things are being done. How to determine the right things to do – a management responsibility – is our concern in Part II.

In an ideal analytical world the manpower development work of a company would be conducted in order to include and throw light on the following.

1   The present company

Information is required under the following headings:

(a) The present activities and technologies, with details of machinery, equipment, processes, product volumes etc. The current need for employees, by number and quality, to satisfy the activities and technologies.

(b) The present actual manpower, with detailed age structures, occupational details of skill and experience, employee wastage patterns and rates, organisation and hierarchies.

Thus we have a picture of what the company does, makes etc.; of how it does it, with what equipment, plant and methods; and of the manpower required, together with its ageing and wastage characteristics, and quality.

2   The future company

At a specified date in the future, e.g. in five years' time, the company will be different. One would like to know such things as

(a) The future activities and technologies, with details of future machinery, equipment, processes and product volume.

(b) The future manpower, with details of the future organisation and hierarchies, and numbers; the distribution of skills and qualities across the organisation, required by 2(a); the future desirable age structures.

3   The manpower objective and strategy

The manpower objective is to achieve the future manpower as specified in item 2(b). The manpower strategy will define the types of actions, in broad terms, which are to be taken in order to meet this objective. The strategy will embrace

Employee retention, redundancy and recruitment
Promotion and transfer
Education and training and job experience
Organisation development

4   The manpower plans

These will provide statements of the details of action to be taken by the subsidiary manpower functions of education and training, recruitment, personnel development etc. to meet the manpower targets, and of how these actions interlock in order that the defined strategy can be pursued and the targets met.

From this point on, action is taken by the subsidiary functions and, with sufficient monitoring and co-ordination at a senior management level, the desired manpower structures and qualities emerge in the course of time. *Unfortunately the situation is rarely, if ever, as simple and as clear-cut as described in this ideal picture.* Manpower targets prove to be wrong; recruitment proves to be difficult:

the original strategies are inappropriate. Once again the personnel function is pilloried for neglecting its responsibilities, and urged to improve its manpower capability.

But is it a question of capability? Can you get the 'right' answer by being a better analyst and planner? Or are there factors and difficulties in this work which make precision illusory? We shall look more closely at the problems of the analyst.

We wish to know two things as precisely as possible. First, the details of the future manpower requirement, in quantitative and qualitative terms. We shall use the symbol M_f for this.

Second, we wish to know the extent to which the present manpower will contribute, at that later date, to providing the future manpower. We shall use the symbol M_p for the present manpower, in quantity and quality today. However, if all the normal processes of ageing and leaving the company continue, as one would expect, the present manpower M_p will have become older and smaller, and somewhat more experienced. This older and smaller version of M_p we shall call M_c, the suffix c standing for 'core', implying that there is a 'core' of employees who remain over a length of time, the rest dying or leaving the company.

We can now construct a small equation, of great significance in manpower planning. It is

$$M_f - M_c = M_d$$

which reads. 'The difference between the manpower you want at a future date, (M_f), and the core of manpower you will be left with from your present strength (M_c), is the manpower you have to develop (M_d) between now and that future date.' It is a commonsense equation. Its simplicity of statement must not be confused with the complexity of achievement – when one looks at essential details. We shall consider the three factors in turn.

The future manpower

This will be based, as indicated in 2 (a) above on the trade levels, technology, and manufacturing methods of the future. The questions to be asked in the first instance are

1 What will the company be making and in what quantity?
2 Will there be the same plant with the same manning principles as today, or will there be new plant? What is known of the manning needed for it?
3 Will non-production employment, on administration, computers, research etc. be maintained, or altered?

Some management will claim to know, with precision, their plans for five or eight years hence. Some will be confident about manning requirements. But many will be hesitant about both and with good reason. For any company change, any growth not yet under way, is subject to some uncertainty. This is due to the unpredictability of future markets, competition, finance, automation, take-overs and mergers – to mention a few influences. What is not yet on the drawing board or not yet building, cannot be quoted with full confidence.

Hence the manpower manager, looking for information on the operations of more than, say, two to three years in the future, may not get the precise answers he is looking for. He may even be baffled by the variety of answers he gets from managers of comparable senior responsibility, particularly on projects on which no corporate final decisions have yet been taken.

The manpower core

Fortunately the analysis leading to an estimate of core size contains one element that is unarguable – that of ageing. The analyst can predict the ages of all members of the company x years ahead (assuming them still to be alive) and can account for those who will have retired by that time. What he cannot be so confident about is employee wastage; the loss of employees who leave to join other companies. This loss rate will be dependent on a number of influences, internal and external, some of which can be analysed in greater detail, some of which cannot. If there is a general expansion in the economy there could be an increase in wastage of people leaving to take better jobs elsewhere; if the economy becomes depressed then the wastage may well reduce. A study of business cycles is helpful, and the analyst hopes, in vain, that future cycles continue in the same pattern as in the past.

What age-structure and core-analysis will not reveal is who will leave the company, apart from those who retire. This may or may not be important: it is important when considering the future role of special trainee groups of technical, supervisory, executive or management type, on whose shoulders high responsibilities are to rest. These groups are especially sensitive to internal conditions and opportunities as well as to the higher paid opportunities offered by competitive companies outside.

Whilst core-analysis may produce an adequate picture of the numbers of people in any particular class, a further form of study is required to estimate the spectrum of quality of people in that class. This study, a study of human potential, may be undertaken on two distinctly different bases, as follows.

The first we shall call statistical. That is, if, in the company's 20 years of experience, Y per cent of executives aged 30 have become competent managers at specified higher levels by the age of 37, generation by generation, then it is reasonable to suppose that this development is repeatable given that the latest batch of 30 year olds is of the same general quality as before, and that the increase in responsibilities to be carried is about the same. For example, if during a period of 20 years, of 350 executives aged 30 in junior management posts, 70 have successfully occupied middle management posts, and of these 35 have successfully occupied senior management posts, then one can say there is evidence that 10 per cent of junior managers make the grade as senior managers and 20 per cent as middle managers. A trend analysis would need to show no significant change of type of person or type of work. This does not indicate exactly who is the manager of the future, but it does give an indication of whether the number of people of that quality will exist in the company.

The second we shall call individual assessment. In this case each person is looked at in order to find evidence that he has the character, capability and capacity for development that will enable him to carry higher responsibilities, general and/or specific, in the future. The assessment may be carried out by one or more managers, by specialists, or through the help of specially designed tests and exercises in assessment centres. There is some evidence of accuracy attributable to the use of either unsophisticated or the more sophisticated techniques in industrial and commercial companies; but techniques continue to develop, and can only develop successfully if they are put to realistic practical test. Personal judgement continues to be widely used, and is often preferred despite its acknowledged weaknesses and failures. The search must continue for the appropriate capabilities or competences of importance in management, in terms of which a person's present performance and future potential can be assessed. Some of these will be technical and some will be 'behavioural'.

Returning then to the quantitative and qualitative characteristics of the future manpower core, we find that, again, there is uncertainty about the estimate of both the size and the qualititative characteristics of that core.

The manpower to be developed

We now have to 'subtract' the core, Mc, from the future manpower, Mf, to tell us the size and quality of manpower that is to be developed, Md. Were Mc and Mf single precise figures produced with confidence and accuracy, the arithmetic and the ensuing target setting would be undertaken with relative ease. With Mc and Mf both uncertain, it is imperative to deal with this uncertainty sufficiently thoroughly, to produce valid manpower plans and to enable the subsidiary manpower activities to be planned with reasonable confidence.

We must appreciate that whatever the uncertainty of the future, both in the environment and within the employee groups, it is unacceptable for this uncertainty to become a psychological lack of confidence in those who have to approve manpower actions, and those who have to execute them. These managers and executives should fully understand the probabilistic nature of future prediction; and they should be knowledgeable and confident about the rationale which produces the final executive decision.

Dealing with uncertainty

One way of dealing with a number of uncertain predictions or outcomes, is to examine each outcome in turn, assess what action is required of the company in each outcome and then see what the variation of those actions is going to be. Within this range of variation of action there may be some which are practical, some of them similar. There may be one or more actions which look impossible, or are too expensive. These will cause management to rethink their operating objectives, provided they believe that those particular outcomes are reasonably likely to occur.

Two frequently used methods of analysis are based on the use of alternative scenarios and the use of sensitivity analysis. Both are used by economists in company and national forward estimating and planning, and their use in manpower planning is increasing. An outline of their methods will suffice for this text.

137

ALTERNATIVE SCENARIOS

When we think of the world as having a particular level of economic activity, a particular level of employment and a particular level of technology, we are specifying and describing a 'scenario'. Against this scenario, or backcloth, we can then describe the response of our company to the influences which act on it, influences which are determined by that scenario. We can create, in our minds and on paper, as many scenarios as we wish, and then estimate the company performance in each. We would not waste time examining scenarios which were, in whole or in part, unlikely to occur, and the use of alternative scenarios demands skill and discrimination in deciding how varied the chosen scenarios are to be, and how far into 'the unlikely' one needs to enquire.

The chosen scenarios might be based on the following factors

1   The economy, national and/or international may be (a) vigorous (b) average (c) weak
2   The company's growth may be (a) high (b) low

Thus we have six, i.e. 3 x 2, scenarios against which to estimate the demand on company manpower, and against which to make propositions on the steps to be taken to provide Md, i.e. the development of manpower to deal with the company's business in each particular scenario. One of these scenarios is that chosen by the general manager for the establishment of overall corporate trading and operating objectives.

In the examination of manpower, in each scenario there will be values for Mf and for Mc appropriate to that scenario, e.g. the wastage rates will differ from scenario to scenario and will produce different manpower cores: the company's need for executives, technologists, researchers, could be higher in a time of high company growth and produce, therefore, a larger value for Mf, the manpower required in the future.

We can estimate, therefore, for each scenario, a value for Md, in numbers and types, in quantity and quality, that have to be developed during the period of time between now and that future date. We now have to propose how each development of manpower is to take place.

The development will be based in each case, on

(a) The behaviour of the core, already allowed for in our estimates, but for whom continuing developmental provisions may be required to achieve the new qualities required.
(b) The recruitment of extra personnel to achieve the planned size and the required age, grade and skill structures.
(c) The training and development of the new recruits, initially and thereafter, to achieve the qualities required.

There are four major constraints which have to be taken into account

(i) the development of individual and team capability will be based on learning through work, on-the-job exposure and instruction, movement through 'progressive' responsibilities, as well as by attendance at courses, seminars etc. and reading. The organisation and execution of the above, particularly the job movements, must be undertaken in such a way as to allow the company's work to continue smoothly and efficiently as well as to provide suitable developmental experience for the individuals.

(ii) recruitment plans and action envisaged must be realistic, taking into account the likely state of the labour market and availability of suitable recruits in the scenario under consideration.

(iii) there will be wastage amongst those newly and recently recruited: this will probably be higher than for the existing manpower and needs separate wastage estimates.

(iv) there needs to be compatibility between the company's plans for moving, training and progressing the career of individuals, and the interests and ambitions of those individuals. Steps must be taken to bring about pay, work and career satisfaction, as far as this is possible, for all employees both inside and outside the manpower development network of plans and programmes.

Alternative manpower development strategies

We now have, for each scenario, a strategy for manpower development. Each strategy contains a statement about

Recruitment   – by number, type, work area
Transfers   – into new work areas, either for or not for planned development
Promotion   – into new/old work areas, either for or not for planned development
Training   – by types; training objectives/corporate objectives

and an indication of the way that these are intended to interlock to meet the manpower requirement for that scenario. They are interdependent and contribute to a specific manpower objective. They can only be fully and professionally understood by referring to the details of, and assumptions about, the scenario itself.

Which scenario?

Merely having a number of scenarios, each with its manpower requirement and strategy proposal, might be little more than confusing. Someone has to decide which scenarios to go for: that someone may be the general manager of the company or the managing directors. It is not the personnel manager or the manpower manager, for the scenarios must be the same as those chosen by general management for planning future company operations. Thus the choice of scenario and the 'preferred' manpower strategy is made by line management.

Account must now be taken of the future being uncertain. No one will wish to proceed on the basis that the future will precisely correspond to the one chosen scenario. It is believed, or hoped, to be the most likely one, but precautions must be taken for the occurrence of the less likely. This is achieved by examining the alternative scenarios and the alternative strategies, and comparing the preferred strategy with the alternatives. This comparison enables the company management to estimate the error of the preferred strategy if, in the course of events, the world follows the course of a different scenario, for which a different strategy should have been prescribed. A number of answers will then come to light to the questions

(i) What are the differences between the preferred manpower strategy and the other strategies?

(ii) Are the differences great or small, important or unimportant?

(iii) Will it be possible effectively to change from the preferred strategy to that which is required by the actual future situation?

(iv) Can contingency plans be drawn up now to deal with the changes in strategy at any point?

(v) What is the cost of pursuing a 'wrongly' chosen strategy?

(vi) Is there a substantial common element to all the strategies? If so can a 'common strategy' be defined, based on this common element, with small additional strategy items to be added to it according to which scenario is enacted? As an example, it may be possible to say that irrespective of which strategy we are considering, 42 men must definitely be upgraded to junior supervision and then add to this number 0, 3, 6, 7 extra for strategies A, B, C and D. Thus, with a well chosen common strategy one can proceed with confidence that the ultimate error is unlikely to be great – and later corrective steps may be possible in good time.

SENSITIVITY ANALYSIS

The selection of a common strategy is very similar to the first step in sensitivity analysis. In this, a single scenario, or a single set of assumptions about the economy and the company's trading activity, is drawn up. From this the future manpower requirement (Mf) and the manpower development to be undertaken (Md) may be estimated, as in the instances above. From this a single manpower strategy is devised, plus action plans.

Any likely variation in, for example, company growth, or the availability of external recruits, which are different from the figures put into the main calculations are then, in further calculations, given greater or lesser values, and the change in the resulting manpower requirement is calculated. Thus, for example, having assumed an executive wastage rate of 7.2 per cent per annum for the main calculation, we answer the question 'what if it is 10 per cent' by replacing the 7.2 by 10 per cent in the computation. The impact of this on the creation of vacancies, on internal movement and promotion requirements and on external recruitment requirements will be calculable. One will see precisely how sensitive the company's manpower is to variations in executive wastage. The manpower plans may have to be amended if it is shown that the company is seriously sensitive to variation in any one or more such factors.

The use of sensitivity analysis is not the same as use of scenarios. Each scenario represents a state of the world and includes judgement on the interdependence of the various factors which go to make up that world, scenario by scenario. In sensitivity analysis one is merely looking at the effect of change of one or more detail, the rest being assumed stable. The use of sensitivity analysis may be preferred where it is believed that the future is reasonably predictable. Scenarios will be used where there is a wish to understand better the interaction of factors in widely varying future economies and trading situations, and where management have to make significantly different decisions on money, plant, manpower according to their belief about the alternative futures.

17 How much planning?

The processes of forecasting and manpower analysis described in the preceding chapter represent a great deal of work, and must evoke the question 'how much of this is really necessary?' The combination of in-built uncertainty in connection with the results of such analysis, and the expense of maintaining a team of people for the purposes of manpower analysis, throws doubt on the worthwhileness of some of the more sophisticated parts of the processes. Yet, as we have seen, it is a commonsense activity, and merely attempts to deal thoroughly with points which might otherwise be overlooked, ignored deliberately, or approached simply by inspired guesswork.

The counter-question might be asked 'given the importance of manpower, can the company afford to approach its manpower problems other than thoroughly?' And to this one can add the question 'is it right to forgo meticulous planning when employees' jobs and careers may be at stake?' In most companies the ultimate question is not likely to be 'should we do manpower planning?' but instead it is likely to be *'how much* should we do?' This is a question on which the personnel function has to advise the company, and we shall devote some time to it, for the factors which are to be considered in answering this question are the same factors which help or hinder the actual plan, at a later date, when it goes into action.

Let us remind ourselves of the whole analytic and design process, step by step. The four steps are, in outline

1   Produce a statement of the present operating and manpower position of the company
2   Produce a statement of the future operating and manpower requirement of the company, with allowance for uncertainty.
3   Estimate the deficiency in quantity and quality likely to be present in the remaining future core of the company – this deficiency to be made up by recruitment, training etc.
4   Produce plans for the forthcoming years covering all aspects of manpower,

together with such contingency plans as are necessary to cope with likely internal and external upset conditions.

The readiness with which line management and personnel management will take the four steps will depend to a large extent on the type of company, its economic health and plans and the anticipated changes in the environment. Three short examples will illustrate this.

1   A medium sized company manufacturing components for the motor car industry, with a considerable capacity for increasing production by overtime working, is operating profitably whilst the economy and general trading levels of the country are at an average level. The age structures are favourable, the apprenticeship schemes are full and successful, and there is no problem in recruiting to replace either the fairly heavy unskilled labour wastage, or the skilled craftsmen and professionals. All of this is common knowledge in management circles. The future plans are to increase production slowly to maintain about the same share of the automative component market as that market grows; this will mean from time to time introducing additional plant for which there is plenty of room on the one site for at least the next 15 years. There is no impending manpower emergency or deficiency as far as can be seen, provided the external world continues to behave in the way it behaves today.

The management of the company decides that there is no need for a manpower plan; instead it is enough to carry on as at present with the recruitment, promotion, and training arrangements now in force, adjusting them from time to time according to any change in circumstances and need.

Of course, the company *has* a manpower plan of sorts, implicit in the present practices. But as the company is operating in what are almost 'steady-state' conditions, the impression is gained that there is no need for planning. We must note that steps 1, 2 and 3 have all been taken, as far as was regarded as necessary. The present position of operations and manpower is known and understood, and well documented. The future position of operations and manpower is less accurately understood, but is seen as a continuation of the present steady and slow growth with which the company is very familiar. The additional manpower requirement does not need to be anticipated and planned for, more than days, weeks or several months in advance, as is the present practice.

2   Part of a government department is to move from the capital to a small town in the provinces. This means that only some of the present staff of 1,200 people – clerks, supervisors and managers – will move with it, for some will prefer to stay in the capital city and find other work. Together with the move will come the introduction of new types of office equipment for handling and processing data. The replacement of those people who choose not to go, will be done by transferring into the department members of other departments who wish to live in the provinces, and by local recruitment in the new town. Further recruitment into the office will be largely from the new town, with some jobs held in reserve for high flyers and senior administrators from the capital and elsewhere. It is planned also to enlarge the new office to cope with entirely new work, arising from new legislation, in four years' time.

In this case all four steps are taken with great thoroughness, step 4 producing plans covering a total of six years, in order to outline the actions that have to be taken during the expansion in four years from now. In order to produce this strategy and planning, it was imperative to examine the provincial labour market and its future trends, and the output and capabilities of the schools and colleges in the vicinity. Included in the analysis was sensitivity analysis covering reasonable variations in the volume of work to be handled, and a withdrawal at the last minute of an additional percentage of people who do not want to move house to the provinces, or who find increasing computerisation unacceptable.

The plans for recruitment, transfer, promotion, and training, were produced in the form of objectives, confidently attainable, to be acted on by the subsidiary personnel functions, and by line management.

In this case it was clear that the move constituted a colossal manpower disruption, which could only be tackled by careful analysis and planning, with all managers and supervisors and employees informed and involved. This is an emergency, of sorts. There will clearly be a mix-up somewhere unless someone directs the activities of the personnel function beyond its normal day-to-day role. When this is done it is welcomed, although not by every manager and employee, for no employer can fully satisfy everyone in such circumstances. The chapter on 'corporate change' deals further with major reorganisation.

3 A large engineering company, operating internationally, and with a great strength in its design and consultation-professional staff, plans to expand its business by some 30 per cent during the next four years in order to take advantage of the upturn in overseas opportunities. The management knows clearly the sort of business it will be looking for, in which it is already expert and well known. Plans must be laid now for expansion of staff and premises. Finance and contracts are already under consideration.

Again there is a clear need for analysis and planning on the manpower side and step 1 is undertaken, to produce a statement of the present position. The personnel manager discovers that, when subject to analysis, the age structure is very worrying. Up to that moment the grey heads and the middle-aged appearance of the greater part of the population of managers and professionals was taken as a sign of experience and strength, as indeed it was. But only for the time being; for the next eight years would see 60 per cent of top people retiring or dying, and a lack of younger men to follow on. With the expansion programme to deal with at the same time, with possibly conflicting objectives, there was a lot of hard thinking to be done.

Steps 2, 3 and 4 were taken, with alternative strategies produced in step 4 to allow for different levels of expansion, and the introduction of a delayed retirement scheme. By this time the whole situation had become much less clear for most people in management. Age structure analysis and its implications was new to them and difficult to introduce into their decision-making; their main impulse was 'to get the job done' at almost all costs, and restrictions on staffing moves or recruitment were very unwelcome.

However the directors, responsible for the company's more distant future, fully recognised the problem and agreed one of the strategies. They also had to agree to the introduction, over their signature, of rules relating to recruitment and transfer and promotion which would protect the longer term interests of the company. Without these rules the immediate demands of managers and supervisors would lead to an even worse imbalance in the age structure, and even greater ageing, loss and replacement problems in a few years' time.

SOME CONCLUSIONS

From these examples we can see the place of certain basic practices in all companies, i.e.

(a) all companies must know the facts concerning present production, facilities, and its manpower. The picture of manpower must be qualitative as well as quantitative, and must be drawn up and structured in whatever ways are required to illuminate present and future situations and trends.

(b) all companies must know which way they are going operationally – that is a normal responsibility of the directors. They must also know the sort of manpower required to conduct future operations, whether there is a great or little change envisaged in the future.

(c) all companies must estimate, even if only as a first approximation, the deficiency in future manpower consequent on the above; ideally, estimating what will be required beyond the remaining core, as distinct from estimating what will be required beyond current recruitment levels.

  The amount of work needed to produce (b) and (c) will depend on the size and complexity of the changes proposed for the future, the revelation of the manpower structures, and how stable the environment is now and in the future.

(d) strategies must be decided for an agreed period of time on all aspects of manpower, to meet agreed objectives. The plans then to be produced may be very simple, or very complex, depending on the extent to which the objectives and strategies deviate from the present objectives and strategies. There may even be no change in manpower plans and activities. But in all case the *decisions on objectives and strategies and the rationale behind the decisions should be understood by members of line management, personnel management, and by the employees in those areas affected by the decisions.* The decision that there is to be no change in the levels and targets for recruitment and training, should not mean that there is no plan. There must be one, and it must be communicated in such a way as to show its relevance to objectives.

18 The economic and political context

It was said earlier that the many considerations, and types of analysis, which enter into the production of a manpower development plan should be known to the managers of recruitment, training, and other sections of manpower activity and control in the company. It goes without saying that these specialists will provide information on their specialisms, on which the analysis and plans will, to some extent, be based. They will also hold opinions on the practicability of such plans as they emerge, as well as on the assumptions which have to be made in order to create the scenarios and manpower models needed for analysis and prediction. All of this implies an ongoing dialogue between planner and personnel specialist, which should prove helpful to both, in creating mutual understanding and in producing acceptable and practicable plans.

There is a further way in which knowledge of the basic assumptions made during planning, proves to be of value to those responsible for its execution. This knowledge enables the executive to see for himself whether the world, inside and outside the company, is behaving as predicted, as the months and years pass by. Some of the variables he deals with in the course of his daily work on behalf of the development plan are sensitive to the impact of major internal and environmental factors. The planner will have assumed some of these factors to be active during the design and the subsequent operation of the plan. In the event, a particular factor may, indeed, be active. It may be benign and pass unnoticed by the personnel executives; or it may seem to be menacing, and cause worry and a local change in tactics which should not be introduced, in view of the fact that the upset presently being experienced has already been allowed for in the plan.

On the other hand, a factor may, in reality, not be active, or may be less active, and the plan is rendered to some extent inappropriate. Further, new factors, not allowed for at all in the plan, may become active. How does the personnel executive know that these are changes in circumstances demanding new planning attention, *if he does not know what the original planning assumptions were?* This sort of oversight can and does produce problems in companies, and before we go on to look at the more powerful factors in some detail, an example will illustrate the impact of such factors where full information on assumptions previously made is not given to the executives responsible for day-to-day activities.

A chemical company establishes a new factory on the northern seaboard of Europe and invests in commissioning training along the lines of the example called 'New plant commissioning' in Chapter 12. It is intended that after commissioning and the completion of initial job training, there is to be a new phase of employee development for which a plan is drawn up. This plan contains what is known as flexibility training, which enables operators to acquire knowledge and skills that are required for working on other parts of the plant. This makes it possible to move operators into work beyond their present responsibilities, at very short notice. It makes shift-work organisation, promotion, and the handling of emergency situations on the plant much easier and more readily dealt with.

This training proceeds smoothly, but within six months it is clear that all is not well. High losses in operators become noticeable to both the process superintendent and the training officer. The plant manning and the continuity of the flexibility training are suffering. A great effort is made to examine the rate of loss of operators and, wherever possible, stem the outward flow. But it is of no use. At the end of 18 months the rate of loss of locally recruited operators is calculated at 41 per cent although it is improving. There is considerable distress amongst management, and amongst those responsible for the flexibility training. There is also a sense of failure, and, to a small extent, an element of recrimination in the discussions which take place on this point.

The matter is raised with the Head Office specialists responsible for the overall planning of this new factory. It is then announced by the planners that the anticipated wastage for the first two years had been 46 per cent, this being the estimated figure provided by the local employers' federation for new process shift-work on a seaboard in a vicinity in which there is a sizeable fishing industry of a seasonable nature. 'You are to be congratulated', said head office, 'for keeping the wastage down to 41 per cent.'

Whatever the sense of relief may have been in the factory at learning this news, it could not compensate for the inefficiency of the previous 18 months. There would have been a totally different pattern of recruitment and training after commissioning; there would have been no time wasted on examining and prescribing for a wastage rate that was unavoidable but, if anticipated in time, manageable. The information had been available; it was used by the planners in the centre, but it was not passed down the line. The reality proved to be very much as the planners anticipated, but when it happened the local executives, not forewarned, found it unacceptable and reacted against it.

It is a factor such as this, i.e. an unusually high wastage rate, that obliges management to take a rather more carefully calculated step in drawing up its manpower development plans, producing often a proposition that is not the same as otherwise. One can envisage the situation in another factory in which the actual wastage rate is a mere 5 per cent per annum. This would mean, wastage patterns being what they are, that after the first three years there would be a large enduring core of operators. If the age structure is right, succession planning and promotions and associated training would be relatively easy to design and execute. With

147

a plant and manpower expansion every five years or so there would be room in the future for all competent and ambitious employees.

Knowing this the factory management could well say that they have no particular planning problems in manpower. They can deal with each situation, as it arises, in good time. There are succession plans for senior posts and key posts, and any deficiency is made good by outside recruitment. 'There are plenty of good people in the town who would like to work for us. We are regarded as a very good company, you know.' Lucky company that they are. But not all companies can make these claims, and for no fault of their own. Will the luck last forever? Will the various external factors which influence the future of manpower, always remain favourable?

The answer to this question must be that these factors *will* change. It is vital that management understand not merely that there is a wide range of factors that have a bearing on manpower, but also that changes can take place in these factors and their impact on the company. There is no standard list of factors and changes and impacts, for the consequence of changes varies from one situation to the next, sometimes for good and sometimes for bad. It is fundamental that management acquire the ability to perceive these factors, and to understand the dependence of their personal success on variations in them. We shall examine some of the more typical factors, and the effect of variations in them.

TRADING STABILITY

This does not at first sight look like a factor that influences the successful implementation of manpower development plans, but it is the most significant of all. Its importance is perhaps most readily appreciated in cases of instability or upset in the company as the result of a sudden and unfavourable change in external financial, marketing, or political circumstances. Obviously the loss of a large government contract, the inability to extend the borrowing of money for capital development schemes, or the overnight change in consumer preference for a previously much sought after product, creates an atmosphere of uncertainty and anxiety in the company that is often followed quickly by decisions and actions designed to save money, or reduce losses. But there is more than money saving involved. A management which feels itself menaced, is a defensive management, and defensiveness often leads to a withdrawal from anything, activity or expenditure, that is not immediately necessary. It is not unusual to find a slowing-up in training and development work in such circumstances, even though the company concerned can still afford the money, the time and the effort demanded. The reason for the withdrawal is, in effect, often of a psychological nature and may affect the wealthiest of enterprises.

The form that the withdrawal from manpower development takes is familiar. The first to suffer will be the apprenticeship and traineeship schemes, with recruitment stopped or cut back. Then will come the use of external courses, with cancellations and a reduction in the rate at which people are nominated. Then a slowing up in the posting of people into jobs identified for development purposes. It requires a strong and clear headed management to see, and to declare, that not only are such economies not needed, but that they are also harmful to the company's longer term interests. Each withdrawal action is, in terms of immediate cost saving, apparently justifiable. What is of interest to us is to recognise that at the time the manpower development plan was drawn up, at some earlier date, it will have been known that the company's fortunes were bound to fluctuate; but it was not at that time prescribed that there should be a cut-back in development each time a downward fluctuation took place. In times of relative prosperity such cut-back proposals are seen to be destructive, and counterproductive for the long term.

At the opposite extreme we have the company that is very securely placed in a very favourable trading position. Its products are easy to make, they are in great demand, and there is no important competition. This position has been held for many years, and, apart from wars and political crises, could go on indefinitely. Although these benign factors do not ensure easy and manageable development programmes for company manpower, they do influence the quality and form that they take, in an important way.

First, the company in a sense is successful and, although the success may not be due to management and executive vitality and creativity at all, there may be present in the company a feeling of self-sufficiency and capability that is only valid whilst these favourable external circumstances remain. There may be actually a marked level of inefficiency in management, executive or operational activities, which passes unnoticed; or noticed, is regarded as part of the culture of that company. Which it is, of course. During this period of company existence it is seen that development programmes have certain characteristics. Whilst they may be effective in ensuring that future vacancies, particularly in management and key posts, are never in want of people to fill them, (there is always someone available in the development process), the question of high quality and capability is relatively unimportant. For in companies in which management is under relatively little strain, and can cope with the bulk of its problems by using a little commonsense – no matter what minor inefficiencies ensue – there is little interest, or incentive, in accumulating increasing management expertise, or in teaching it.

So we suggest that the environmental factors which present favourable or difficult trading conditions, have their influence on the patterns of manpower development, and that this influence is not always properly recognised. The company behaves as it does, not only because of rational decisions, but instinctively or intuitively – there is no suitable word for a corporate response of this type. We now have to look at the impact on the company of a change in this external factor.

The first of our two example companies now finds that, instead of being in an adverse trading position, its situation is markedly improved; substantial long term contracts for the manufacture and supply of goods on an increasing scale have been signed, and should keep the production line running and expanding for a predicted five years. Cheaper capital and government subsidies make it possible to develop the plant and improve all facilities very quickly. The 'future' for which the forward plans were drawn up three years ago has arrived, and looks very promising.

However the manpower position is not satisfactory. Although the company directors have worked hard to get the business opportunities which have now materialised, they have failed to maintain the rate of development of the manpower needed fully to exploit these opportunities. There is a shortage of skilled men in the tool room, of technicians in instruments and controls, of supervisors ready for movement and promotion, of executives with sophisticated skills in project development, and of senior managers capable of controlling everything from cash to labour relations in the most complex growth the company has yet undertaken. Some aspects of company affairs may suffer as a result: too much money may be spent on expansion, inadequate reorganisation may lead to labour troubles and wastage, lack of leadership can demotivate the research and design staff, and false economies on equipment and tooling will lead to unnecessary obsolescence. These are all failures ultimately in human capability, a capability that was not developed in time.

There are many companies who are in this position from time to time. Some fail and go under. Others survive, even flourish. In some cases the loss of efficiency is not recognised as such, for if things go badly they may still either get straightened out or be accepted as a hazard or a difficulty, and not as a sign of incompetence in the executive, manager or director concerned. Shortages of skilled men, technicians and professional staff, reliable and well versed in company practices are, on the other hand, readily recognised as such, and are a failure by the company to plan and develop its manpower effectively. The same upturn in the economy that has helped this company to get back on its feet has generated business and expansions in other companies also, and the recruiters are not going to find it easy to get the required personnel in the numbers and quality required from the outside market.

The second of our two companies is in an equally difficult position when its trading position suffers as the result of an adverse change in the external economy. Its culture and its manpower development plans have produced managers, executives and technologists whose outlook has been unimaginative and relatively non-competitive, but fully able to run the company as it was; these same people now have not only to determine how the company should run in the future, but have also actually to run it in this new way. This is an important distinction to make. Determining that the company must be from now on competitive, creative and aggressive in its approach to everything from organisation to advertising, is little more than an intellectual exercise. Actually *being* competitive, creative and aggressive when previously you have not been, is vastly more difficult, perhaps impossible, for those same people.

The point of importance for manpower development is this. It has to be recognised that although the strategies and objectives and actions embarked on were right for the company as it was, they are almost certainly wrong and unacceptable after the trading and economic upset, if we assume that things will not revert to what they were before. Moreover the new requirement of the company is not likely to be met purely by increasing the amount of training and development as conducted earlier; the objectives and the required quality now have to be changed, and quickly. This merely reflects the position in all the departments and functions of the company in its day to day work. The old style, tempo and criteria may have to go, along with the actual pre-crisis plans. There is no sense in allowing the development plans and training activities to drift on as though nothing had happened; they must be recast to help bring about the regeneration of the company.

It is easy to criticise the manpower development plans, and the planners themselves, for having adopted a blinkered outlook towards the requirements of the company's present and future manpower, for having failed to produce the capability to deal with the new situation. Criticism will be levelled at any part of management which is held responsible for the damage now visible in the company, and the unhappiness and uncertainty experienced by its members. It is understandable, particularly when there are quick reductions in personnel, a freeze on expansion, and an anticipated loss of promotion opportunities for many ambitious members of the company; but not always justifiable, for there can always be changes in the economic and political environment which will defeat the best run enterprises.

What is open to criticism is the thoughtless assumption that the environment will never change for the worse; and the failure to equip the company's managers and professional staff for such an event. Hence the training and development objectives and activities must always deliberately embody elements which produce vitality, even though such vitality may at any one moment appear to be absent from the ongoing secure company, well placed in trading and economic terms. How this is to be done will depend on the particular company, but it cannot be introduced merely as stimulating and thought provoking material in company courses and seminars. It has to have a real opportunity to express itself in the day to day work of the company. Developments must be encouraged, even if with small marginal pay-offs, in such companies because they engender the creativity, adaptability and the continuous learning which are essential for healthy survival in the longer term.

Thus the culture of the company itself is changed, and as a result the development of its people changes. On paper the development programmes may look the same from one company to another, from one culture to another, but what is experienced may be fundamentally different in content and value. Continuous learning and development and cultural changes are discussed further in later chapters.

POLITICAL OBSTACLES AND INCENTIVES

We move now from the problems posed by changing external economic circumstances to those created by politically inspired actions and schemes. During the past 25 years the direct and indirect effect of actions and rulings of the government of the country have become increasingly noticeable, and, in some instances, of prime importance. Whatever country one is in, one has to take account of legislation concerned with manpower and employee relations, and of the schemes and financial rewards and penalties presented by the government. No discussion of factors influencing manpower development can be adequate without the inclusion of the way in which a company can use the facilities offered in that country; nor without taking into account the way that powerful and persuasive government action can shape or warp the progress of manpower development in that country.

In Europe there has been considerable advance in legislation concerning the employment and the training of employees in industry and commerce. Each country has afforded greater or lesser authority under these headings to the employer, the employee, the trade union or other employees' representative bodies, and to the government itself. The differences are too numerous and too complex to be discussed in any detail in this text, as are the resulting benefits and costs of these new measures. One thing is clear however in all countries: no matter how vigorously the government legislates for further advances, there can be no sudden improvement in the quality of the development work undertaken, and there will be education and training only as good as the quality of the resources available in the country and in the companies. These resources, the industrial managers, the business school teachers, the development programmes, can only improve slowly.

During this slow improvement we witness another phenomenon. It is the devotion of considerable effort to meeting legislative requirements, and, where possible, to beating the system. That is to say, the requirements imposed by law on a company, which define that company's obligations, make it necessary for the company to spend time and money in meeting these obligations. These obligations are not necessarily the same thing as the development requirements of the manpower in that company, although ideally they would correspond quite closely. As a result we find amongst company managements, particularly in countries in which the legislation is powerful, a tendency to drift into a form of management schizophrenia. Whilst speaking the language of training and development, they are at the same time increasingly concerned with the fact that they have to act according to regulations which they wish to reject, and have to take training and development actions which may not be best for the company's real requirements. A company which has to spend a certain percentage of its payroll on training might easily find itself embarrassed by underspending in a particular year. It then hastens to find ways of quickly spending more, or of presenting its accounts in a more favourable way. It is thus on the edge of corruption; not, perhaps, very serious corruption, but which will bias development decisions towards financial expediency.

For the moment we are concerned with recognising the impact that action, taken by the government, has on the course of manpower development within the company, on its control and on the ultimate achievement of objectives. We see that there can be a complete destruction, in some situations, of the progress of training and development, not because of deliberate intervention but because of the unforeseen consequences of governmental actions, even of a benign nature.

The questions for management to deal with are:

1 Is it possible to predict what legislation or action will be undertaken in the future, that will have a significant impact on company manpower, with particular reference to its training and development?
2 Is it possible then to estimate the precise effect that this will have on the company manning and efficiency?
3 If the effect is unacceptable can the government be persuaded to modify its actions in such a way as to satisfy all concerned?
4 If the government cannot be persuaded, what are the choices left to the company, and which should it take?

In some countries the experience of the past plus the sophistication of social and economic analysis undertaken by both the government and by independent bodies have shown the complex interactions between government action in tax and monetary control, and the national level of industrial output; between economic growth and unemployment levels; and between unemployment levels and human health and vitality in the local communities. Within the companies themselves it is recognised that legislation does not merely affect unemployment; it affects internal organisation and career prospects, although with less predictability. It affects not only the manpower development requirements, but also the ability of the company to meet these requirements.

In the developing countries this is equally true, and as elsewhere there must be some consideration of present and future legislation in drawing up manpower and manpower development objectives and plans. It requires the development of mutual confidence and rapport between industry, commerce and the government, if there are to be the earliest possible discussions on the subject of future legislation and its effect on manpower. It requires also that within the companies there are managers with external political responsibilities who understand the manpower implications of legislation, who can bring their anxieties to the attention of general management in good time, and influence the decisions on the ultimate form that manpower plans are to take. At the same time, it would appear reasonable that government representatives are presented with the information concerning the impact of legislation on the ability of a company to meet its development requirements, and that these representatives are able fully to understand and appreciate this information.

Training and development in developing countries is given further attention in Chapter 31, 'The international context'.

19 Planning and the individual

There are two distinct and different ways in which manpower and its development may be thought about, which are complementary to one another. One is concerned with the various structures within the company of a static or dynamic nature; the other is concerned with the quality of the individuals and with the specific characteristics of the jobs which have to be filled. The structures are revealed by the analyst working on problems of age distribution, skill or qualification distribution, costs of employment, wastage incidence and variation and so on. Within this work the individual, by name and by personal identity, must disappear; the material produced by the structural analyst deals with populations of people, with the fact of their existence, their lengths of service, their distribution in space and time, and in any other social dimension which he chooses to consider.

On the other hand in dealing with quality and specific characteristics, we are immediately concerned with the person as an individual, or strictly speaking, with our view of that person. We are also concerned with particular jobs, where they are, the skills required, the sort of person needed to fill each one – again, in our view. This is much more like a close up on life itself than the structural picture presented by the analyst. Sometimes these two views of the whole situation produce conflict and misunderstanding, and problems for manpower development, and it is important to stress not merely the complementarity of the two, but the need for management thoroughly to understand this complementarity in human and structural detail as well as in principle. If the detail is not understood then, despite a general understanding of the quality/structure relationship and interaction, decisions and actions can be taken, which, although well intended, conflict with agreed policies. Moreover without this detailed understanding it is possible, whilst considering the individuals, to draw up policies for their development which are structurally impossible to achieve. We can illustrate this by an example.

A company decides to rationalise its organisation and manpower in order to improve communications and management efficiency, as well as to improve the effectiveness of its manpower. There is to be no cut back in personnel, but there will be a deliberate control on a lower growth rate in personnel during at least the next five years; the recent growth rate has been approximately 8½ per cent p.a., and the new target is to be only 2 per cent. At the same time there will be a growth in output and sales of 6 per cent p.a. and this will be achieved by the increased productivity brought about by regrouping and some changes in working methods.

The management declare that not only is there to be no redundancy, but that these decisions herald the beginning of an even more prosperous era for the company and for those who work in it. Training and development will continue as before, and the career prospects within the company are unaltered.

Let us look at career prospects first. For most people this means, within the one company, promotion with commensurate pay increases, not merely pay increases. The structural analyst, looking closely at the actual age and hierarchical structures and the way in which people have been advancing into vacancies produced by expansion, death and other wastage, discovers that in this particular company, by reducing the personnel growth rate from 8½ to 2 per cent p.a. (not, remember, the total size of the company) the number of vacancies occurring per annum that present promotion opportunities will be halved.

This means that the career prospects are definitely altered. The chances of being promoted are now half what they were. This was not the intention of management; it was implicit in the structure of the company. This information presents management with an entirely new problem to solve, for the probability is that once the truth is generally realised then the more ambitious and perhaps the more competent professionals and junior managers will leave to seek their fortunes elsewhere.

Let us look at the implications of this for manpower development. If the frequency of promotion vacancies halved, then the numbers of people under development and consideration for promotion during the next few years should surely be either halved or otherwise reduced. Therefore the various plans and activities of the development specialists in the company must all be reviewed, and new targets and plans set and drawn up. Should the employees be told? Can it be kept secret? Or should the plans continue as at present?

It can be quickly pointed out that running a development scheme which has an 'output' far in excess of the company's promotion requirement can magnify the disappointment and frustrations felt in the company. The management is left with a difficult decision to make.

Those who are responsible for the planning and assessment of the individuals and their careers and promotions, are likely to be as disappointed and frustrated as the individual employees. As the guardians of quality is it not their responsibility to ensure that people of high ability and potential end up in the job that matches this ability and potential? In the company in this example, the quality specialist can view the change in company growth rate as nothing short of a disaster. The structural analyst regards it as a triumph for rationality.

Bearing the above points in mind let us now look separately at questions of quality and structure, and consider how they influence the form that manpower development takes and how changes in them can produce problems for the management of a development scheme. First we shall look at quality, but, of course, referring to structural points whenever this is necessary.

Within any company there are a whole range of jobs to be done, and for which posts have to be filled. Within this range there are jobs which vary in difficulty from the simplest to the most complex, demanding simple commonplace skills to esoteric sophisticated capabilities. This range, from simple to complex, represents one important axis of employment requirements, and, at the same time, job and career opportunities.

Within any population there exists also a range of personal capability, not uniformly distributed, from those with only the simplest capabilities to those with the most complex. The reasons for the variation are many: the genetic inheritance of the child at birth, upbringing and health during growth and development, schooling, and the opportunities presented by choice and by chance, during the whole lifetime, to develop an otherwise latent capability. Within these capabilities are those of literacy and numeracy, on which so much other learning can depend, provided through the medium of schooling; and others, totally different, such as intelligence and stamina. The list is long, and our crude summary is offered only for the purpose of this immediate argument.

No individual is limited in his capabilities to those things which he is presently doing. It is now a conventional assumption in manpower work to speak of both the present skills and capabilities of a person; and of the skills and capabilities usually of more complex nature, that he might reveal in the future. The latter are referred to as potential. Sometimes the meaning of potential is glossed over, with the result that manpower development is organised without sufficient understanding of the processes of human development, to the disadvantage of the company and the individual.

Potential can be better understood by simple illustrations. If a person can today do, in mathematics, square-root calculations, and has also a fair understanding of elementary geometry, then it is reasonable to suppose that at some moment in the future he will quickly master calculations on right-angled triangles according to Pythagoras's theorem. This represents a potential which he has, which could be best described as the wider exercise of a present capability. On the other hand it would not be reasonable to suppose that he would quickly master elementary differential calculus at any moment in the future. He might, but many people do not. That step entails the use of quite different concepts and ways of thinking. If he is going to master them, he will require a potential of a different sort from that needed to move on to Pythagorean calculations.

There are then two broad types of potential, both expressing themselves in the doing of 'new' things at some time in the future. One, we see as the wider use of present capability, which we shall call capital potential, and the other we see as the emergence of a new quality in that person, which we shall call development potential. The assessment of capital potential demands little more than the study of present capabilities in a person, and then seeing if any particular combination will equip him to deal with a situation with which he has not yet been confronted, i.e. seeing if he has the potential to deal with that new and perhaps more complex task.

This, we must hasten to add, cannot be a fully reliable approach to the assessment of capital potential for though the analyst may undertake an accurate estimate of the things that make up the new job and its responsibilities, the job-as-a-whole is something that that individual has not previously been confronted with, and may actually constitute a challenge to his own development potential. Nevertheless, one can regard this approach as providing a fair first approximation.

The assessment of development potentials is much more difficult, for one is trying to predict the performance level of a person in an activity or a skill which contains elements which he has so far never exercised himself on. Moreover one is not concerned merely with the question 'can he do it?' but instead 'can he do it well?' knowing that failure by him to cope may be masked by him for a long time; and that during that time he, or his subordinates, may have to endure anxiety and even psychological damage. There are predictive tests produced by psychologists and used by some companies and the selection boards of governments and the armed forces. The more precise the conditions of the future job, and the more mature and extensively educated and experienced the candidate is, the more material there is for capital potential to be appraised and matched against the posts under consideration, and the less one depends on the assessment of development potential.

Once he is moved into a job of more testing responsibilities, the individual is subject to further appraisal, and the picture of capital potential is brought up to date, providing a fuller picture of the person against which to consider even further moves.

The problem for the developer is to know what progress in career a person has made, and might make, drawing on capital; what he has achieved through the expression of development potential; and then what he is likely to do in the way of expression of development potential in the future. This question is not often regarded as a major one. With the preliminary sorting out of people through the education system one major classification of human resources has been undertaken for the employer, although it may be an inaccurate and even unjust classification. The schools and universities produce people on whom one can make quick judgements about intelligence and academic knowledge. Both are of high immediate value to the employer; academic knowledge, particularly at about graduate level, will be the material of capital potential for some years; intelligence plus literacy and quick learning ability help ensure that jobs and tasks, the facts and figures, are learned quickly in successive jobs, but little more.

Whereas the use of capital is one of exploitation, the processes of development potential are essentially ones of cultivation. In the appraisal of a person's performance, and in the consideration of his further potential the questions asked differ according to whether one is concerned with capital potential or with development potential. To estimate capital potential one needs to know the person's capability in given and definable tasks and skills. Consequently the level of performance in bookkeeping, or in chairmanship, or in computer programming has to be focused on. If they are imperfect in any important way they can be polished up. They can be used in other jobs and represent a great resource in the company. However, in attempting to appraise a person's development potential, and in handling a development programme based on and concerned with this form of potential, a fundamentally different philosophy has to be adopted.

We are confronted by a higher degree of uncertainty as to the outcome of moving a person into work to which he takes a relatively low capital potential, thus

157

obliging him to undertake a much higher proportion of learning in areas which may be very unfamiliar. This uncertainty is not to be confused with 'lack of confidence', nor is the inability of a person to adapt himself to some of the tasks now to be undertaken to be regarded as failure. Within such a programme despite the fact that executive, supervisory and all other types of work still have to be done efficiently, the people involved are engaged in important learning and growth processes, from which the manpower developer can learn – and there is no other way – something about the future capabilities of those people.

20 Philosophies of development

Consciously or unconsciously, management conducts its manpower development in a particular style and according to certain beliefs and principles. The adherence to a belief, appropriate to the company's requirement and situation, is a management prerogative. Techniques are common throughout many companies, but all hold somewhat different beliefs about their best use. That is to say that such things as appraisal, selection, job rotation, special projects, internal and external courses, are ingredients to be found the world over, and do not indicate in themselves the strategy into which they fit. Nor do they indicate the assumptions which have been made, or which are implied, about why that particular strategy will lead to the realisation of manpower objectives, whereas another strategy will not. Inevitably, in dealing with long term human affairs and the prediction of outcome some years into the future, personal belief and conviction must enter into the final decision on strategy, and hence the word philosophy does not seem to be out of place.

Strangely, even a philosophy which is without any real supporting evidence may be adopted and maintained, simply because it remains untested. Consequently, we are interested in the basis for, and evidence in favour of, the adoption of any particular philosophy. It must of course be practical, lead to economical operation, and simple in concept so that those who operate it and work in it and alongside it can understand it. But there have been some development schemes which have looked good on the drawing board, and whose philosophy and strategy have seemed admirable, but which have 'got it wrong' about the human being. How can this come about?

There are three main principles on which beliefs, philosophies and strategies can be based. They are the deterministic principle, the probabilistic principle, and the heuristic principle, and we shall define and discuss each of these in turn, and see how they lead to different learning processes, administration and results.

THE DETERMINISTIC PRINCIPLE

When the company chairman decides that his nephew, who has just left college, will become the managing director in ten years' time, he is employing the deterministic principle. Whether or not this appointment ever comes about is open to doubt and in this sense we are not using the word deterministic in the same way as it is used in the mechanical sciences. In our case it means that a decision has been made, an intention has been stated; and moreover there is a belief that in some way this is the right decision to make. The deterministic principle is not confined to chairmen and their nephews, for it appears over and over again in a wide variety of decisions. It has to, because sooner or later someone has to decide what is to be done, and issue an instruction.

When Jack Smith is told by his branch manager that he is to become the next section leader, as from Monday fortnight, this is taken as a normal and correct use of authority and judgement. Monday fortnight is sufficiently close for the decision to be made with a feeling of total confidence; Smith is the best qualified and experienced man for the job, and it is very unlikely that anything will alter that within the next two weeks. However, if the branch manager tells one of the juniors, Bill Jones, that he will be the successor to Smith when Smith retires in five years' time, this news would lack credibility. Jones is inexperienced, not yet fully qualified, has trouble with his wife and suffers from asthma. All of these are reasons why such a deterministic judgement seems unreliable, even unnecessary. It is too soon to predict whether he will prove to be suitable such a long way into the future, and with so much still to learn.

The deterministic principle, according to which it is determined today that a particular individual will be moved into a new post on a prescribed date in the future, is more or less reliable, more or less valuable, depending on the length of time between today and the date of the commission, and the new capabilities which that person has to acquire in the meantime, or demonstrate shortly after moving into the new post.

The longer the time that has to elapse, the more chance there is for something to intervene, and to make the move undesirable or impracticable. The person may leave the company, or become mentally ill, or there may be an unpredicted reorganisation and his company career has led him in a totally different direction. Or his personal maturing has not continued as hoped for; the early signs of brightness were misleading. He can no longer be considered. The greater the development in capability required of a person, obviously the greater the risk that he will not make the grade on the day. Clearly this risk is minimised if we are concerned with people who are well endowed with capital potential and if they are able to draw on that capital potential to meet the requirements of the new job.

Whatever the ultimate outcome of the use of the deterministic principle, whether the decisions are put fully and successfully into action, or whether people fall by the wayside, we recognise the use of that principle. Successful or not at a later date, it is the way in which the question of filling the post was approached; it is of interest that there will be a percentage of failures, and that success in such an appointment process has a probabilistic aspect.

THE PROBABILISTIC PRINCIPLE

Everyone knows, of course, that the future is unpredictable to some extent, and that any attempt to base long term manpower planning and development on the deterministic principle will fail, although it will be possible to keep the company running by taking corrective steps each time a long term deterministic decision proves to be wrong, provided there are time and resources enough for this correction. In using the probabilistic principle one builds in an allowance for failure, and sufficient cover to ensure that despite failures there are people of sufficient calibre to fill the more senior jobs in the future. It works like this.

The senior mechanical engineer in the engineering department will retire in about seven years. Who should replace him from amongst the 12 or so capable junior men, one or two rungs down in the organisation in that large department? Of these the directors identify four who are most promising, and are tempted to select one of them now, in secret, in order to groom him for promotion at a later date. This would have been straightforward deterministic selection. It is decided instead to provide all four and one or two others with opportunities for more complex responsibilities, watch them carefully, and see how they turn out. The probability of one of them, perhaps even two or three, making the grade, is much higher than that of one person doing so. This is a very simple principle, and often used, but also often abused. One is playing a totally different sort of probability game if only one person is under observation over a long period of time. The probability of success is less than satisfactory; the object of the probability principle is to maximise the probability of having a good person available for the vacancy, not merely to take a risk.

It is a principle that may be consciously employed in initial recruitment of qualified staff. Although no attempt is made to predict which five out of 25 recruited each year will be promoted into junior management in about six years' time, the probability is high that there will be five or more fully suitable people from this year's group of recruits. They do not have to be personally identified by the recruiter; he could not do it, and he is not expected to do it. What he is expected to do, and this is the essence of probabilistic planning, is to make sure that the attributes of those recruited today are such as to ensure that a given proportion of them are suitable for promotion in five years from now.

Two points stand out. The probabilistic principle is good cover if one is seeking development of people according to our definition of potential development. Potential development pushes into the unknown, the uncertain, and there is safety in numbers. The second point is that even the well trained recruiter will be tempted to make his predictions of the development of each person taken on; he may feel himself obliged to do this should his directors ask if the quality and potential of this year's recruits is sufficient to ensure a sound junior management in five to ten years' time. It is to be hoped that the directors understand the probabilistic approach and the high confidence which it produces – if it is understood.

THE HEURISTIC PRINCIPLE

First we must look at the word heuristic. It comes from the Greek *heurikein*, which means 'to find'. It has acquired a number of uses and slightly varied meanings, all relating to the idea of 'finding out'. In education it refers to a method of education by which a pupil is set to find out things for himself; in the management sciences it refers to decision-making in situations in which all the moves and consequences cannot be foreseen, and the decision has to be taken in steps, by trial and error, so that when one step is taken you see where you have reached, and only then decide on the next step, and so on.

We use it in the following way. When a person is confronted with things to learn and to do that are new to him, he undertakes only that learning and action which he is capable of achieving with some confidence. When he has acquired the ease and facility suitable for its use he then undertakes learning and action in further new skills and knowledge. When this is achieved he moves on again. At each stage he experiences interest and satisfaction. He does not move on into areas of more advanced learning if he is inept and disinterested; he moves on only where the interest and, of course, the opportunities lie. The task of the educator is, amongst other things, to provide the breadth of opportunities, sufficient to keep the learning and action on the move, and, in an industrial situation, which are of relevance to the content of industrial occupations and technology. Thus the learner moves forward step by step and is limited mainly to his own learning capacity and not by the difficulty of lessons or training or instruction which are beyond his immediate reach. It is a very powerful educational method, but is not commonly adopted in schools, as it is difficult to administer.

In another sense the word heuristic is appropriate. The educator or supervisor is learning also about the abilities of the pupil as he goes through this step by step learning process; he cannot predict the full range of knowledge and skill that any one person will develop during the educational process, or what the particularly strong points in his achievements will be; he has to go along with the heuristic development of the learner and watch the potential unfold, a direction largely determined by the learner.

This may be a new word for many readers, but it will not be a completely new idea. Even in industry it has been recognised that the beginning of an apprentice-ship in, for example, machine shop engineering, should include a variety of opportunities to try different skills and materials to work on, different hand and machine tools to get the feel of. This is simply to find the initial likes and dislikes based on a little experience, before launching into several years of specialisation. It is not the full educational process for the apprentice, but is intended to provide a basis for decisions on 'what next', using what the learner himself has found out, and then what he is interested in pursuing, what he is good at.

Heuristic learning is likely to be a prominent feature of potential development as we defined that term earlier, for it is concerned with the realisation of abilities which up to the present have not been expressed by the individual. It is not concerned with the expression of capital development, for this form of develop-ment is little other than the use of already developed skills, but in a different combination or in a different situation from previously.

One can see immediately that the extensive use of the heuristic principle becomes something of a problem when one is considering a normal industrial or commercial organisation. If we consider first of all the development of children, and of young adults in a company training centre, we recognise that it is possible for the environment in which these young people grow and learn to be such as to support the heuristic principle in action. There will be a diversity of opportunities for things to do, whether in the home, the play group, the junior school or in the appropriately designed training centre. Moreover there is acceptance on the part of those who are in charge, that personal interest and personal dedication to chosen pursuits is important. There is no output target to be reached, and no deadline for its achievement; the object of the activities, from the point of view of the organisers, is the development of the people involved in the activities, each according to his own potential.

Inside a company, at normal employment levels, it is overwhelmingly typical that the work undertaken by employees is very tightly defined and controlled, allowing little if any room for the exercise of personal interest and flair, or for dropping those tasks in which the employee has neither interest nor marked capability. Adjustment may be made to suit the individual only if the efficiency of the work is not impaired. Heurism has little room for expression, and we would, generally speaking, not expect it to be otherwise. However, jobs in which there is the possibility of working 'your own way' and of pursuing goals according to your own judgement, can offer a lot of heuristic scope; that is to say, scope to encounter and try your hand at things which are new to you, but which engage your interest, and which, at the same time, may offer some economic benefit to the company. Those who work in the professions or in management, and who are concerned with the development of their work area, or with design or research, may be stretching themselves into new fields of knowledge, and developing according to the heuristic principle.

If one wishes to employ the heuristic principle, therefore, one has to see whether or not any particular job contains heuristic opportunity, perhaps suitable for the individual under consideration. If it does not, then the movement of the person across a number of jobs may provide sufficient opportunity for him to encounter tasks and ideas which strongly motivate him, and in which he may then develop otherwise unexpressed potential to a level of capability significantly higher than what is acquired when a high level of interest is lacking.

For the manpower developer there are many difficulties at this point. He has to find a way of discovering which of the newly developed abilities are mere rote learning, and which are based on a feeling of marked interest; which are a combination of old skills and which are dependent on some new ingredient. To try and find out by searching through records would be, even with computer assistance, unreliable. The best source of information would be the individual himself, and then his supervisor.

To summarise, the heuristic principle does not imply simply teaching a person a range of new tasks and seeing which he is best at. Although this has a definite short term value, in that you may then be able to use him in these things he is best at, you may be merely using existing capabilities in a new combination. The principle asks that the person pursues those things in which he shows marked interest; and to find them there has to be a certain variety in the opportunities offered and the freedom to pursue the thing which interests him. In a suitable environment the activities which he chooses to follow are not merely interesting; they are also do-able for people of his stage of development. The usual finding is that the standard reached in this way is above the normal, and that the sense of responsibility shown by that person is markedly high.

THE THREE PRINCIPLES IN ACTION

For the manpower developer these principles are not mutually exclusive within the organisation. At any one moment short term promotions will be deterministic, long term promotions will be probabilistic. Of course all future moves are actually probabilistic, by the sheer nature of things, and we must remember that determinism and probabilism are philosophies adopted by the management, to be used according to the nature of the decision that has to be made about the future. The closer one is to the future event the more confident one may be in making decisions about that future event, and despite some inevitable uncertainties, the more likely one is to be deterministic. The further away the future is, the less confident one can be, and the more likely one is to be probabilistic.

Between them, the probabilistic and the deterministic principles will provide people to fill the posts in the future, good, bad and indifferent. The quality of all can be enhanced, and the outright failure rate can be diminished by planned moves for some, perhaps for most, ensuring that sufficient breadth of experience is acquired prior to higher appointments being undertaken. This planning of moves can be done within both the principles. For example, the deterministic decision is that Jack Smith will be sales manager in four years' time; but before then he will work in finance and accounts for 18 months, followed by two and a half years as manager of the southern region. These are training moves; they give him knowledge and skill required for his ultimate appointment; there is no heurism intended and no probabilism.

As a second example, the eight best sales branch managers will all during the next seven years work in posts offering experience in accounting, market research, and new product development. At the end of that time the company will have – of those who are left in the company, for some will have left – men better equipped to become regional managers from whom then, at an even later date, the sales manager might be selected. There are no names written firmly against future posts as yet. The above moves, still to be planned in practical detail, are simply training moves in objective. In the course of time the most suitable men of the eight will be chosen for promotion. The deterministic principle is being deliberately avoided for the time being, in favour of probabilism plus training.

In the above two examples the heuristic principle is not fully engaged, nor is it fully ignored. To engage it fully would mean, for example, enabling each person, in either example, to undertake work in the near future where his own interest took him. His interest would be the net result of his skill interest and his career interest, but he would, we suppose, make a reasonable decision. As a result he would then move at a mutually agreed date to, shall we say, economics research, where he would fill a post for which he was sufficiently suitable, and which gave him the chance to develop his interest and skill in mathematical programming of marketing decisions. He would then find that his work was absolutely engrossing, particularly in the relatively new field of interproduct economics. After two years of this he is ready to study for a diploma and move into a specialist career in marketing economics.

What happens then? This depends on the company philosophy and on the company manpower requirement. The answer given to him might be, 'Yes, by all means do these things. We believe that people should work in things in which they have strong interest and skill; you obviously have both. We also have a need in this company for people with ability in marketing economics. And we are prepared to pay them as well as any other senior appointment'. This is the most favourable company attitude and answer from the man's point of view. But he is lucky. There might be no real philosophy of a heuristic nature; instead, merely a preparedness to compromise in the face of pressure from a promising employee. There might be no need for marketing economics, or for his continuing work in it. There may be a desperate need for good sales managers.

In consequence one can sympathise with a hardening management attitude against the heuristic principle, except where there is nothing to lose. To abandon the control of determinism and of carefully thought out probabilistic planning, and inject a large amount of employee choice and self determination into the picture of future manpower development, would be an act of faith of an exceptional order.

And yet, no matter how difficult it is to administer, particularly at levels above the most junior trainees, *it is a principle with enormous potential;* it is also a principle which operates as best it can irrespective of the philosophy adopted by the company, for *it is a natural principle of learning and development,* not an artifact of administration. It shows itself in the success stories of men and women in companies (and outside) who have found and followed interests, irrespective of the norm of behaviour and progress in companies and other organisations. Companies actually benefit by it as and when it expresses itself through the initiative and persistence of individuals, although the company's policy and manpower expertise is unable openly to embrace heurism.

In companies which are endowed with many people of well developed ability, through good initial selection from an educated population outside, the heuristic principle may operate mainly through employee initiative and employee pressure. Individual interest will be aroused through the courses attended, professional reading, conversations with friends and colleagues, and sustained by that person in his choice of future domestic and professional action. He will then, with some confidence, knowledge and understanding, take steps to get himself into the sort of work that matches these growing interests – provided, of course, the money is right. In this way the company willy-nilly is gaining from the inherent energy and capability implicit in the heuristic principle.

In some companies, short of engaging in a complete revolution in manpower planning and development some more discreet steps are taken to capture the capability which lies within the heuristic process of development. It is not unusual to find that at regular intervals employees are asked, individually, to indicate where their interests lie, and what work they would particularly like to move into. It is then possible to develop personnel movements in the company which take account of these interests.

There are, however, problems to be faced even in this simple-looking practice, for not all moves asked for can be accommodated, and nor is all interest expressed by people heuristic in origin or outcome. It is worth elaborating a little.

The possibility of being moved into a work area depends on there being a vacancy there; on the applicant being approved by the receiving management; and on there being no other more suitable person waiting in the queue. One can see immediately that there are reasons for approaching such a scheme with some caution, for the failure to move a person within a reasonable length of time into a job for which he is suited, and which he has asked for at the suggestion of management, is likely to produce individual and collective frustration. This may be followed by a lack of confidence in the management and in the company, on the part of the employees, if it happens often.

The reason behind a request for a transfer need not be an interest in the work itself and the skills and knowledge, or even the context, of the work. The applicant may wish to be nearer to a friend; or may think the new post more prestigious than the old one; or he may be fed up with the old one. These are probably good enough reasons in themselves for seeking a move to different work, and they may provide extra motivation and even improved work, but they do not present the same possibility of development of potential as do interest based moves of heuristic nature. The problem for management is to distinguish one from the other, and to decide how to deal with each.

CONTINUOUS DEVELOPMENT

This chapter has looked at the application of deterministic and probabilistic principles to structured planning. We have seen that the heuristic principle is one of great value but can be applied, on the whole, only when the planning structures permit. In the next chaper we shall look at the possibility of continuous opportunity for employing the heuristic principle, irrespective of structure.

21 Continuous development

Up to this point we have explored:

1 Manpower planning.
2 The opportunities for career development.
3 The limitation on career development.
4 Management's obligation to accept employee career development as a social responsibility.

The overall picture, from management's point of view, is a complex one. Their objective is to staff the company with competent people now and in the future. The company has the systems that will help ensure that this is done. At the same time, steps will be always be taken to maintain an acceptable pattern of job moves to help meet the career needs of employees as far as this is possible.

Management, and their planners, are aware of a great deal of development activity – analyses, forecasts, planning meetings, reorganisations, promotions, transfers and so on. But the view of the future for many individual employees, at almost any level, may be lifeless, dull, blank, their career prospects are vague: the present is 'all right', but not particularly interesting.

For many people the experience of getting into a job has an almost classic pattern. At first everything is new – a new place, new colleagues and manager, and new work. This has its interest. Then comes the task of learning the job, becoming proficient in it, and understanding how it fits into the wider company. This has interest and some satisfaction. Then comes a period of application of the new skills, dealing with irregularities and hiccups in the work, learning to recognise and sort out problems.

This is a period of discovery, of learning new skills, and, probably, of personal creativity. For many people it comes gradually to a close, and the job becomes 'routine'. The employee is, of course, expected to keep his eyes and ears open, to spot irregularities and deal with them. But the newness and creativity have gone: irregularities have lost their novelty. This is likely to be management's intention: things should run smoothly, systems should be immaculate because this leads to efficiency and high quality work and products.

At the same time, however, it is known that reiterative work can, for many people, produce a lessening vitality and motivation, and an increase in error rate possibly with an increase in sickness and in sickness absence. There have been considerable efforts by some employers to improve motivation: for example using job-rotation. The use of 'semi-autonomous' worker teams in Britain, then in Sweden, led to the development of quality circles in which there is sufficient freedom to enable the workers to make many decisions of their own, and meet workloads and challenges their own way. For its successful operation, the team's members need, of course, a high level of training and information about the work which has come under their control.

It is worth noting that researchers in both USA and Sweden have shown that there has been a measurable loss of health of workers employed in dull and unsatisfying work, over which they have little control and in which there is virtually no possibility of using other capabilities which they have. This is consistent with other findings of a socio-medical nature. In 1938 Dr Scott Williamson published findings about the Peckham Experiment. These showed that by changing the social environment, and increasing the opportunities for people to develop their potential for social, intellectual and physical skills, those people distinctly and measurably improved in physical and mental health. Today the work of researchers points to the fact that, in the words of the World Health Organisation, one cause of 'inequity in health' is the lack of opportunity for people to use their initiative to develop their human potential in a creative way, either as individuals or in a community setting.

So it would seem that the social responsibility of corporate management does not apply purely to its impacts on the world *outside* the company: nor merely to making sure that work is safe and in compliance with the law. Social responsibility extends to the organisation of work within which certain social and individual developmental needs of the employee must receive full consideration, not once every few years, but continuously.

This is not an easy challenge for managements to meet. All managements give, and always have given, a high priority to production quality, to the development of technology and to the ultimate profitability of the company. Considerations of human health and quality of life are secondary although often sincere. Much re-education and self-examination is needed before an appropriate management style can evolve. Fortunately, there is enough evidence that, as we have proposed earlier, the release of human capital and development potential can produce organisation, work methods and individual contributions that are of net benefit to the company.

The continuous release of human potential, in both learning and improving work methods, has to be offered to management as a 'system' that leads ultimately to improved performance. The improved performance, of the individual and/or of the work team, is achieved by continuous learning and the application of this learning to the work they do. To help bring about this learning there have to be resources to help the learner. There is also a need for the employee/learner to sustain his own initiative in learning, i.e. his own self-development on and off the job. All members of the company, from the board downwards, have a place in this 'system' and all have their individual needs for continuous development, whether they are director, functional heads, supervisor or assistants. Management has the responsibility for establishing 'continuous development' as part of the company's policy, of defining or agreeing methods, and monitoring progress and results. But how do we move, as managers, from merely agreeing that continuous development is a 'good idea'? How can we promote and manage it?

OPPORTUNITIES FOR LEARNING AND TEACHING

How can learning and development be continuous? What are the opportunities for learning and for teaching? These questions have been given close attention in Chapters 4, 5, 6, and 7 which dealt with training opportunities and the opportunity matrix, notifiable and non-notifiable training. All of the 'training opportunities' can be seen as learning and development opportunities. For example, John Smith joins the company as a new recruit, is later transferred, and then promoted. These are three major learning opportunities under the heading of notifiable training. Training is virtually unavoidable: it will be mainly on-the-job, given by his superiors, with some off-the-job excursions and special instruction on sophisticated processes or procedures.

However, there are breaks between these learning opportunities. How are they filled in? How is continuity achieved? This is where training and learning become much less certain. On the training opportunity matrix we have new plant, procedures, standards, rules, relationships etc., as providing further opportunities. These are non-notifiable and the opportunity for teaching and learning may be neglected, unless there is a high level of training consciousness in management, and good relationships between line management and training management.

Regarding those entries in the training opportunity matrix that are concerned with the maintenance of standards and of adaptability – 'standards' concerns quality of work and of product; 'adaptability' is important because future learning and the development of potential are at risk if adaptability is diminished.

All of the above types of learning opportunities are dealt with in some detail in Chapters 4 to 7. So far, John Smith's learning opportunities, spread over the years, amount to infrequent job changes, occasional operational changes at his work place, in other functions or outside the company, and retraining or refreshers for maintaining standards and motivation. Any of these may happen with long intervals between them. What of 'continuity'?

In the John Smith example a further 'opportunity' for learning is when he takes the initiative himself. We have met this important factor in learning, earlier in the text, in Chapter 1, with reference to 'learning through experience'. Personal initiative provides the underlying *continuation and drive* in learning and development but it requires a work environment that is favourable to the development and expression of interest, and to the exercise of initiative. It is very much a responsibility of managers and supervisors to maintain a favourable work environment. Let us take an illustrative example.

Peter Wells entered the company after graduation and started work in market research.

169

His first job was to search through the huge volume of records, extract the annual sales data in Europe, country by country, product by product, for the previous 6 years. He then gave them to someone else. And that was all. After three weeks he complained to his manager, who listened somewhat unsympathetically and told him to be patient. Peter was patient for a further month, and then went to see T & D. T & D talked with the branch manager, and persuaded him that:

1 Peter Wells should be given the whole picture of the sales and manufacturing forecasting which the branch was working on.
2 That he should see the sales trend analysis that used his data: and see the forward projection calculations of future sales.
3 That he should be encouraged to talk with the branch members doing this work, and vice versa.
4 That the members should note his interests and provide work that matched his interests.

The branch members had no objection at all to this, and soon Peter was involved in helping with the analysis. *He had a couple of ideas that were listened to and incorporated.* He was pleased, felt at home, and stayed.

This illustrates the classic case of how to lose new and demotivated graduates: and of the useful intervention of T & D, who encouraged intelligent and sympathetic listening by supervisors, and a willingness to evaluate, on their merits suggestions by juniors.

The above example is really a 'special case'. Peter Wells entered the company as a graduate through a training scheme, specially administered. The learning and career needs of the graduates were given close attention by T & D, as well as by line management. T & D had an acknowledged authority to monitor the work and the progress of graduates for the first year or so after recruitment, and to investigate cases that looked to be, for some reason, unsatisfactory. But what of the rest of the employees? What of *their* interests and ideas, and their initiatives? Who looks after them?

It is management that is responsible for objectives and strategies; and carries a large responsibility for detailing and teaching. Training and Development is responsible for monitoring progress, for recommending and designing schemes and, for advising on teaching and learning.

What is required, in principle, is:

(a) The active engagement of supervision and management in the continuous response to the interests and developmental need of individuals in their workforce.
(b) The improvement where needed, of listening, coaching and consultative skills to make (a) above effective: and the development of managers' and supervisors' ability to use these skills at the workplace.
(c) The introduction of top management policies giving encouragement and authority to the above.

Clearly T & D will be involved in all three of (a), (b) & (c), as well as in monitoring progress in the application of any new measures. This latter is likely to be the most difficult. There will be problems in getting information on whether the new style of management and supervision is actually being operated: and further problems in measuring and accounting for improvements in performance – which is a target of the whole exercise.

Finally, a few thoughts on the realities of efforts to change management/employee working relationships, in this particular way.

1   The idea of continuous development (CD), including its practice at the workplace, may be acceptable to most managers and supervisors as a good principle. But less acceptable to many will be the 'obligation' actually to alter their style and habits of relationship with their staff at the workplace.

2   The introduction of workplace CD will need to be handled, therefore, taking full account of the style and temperament of managers in the various areas of the company. It is better to go slow, to first raise interest amongst management, than rush in and raise resistance. But, one should aim at collaboration with managers, using their ideas and initiatives.

3   Some managers, perhaps some departments, will already be practising workplace CD, without even being highly conscious of it. It will be a part of their culture. Others will have traditions that are counter to CD and will hinder its introduction. There is great value in using the experience of the practising department and managers as an illustration of the value and practicality of CD: the practising managers may be better salesman than either training staff or outside consultants. They can add a touch of reality, and they can confess to difficulties that will be recognised by the other managers who have yet to change their style.

4   Once 'workplace development' has become accepted by managers, supervisors and the staff of an area of the company, and is being practised, it can be both self-sustaining and infectious.

The last point can be illustrated by the example which follows, taken from the head office of a large company.

Eric Hill was a new training officer allocated to the Technical Division of the company. After a few months he dropped in to chat with the manager of T & D. The conversation went something like this:

MTD: 'How are things going?'
EH: 'Quite well, I think.'
MTD: 'You don't seem sure.'
EH: 'I'm not. There has been a lot of discussion, even argument, about some product quality. The managers have organised a meeting to thrash things out: they are calling it a workshop: it will last almost all day.'
MTD: 'Who is going to it?'
EH: 'Members of Technical Division, at different levels, all connected to the problem. Quite a few of them, about ten people in all.'
MTD: 'What's the purpose?'
EH: 'I understand that it is to give everyone the chance to say what they think ought to be said: and hear the others. They've invited someone from Production and someone from Marketing. And one or two other departments want to send someone.'
MTD: 'Sounds very good. Congratulations.'

EH: 'But I've had really nothing to do with it: it has all come out of their work-a-day business. *But they've invited me to attend: they say I ought to be there.*'
MTD: 'Sounds even better.'

This was all in the day's work: it was not regarded as anything special and had no special title. It was the consequence of policies and practices encouraged by top management and T & D. The organisation of such meetings, of which there were many variations, was initially in the hands of the company training officers but was adopted and adapted by line management. The identification of matters which lent themselves to workshop/seminar treatment followed the style of company and department courses organised, as a service, by the training department. These in-company courses always had a high level of company day-to-day work content. Managers, supervisors and staff came to see the courses as places where company matters could be questioned and debated, where you could learn the things you wanted to learn.

Gradually managers took a new role in this sort of learning opportunity – they developed their meetings, their chairmanship, they became more prepared to take a hammering and became aware of the virtue of teaching and of listening to many voices. This takes some skill, and some time to master, and they turned from time to time to Training for help in developing these skills, which they needed and wanted.

22 Manpower development and organisation development

Although it is not the intention to deal with the principles and practices of organisation development in this text, it would seem important to emphasise certain relationships between OD and manpower development, which indicate the need for manpower development to be conducted with full awareness of its organisation implications. It can be claimed that the most effective manpower development can only be achieved if the two functions work in close collaboration, and if at the same time general management are fully aware of the overlapping interests, and the interactions, of the two.

It is recognised by those who actually watch organisations at work – as distinct from writing or reading books on organisation – that, whatever the formal nature of an organisation, as reflected in the organisation charts, the job descriptions and accountability statements, the way it works is dependent on the capabilities, relationships and agreements amongst the people within the organisation. Sometimes these interpersonal relationships are in conflict with the written organisation definitions. Sometimes they are not. Whoever writes the definitions cannot think of everything.

It is also recognised that the people within the organisation must have freedom to adapt and change, according to their strengths and weaknesses, preferences and dislikes, if that organisation is to keep going in the constantly changing human and economic world in which the company operates. Rigidity beyond a certain point is not desirable if managers and executives are expected to respond rapidly to changes in their workloads and problems. Our interest at this moment is to see the way in which organisation and changes in organisation, formal or informal, affect the manpower development work which is being carried out within that organisation.

A common impact of manpower development on organisation arises from the deliberate provision of places for trainees. The apprentice requiring real shop floor experience, the graduate who needs to gain wide experience with minimum delay, the supervisors designate who require exposure to apposite aspects of company work, the thin stream of high flyers who must build up expertise faster than anyone else; all of these people may only get what they require in the way of work experience by a special provision. If they all have to wait in the queue all of the time, the training and development may be impossible to achieve. Some will be possible through normal internal posting and transfer mechanisms, but not all. Indeed, it may be seen as undesirable to maximise the movement of trainees through the normal internal vacancy opportunities, for this might block many opportunities for those who were not members of development schemes but who nevertheless merited a transfer or a promotion.

So some posts or workplaces may have to be created or isolated for development purposes; and this has an effect on organisation structures and the distribution of responsibility. The first effect is the likely increase in the numbers of people in the particular work area, although this need not always be the case when introducing trainees of high calibre. The second effect may then be to create increased supervision, because there are now more employees and the additional ones have an exceptional need for being taught. This is common within apprenticeship schemes, but not so common and not so readily accepted in other schemes. The older and the more sophisticated the learner, the less inclined management are to create new workplaces, and the less inclined are the people already in that work area to accept a stranger in their midst, a stranger who is there to advance his own career at, they may believe, their expense in time and effort.

If the trainees thus posted are good and hard working, and, above all, interested in what they are given to do, they might be quickly assimilated. They may even become indispensable; and this can lead to problems of manpower growth if a strict watch is not kept on the nature of the work undertaken by both trainees and regular employees. A popular trainee group may even create a subtle expansion pressure in the company, should line and manpower managers both prefer to take into their growing establishments such people, beyond their real needs, but too good to let go elsewhere.

Jumping to the other end of the scale we find, for example, the creation of understudy posts at high levels in the hierarchy, in order to provide an insight into more rarified aspects of management for one person, or for a procession of people. Understudy posts can be most successful, it is generally found, if the bulk of the work to be done by the understudy is real and responsible work. Otherwise he is unable to penetrate into the problems and the minds of people around him. If the understudy is given real work to do, where does it come from? From the boss's workload, or from people around him in the organisation? Will the incumbent then inflate the importance of his work until the work becomes recognised as being necessary to the area in which he is working, and so critical that it can never be handed back to those who lent it to him in the first place? Such things do happen. The company may now find itself not only with an extra permanent post, but also with a new division of responsibilities between a group of managers or supervisors in that part of the organisation.

Although these problems may rarely be serious in well established companies in the West, their importance is much greater in companies starting up with inexperienced local labour, or undergoing rapid localisation and growth as in the developing countries, and as will sometimes be the case in countries in Eastern Europe undergoing economic reform. In these cases it would be often unrealistic initially to create hierarchies, structure and job responsibilities based on the Western patterns, although the temptation to do so is extremely great.

The existing levels of knowledge and experiences are relatively low, and therefore the capital potential and ready adaptation of people into new work somewhat unreliable. The capability of anyone to teach his colleagues or his juniors much may be also low and therefore organisation and relationships must be developed in some way that will enhance to a maximum the learning opportunities. These should include heuristic principles if this learning and the accompanying interest growth is to be made the most of. Deterministic planning, and manpower development to suit, is most effective where there is high confidence, with evidence to support that confidence; and such planning demands reasonably well worked out structures through which those chosen can work their way.

Thus organisation development and manpower development must, in these grass roots circumstances, go hand in hand. The work for any individual must not greatly exceed his initial capability, yet it must provide room for 'stretching' and the development of new interest. This may mean that there have to be six in a work unit where otherwise four would be sufficient. But if there are six, with the need for even more supervision than otherwise, attention needs to be paid to the number of supervisors needed, and the levels and sorts of responsibility they are to carry. Clearly their training and development responsibility could be greater than in other older and more experienced companies. With the increase in numbers of supervisory roles at the lower edge of the company, there is an increased pressure on promotion vacancies a little higher up. Does this mean an automatic increase in the number of posts at that higher level? Maybe this is in any case desirable because of the problems for the inexperienced in handling the management workload. Thus one can see a total inflation, vitally necessary perhaps, throughout the company. This increases the fragmentation and decreases the spontaneous communication in the company, both of which are counter-productive and it adds, of course, to the normal manpower control problems of wastage and replacement.

In companies like this, in which a great deal of teaching, learning and personal development is taking place, it is usual to expect to find not only the growth of personal ambition, but also the assumption of a great deal of personal expectation. Socio-economic studies show how expectation provides incentive to action for some, and a mere demand for satisfaction for others. When the growth rate in the standard of living in any country slows up then dissatisfaction will be felt and expressed, even though there may be no actual decline in the absolute standard of living. Similarly in companies; if the rate of advancement of employees slows up noticeably as the company reaches the end of a growth and promotion phase of localisation there will be a sense of disappointment universally felt amongst the employees.

This disappointment will occur at a time when there is every reason to maintain the stimuli of training and other educational processes, for heuristic and work-day purposes; and this may produce in turn a sourness amongst the employees who associate training and education with pretty rapid promotion and salary advancement, which is now on the wane. This now gives organisation development a new objective. Previously it had been concerned with the structuring of an ambitious company in a period of high promotion rates and organisational growth. Now it is concerned with structures of a company in which the growth rate will be much much smaller, where ambition may have turned to cynicism, but even so where the continued development of management, executive, and all other individual capability is vital.

We must add two further causes of problem to the above. Localisation, in developing countries in particular, can run into age-structure problems from the outset. It is not unusual to find there that much of the educational development in the country is recent. Hence the cadre of people in the company who are regarded as being of high technical potential, all fall within a relatively narrow age band, and are probably relatively young. Moreover, those who are the youngest in this group may be the best educated of them all, as a result of the development of educational policies over a period of as little as ten or 15 years.

It would not be surprising to find therefore that there are middle managers in their early thirties, well qualified and trained, who realistically regard their chances of promotion in the foreseeable future as very slight; they know that the ages of those above them are mainly in the middle and late thirties bracket. There must be a very long time to wait before stepping into anyone's shoes unless special measures are taken. Not only has the organisational growth slowed right down, but in addition the natural manpower upward flowrate will in itself be very slow.

This type of problem is met anywhere in the world, and it has become recognised as one which normally needs attention if the resulting stagnation is to be avoided. For the stagnation can produce not merely frustration for the ambitious, but a staleness and loss of creativity and flexibility even in those who are content to accept their lot. At this point organisation development may well become almost indistinguishable from manpower development, for the main question to be dealt with is how to produce structures which provide career satisfaction and progressive work whilst at the same time meet the functional need of the company.

There is a limit to the number of artificial organisation changes that can be effectively made with this sort of objective in mind. Some changes may be accompanied by a loss of self respect, but this depends on the sensitivity of the person then moved or promoted; and there is a loss in working efficiency in areas where one or more of the appointments is actually unnecessary. But fortunately there are other factors at work which can relieve the pressures inside the company. These we shall consider briefly.

Companies which approach their manpower development in a conscientious way may become over-possessive about the people who work in the company, and may regard the loss of people to the outside world as a sort of failure. But however one regards losses, they inevitably happen, and are part of the manpower equations of the company. Losses in personnel, occurring at the right levels of employment, can actually be an advantage to the company. It would relieve the pressure on management to invent organisational ways of sustaining the motivation of junior and middle executive levels if there were sufficient losses in the middle and senior groups. There can be no question of the company's being unconcerned as to how many, and which, people leave; but there is a definite advantage to be considered as arising from losses in certain instances. One device, increasingly used, is 'early retirement', in companies with pension schemes. Older members may be offered, or may volunteer for, retirement a few years before the normal retirement age, with little or no financial disadvantage. For some this can be the opportunity to 'start a new life' before too late: for some it can be a shock and a disappointment. Inside the company career and development routes may open up straight away, or may not, if the purpose of early retirement is manpower reduction.

Fortunately the economic situation which gives rise to the sudden and accelerated growth of a company, may create a demand for skilled and experienced people in the outside labour market. If this is the case then the losses, to other companies, to the government, to education, can be seen as an advantage to the company in overall terms, and might be encouraged through frank disclosure of the limitations to career and personal development in the company, as it is presently manned.

If, however, the company itself envisages a future growth in its own activities then it may be able to use the future growth as a proper means of absorbing that excess fraction of its manpower which, apart from being an extra expense, is impeding its efficiency at present.

THE RIGHT ORGANISATION

We have considered above how the provision of jobs for training and development purposes affects the size, the structure and some of the job responsibilities of a company and how in the extreme a company's structures may be dominated by factors arising from the need to devote so much effort to the employment and development of people of whom a large proportion have an outstanding learning need. We should look now at the question of what sort of organisation is required to best accommodate people who have learned what they have been set to learn, and are no longer considered as predominantly learners, but as doers, as executives or managers.

This may not seem to be an important question to those who believe that an organisation is created by drawing a chart showing the various hierarchical levels, defining the responsibilities of and relationships between all jobs, and then posting people, suitably chosen, into all the positions in the hierarchy. At any time when the operations of the company change, that organisation can be changed in all appropriate details, and those affected can be rebriefed and retrained if necessary. It is the sort of organisation approach that is compatible with the deterministic principle of manpower development, but is not so compatible with the use of the heuristic principle.

We have seen that it is likely that the use of the three principles of development follows the following pattern. For the most junior and elementary trainee and development purposes, heuristic principles may be often used. For middle and junior levels there will be less use of heuristic principles and more dependence on a probabilistic approach coupled with a short term deterministic final decision for each ultimate appointment. At the top levels the deterministic approach will predominate. We have seen, however, that wherever heuristics can be used then the interest, energy and capability levels of those involved are likely to be higher than otherise, as has been illustrated in the chapter on continuous development.

We have been using the word heuristic to apply to a learning method. The principle can be extended, and this was referred to earlier, to include the ultimate selection by the person concerned (the learner) of what he is to do. We have seen that some companies attempt to introduce this element of choice into the career development of employees. What is possible, in addition to the normal use of heuristics for individual learning, is its extension into organisation development. One is getting close to this in the exploratory discovery and learning by the individual, when that discovery and learning is about relationships with other people and other functions in his work area. If the other people at the same time are able to examine these same relationships, then, given senior management agreement, there may be an organisational change or development, albeit a small one.

If this is extended further across the organisation then we would produce organisational development based on the heuristic learning and adaptations of people across the whole network of the organisation. This is familiar concept enough to the OD specialist, who would be interested also in ensuring that the small changes, adaptations and development added up to something that was of advantage to the whole organisation. There are ways of dealing with this, based on providing information that will enable each person to see and understand the whole situation of which he is a part.

What is of significance to organisational development is that the more the company pursues the heuristic principle for its training and development, the more likely it is that those who benefit by this may spontaneously employ it in a search for improvements in organisation. The new forms of organisation will reflect, and use, individual capabilities, with a commensurate release of energy and dedication, instead of persuading or forcing people to adapt into roles created by third party decisions.

The more use of heuristics, therefore, for training and development, the more readily and effectively will that same company, in the face of economic or other environmental changes, reorganise and adapt to deal with its new operational requirements.

23 Corporate change

This chapter might well be called 'all change', for we shall deal with those corporate changes which affect the company as a whole, at many levels, and in many functions, and which call for adjustment in people's work and responsibilities. Corporate changes may also require changes in organisation, in communications and even in attitudes to work. The purpose of corporate change is, broadly speaking, to ensure the success of the enterprise by 'improving' something of importance in its dealings with the outside world: Cost reduction, better quality of goods and services, and more attractive products are the most common objectives and are the most easily understood.

To achieve these corporate objectives, a series of steps has to be planned and undertaken in the company to bring about the necessary changes in many aspects of work. Planning and implementation of these steps will involve:

1 The directors, whose ultimate responsibility it is to set the new direction for the company.
2 Top functional management, who will largely determine the nature of the changes in and between each function, including organisation structure changes.
3 'Operations' managers, who will guide the setting up of new systems, plant and processes within the various functions.
4 The workforce and their supervisors who ultimately will operate, hands-on, the new systems/plant/processes, to whatever new standards are required.
5 The personnel and the T & D functions, who will be concerned with a range of implications of such changes, the more obvious being:

(a) Training – everyone in (1) – (5) has something to learn, some new skill to develop, perhaps a new way of working.

(b) Staffing – there may be adjustments needed in numbers and skills.
(c) Manpower planning and recruitment – these need to take new numbers and skills into account.
(d) Job descriptions, pay structures, performance and potential appraisal; the specialisations in personnel will have responsibility.

The proposals for new corporate objectives, and for the corporate changes required in order to meet those objectives, cannot be made successfully without consultation up and down the line between (1) and (5). The directors need to test out their new ideas on the heads of functions – marketing, manufacture, personnel etc. – before they produce their proposals. The heads of functions will test out some aspects of the ideas on their subordinate managers and specialists, before they can confidently give information to the directors. The heads of personnel and of T & D will need to look broadly into what has probably to be done in recruitment, training, manpower and career planning: at labour relations: and whether the whole organisation has not only the *skill* but also the *will* needed for success.

Let us look at examples of corporate change, and of the factors which help or hinder success, in order to identify the role of the T & D function.

THE CASE OF GOODALL LTD

Goodall Ltd is a medium-sized electro-mechanical manufacturing company. It makes control gear for domestic and small industrial equipment, and sells its products to the equipment manufacturers and to the many service shops and centres throughout the country. Its administration, design, research and development, and manufacturing are all on one site. Everything is there, apart from a few branch offices located in industrial areas, employing Sales and Technical representatives who deal with queries and complaints from customers.

The company's technologists developed a new multiple-function switch: it is very simple, easy to fit or adjust, and reliable. Development work by the production people produced a manufacturing method which demanded some new machinery in the factory.

The management committee examined outline proposals (submitted by R & D, Production & Sales) and offered their recommendation to the managing director, who, in turn, obtained approval from the board of directors *to set up an in-depth study* into what the company had to do to make and sell the new product: its likely cost, sales, and profitability: and the impact on all the company functions and organisation.

A project team was set up. It contained top people from Design, Production, Sales, Finance and Personnel as permanent members, and from other functions as and when needed. Liaison was established also with the Employees Representative Committee, whose chairman was invited to contribute views and information, as the study progressed, on matters affecting employees.

The team recommended that the company commit itself to the new machinery, products and sales: their economic analysis justified this. They also recommended that this new type of machinery should replace some of the existing machinery on other production lines in the near future. They heavily underlined that the new product meant a total change of work for 25 per cent of the production workforce, and a slight adjustment in work content for a large percentage of people in surrounding functions. All of this would throw a considerable extra burden on Personnel, Training, and on managers and supervisors: it could also create uncertainty amongst the general workforce.

The project went ahead. Eighteen months later production and sales figures were on target and the introduction of new machinery on other production lines was beginning. At a Management Committee meeting the project manager was congratulated on the achievement and was asked to comment on the whole process of change which he had helped to manage. He said

'There was a lot to do, a lot of work, and a lot of people involved, but some things were in our favour. In this company, it's a sort of tradition that we work together. If we have problems we say, "what are *we* going to do". Its like that between departments, and on the whole its like that between seniors and juniors. That helps. What also helps is having the Personnel and Training people always working closely with us, and us with them, in the same way.

'So, when the project team had drawn up the outline of everything that needed attention, we turned to the managers and supervisors who were going to be affected, gave them the full picture of what the company was trying to do, and invited them to look at their bit of it and help get the best for the future. They didn't really hesitate: they're used to that way of working. As the project developed and went into operation, they treated it like their own – and it was.

'What also helped was that there was *nothing strange or unfamiliar about what the company was moving into.* We've made new products before, we've introduced new machinery and new jobs before. So, although there were small changes in recruitment, and big changes in job content and job training for some, and although standards, inspection and quality control were tightened up, *we took it in our stride.* It wasn't difficult to understand the changes in the work and the organisation, and it wasn't difficult to learn to do the new work. And nobody got hurt – and that counts a lot'.

What the project manager did not mention was that *the company had not always been like that.* Four years earlier Production Development had developed prototype final assembly benches and equipment for small products. Successful trials led to the installation of an area of benches and equipment in the final assembly shop. The employees were given a quick retraining in the shop and serious work was started. Two weeks later output was 15 per cent down, and not the 15 per cent up, which was aimed at. 'Where's the trouble?' asked the training manager. 'I'm sure it's the assembly manager and his supervisors', said the production manager, 'They resent the intrusion and are influencing the employees. I can't get them to understand. They're a difficult lot. But what can we do?'

In response to this the training manager suggested that a workshop of five consecutive half days should be arranged for supervisors from that area of the factory, as soon as possible. It was offered as an introduction to production efficiency, and would demonstrate the various theories in use, and the sort of work in the company that could benefit from study of methods. The teaching would be by the manager and staff of Production Development: there would be a little exercise work and plenty of discussion time, and the current assembly shop development would be examined.

181

The idea was accepted and the workshop was staged shortly afterwards. The training manager 'ran' the workshop and 'participated' in it to ensure that the atmosphere and discussions were uninhibited and fruitful. It was an immediate success in that, over the five days, it enabled related and unrelated misunder-standings to be expressed and cleared up and it enabled a new understanding between line and specialist staff to be forged. Two days later the output figure had gone from $-$ 15 per cent to $+$ 15 per cent. The workshop had really worked: it had not been merely a talk-shop.

Everyone involved liked and valued the experience they had been through. Gradually this consultative and teaching approach became adopted for handling other tasks or problems, with or without Training Department's help. The princi-ples of collaboration, communication and information were also reinforced by the company's occasional supervisor and executive programmes, and by company information courses. The company was changing. Four years later that company took the major manufactoring development, outlined earlier 'in its stride'. Success was, of course, due to a large extent to the technical and organisational knowledge of the managers and technical specialists. But the ease and thoroughness with which the change was handled was due to the co-operative capability which was now a subtle characteristic of the company. Characteristic – because it was present in many types of problem-solving situations, and because it was part of the style of management from the top down to shop supervisors and their employees. Subtle – because *it was not a doctrine* which people followed. It had become built in to their habits and beliefs, and was exercised almost intuitively, although with discretion. It had become part of the culture of the company, which had developed both *the skill and the will.*

In summary those features of the major project which led to success in the example of Goodall Ltd, are:

1 A clear objective, understandable, and acceptable to all.
2 The required new production technology of manufacture and of quality control was within the technical grasp of production engineers, and the learning capabilities of members of the workforce.
3 Any necessary reorganisation of staff was simple to do, and for people to understand and accept.
4 The company had good two-way communication capability.
5 Being a one site company made for ease and speed in both communication and action: new development was spread companywide by word of mouth, by the company newsletter, and in meetings.
6 The traditional close working relationship of Personnel and T & D, with line management, meant that they quickly serviced every appropriate aspect of the development.

In day-to-day operations the technical and behavioural/cultural state of the company was excellent. It enabled quality to be maintained, minor developments to be undertaken without undue delay, and good management/labour relations to be maintained. When the major development described above was introduced, *the company's resources and culture could deal with it.* More work, of course, for many functions; but the skill and the will was there, and sufficient capacity and flexibility to deal with the extra work during the period of change.

THE FAMILIAR AND THE UNFAMILIAR

Many companies have successfully undergone changes of this type, in which they already have *the capabilities to move into a new but nevertheless 'familiar' pattern of work*. Obviously if a company lacks adequate capability for handling 'familiar' change, it will have problems to deal with. If the change is into new and 'unfamiliar' patterns of work the problems will multiply. Let us look at some possible changes into the 'unfamiliar', and the way in which the T & D function becomes involved.

The most elusive changes are those which require a *change in attitude, in belief, and in consequent action*. The top-level decision, that, for example, Filon Co. will not discriminate against women, or against ethnic minorities, in their recruitment, advancement and career fulfilment, produces applause and scepticism throughout the company. For two and a half years it remains a company policy, but unmonitored. It is then shown that in that time there has been no significant change in actual practices of recruitment and promotion, nor in staff planning.

Top management now make a further decision. A study must be made of present management attitudes and practices: education and training will be provided to help management and supervision adjust their beliefs and actions: and all senior managers will carry ultimate responsibility for ensuring that this policy is implemented fairly. The study team consists of Personnel, T & D, Production & Sales, with help from the university Professor of Industrial Sociology. Their findings lead to special workshops for each layer of managment and supervisors: meetings and consultations between each manager and his junior managers and supervisors: a retraining of some recruiters: and the formation of new consultative committees.

T & D has suddenly entered a new arena. Every item on the above list requires their attention, their advice, or their participation, for everyone involved has new messages to understand, new skills to learn and use. All of this is routine to a well run Training Department: but the scale of the whole exercise may be beyond the resources of the existing training staff. Additional temporary strength may best be found amongst members of other line and service functions: and so T & D have another task – i.e. to plan and coordinate the work of these new members with the work of the central T & D function.

T & D have a further responsibility. They have to understand the basic factors in the problems of discrimination, including prejudice, perception, judgement, relationships, and traditional practices. All of these will feature in the workshops, meetings and consultations, either explicitly or implicitly. All should be undergoing adjustment in the day-to-day work of the company. And all these factors will influence the performance and potential appraisals, and the manpower/career planning. If T & D are to help steer the company forward, then *T & D are as much in need of re-education* as other functions and managements in the company.

We have taken the example of Filon Company's decision to reduce discrimination, as one instance of a company moving into 'unfamiliar' practices. To bring work opportunities and careers of women or ethnic minorities into line with those of white males, one encounters problems which are rooted in personal prejudices and social traditions. Prejudice and traditions against minorities cannot be treated as a temporary or passing phenomenon: they will not disappear when management declares its non-discrimination policies. Moreover, the minorities are here to stay: and they are likely to get bigger. For example, in the USA the US Labor Department reports that the white male share of the labour force will drop to 39.4 per cent by the year 2000, from 48.9 per cent in the year 1976: there will be a corresponding increase in the numbers of women and people of African, Hispanic, Asian and National American origin. In Europe the removal of international barriers to movement and employment will produce population changes in some parts of some countries, in the course of time.

Finally, let us look briefly at two other corporate changes into the 'unfamiliar'. First, *'employee empowerment'* gives the more junior members of any hierachy the right to make decisions, and to take actions, that normally lie solely within the authority of their manager. This is comparable to the principles of continuous development in the encouragement of learning and developing through work-based opportunities. However, whereas CD may be seen as a system for encouraging employees, to their own and the company's advantage, employment empowerment is presented as a step towards the simplification of organisation structure. It can lead to dilution of some intermediate layers of management: it can increase the output and quality of work of the remaining empowered workforce. Its introduction will follow the decision of top management, probably at Board level, and may take one of two forms:

(i) The immediate adoption of new, flatter, organisation structure, to be accompanied by the encouragement of EE; or

(ii) The rigorous pursuit of EE, to be followed by progressive reorganisation as EE makes headway.

Both of the above call for massive corporate re-education and persuasions, much more than is needed for the classic, familiar, forms of reorganisation. Both create uncertainty amongst all levels of employees about their new roles and responsibilities, and some will worry about their future in the company – if any.

The second example of corporate change into the 'unfamiliar' comes with the board's decision that the *quality of products and services* must be improved, in order to meet market requirements externally, and in order to improve efficiency and reduce costs internally. Every function in the company must examine every aspect of its work, from Head Office front door reception through to the delivery of the product to the customer. Industry and commerce are used to hearing management pleas for lower scrap rates, tighter quality controls, better use of time, better interfunctional collaboration. But they are not, generally speaking, familiar with the instruction that every function *will* improve its work quality and *will* report on its achievement by a given date. They have to do something about their performance *now*, and not as and when they get round to it.

As in the earlier examples of corporate change, the board's objective, and the thinking behind the objective has to be understood in the company – by everyone, whether they are directly involved in the changes or not. A high level of motivation and confidence has to be generated, and a watch has to be kept on all actions, changes and improvements to ensure that the actions taken are all compatible with one another and with the overall corporate objective. Within all of this there must be a core of Training and Development involvement in company education at all levels and in the examination and improvement of job training and work standards.

SUMMARY — CORPORATE CHANGE AND THE ROLE OF T & D

1   Corporate change can be into either 'familiar' or 'unfamiliar' types of organisation, practices, relationships and responsibilties, or a combination of both.
2   Changes within the 'familiar' are most likely to be taken in the company's stride, unless they produce unfavourable employment prospects for some people, which cannot be dealt with.
3   Changes into the 'unfamiliar' can produce uncertainty about role, responsibilities, and career for people at all levels. Such changes may well cut across traditions of work relationships and behaviours, and meet with resistance, prejudice and dislike, and real inability to change on the part of some people.
4   (a)   Any corporate change is likely to be easier to handle if: the company is of modest size, principally on one site, with easy management and interfunctional communications.
    (b)   Difficulties can arise with the larger companies, particularly those with many centres. Multinational companies have the further problems of justifying and implementing changes in overseas centres with differing national cultures.
5   Corporate change is a gamble, as are all new ventures. Risks are minimised if the decision to 'go-for-change' is based on sound knowledge, at board level, of all the relevant aspects of the company's capability and potential.
6   Corporate change is easier to approach and implement if:
    (a)   Dialogue and collaboration between functions, and between management and employees, is part of the existing culture.
    (b)   T & D and other personnel functions traditionally work closely with line management and vice-versa.
7   T & D and personnel will be engaged in some or all of the following, in their revision, planning and implementation:
    (a)   *Recruitment* – of people best qualified and experienced, to meet the *new* operating requirement of the company.
    (b)   *Induction and orientation* – of new employees – to give an early insight into the standards of work and relationships now required, and an understanding of the changes currently taking place.
    (c)   *Re-orientation* – of existing employees.
    (d)   *Training and retraining* – of employees on new processes and procedures, and in existing work where standards and quality requirement are changed.
          This must include supervisors and managers, particularly where 'cultural diversity' demands a better understanding by supervisors of behaviour and performance amongst employee minorities.

(e) *Communications* – employees want to know whats 'going on' during major and minor company changes. A natural channel for information is through their supervisors, and their managers. In turn supervisors and the managers need to be given this information. There may be *no* system in place for this information transmission, and one may have to be designed and installed. The employees, managers, and supervisors will have to be given some guidance or training in how to use this system, and to use it with the necessary skills.

Other communication channels may have to be installed or improved, such as the company newsletter, and regular and *ad hoc* information meetings of managers and employees ensuring that there is an opportunity for two-way questions and answers. Without good communication systems and skills, management may not understand the thoughts and feelings of the employees. Misunderstanding and cynicism may grow, with a loss of collaboration between managers and employees.

(f) *Pay structure* – with new production machinery, or a new organisation, some jobs, old and new, require analysis to determine where they fit into the existing pay/grading structure. A radical reorganisation of the company may make the existing pay/grade structure inadequate and a new or modified structured has to be designed, explained and introduced to the company.

(g) *Performance and potential appraisal* – does the change in company objectives, practices and standards, alter the required performance level of employees, supervisors and managers?

Performance is likely to be appraised according to old standards, until the appraisers reset their sights, and until the persons being appraised undertand that there are new standards for their appraisal.

The assessment of potential is also likely to be altered according to the new characteristics, skills and standards required in the company. Potential ratings help to determine who-goes-where on the succession and other planning charts, and it is essential and logical that assessors are capable of taking new potential requirements fully into account. It is also important that these new requirements are catered for in the development programmes of people, particularly those who are entered on planning/succession charts.

(h) *Organisation structure* – if the corporate change is basically one of updating production machinery, quality control equipment and related information technology, then the existing organisation may be 'logically' modified to accommodate these familiar details. On the other hand, if the change is to be driven by the adoption of an unfamiliar management style, practices and culture, then a new organisation structure may have to be searched for.

(i) *Career and redundancy counselling* – all employees will be axious about their future in the company, particularly in those areas directly affected by the planned changes. There need to be policies and guidelines to help managers deal with one-to-one and group discusions: and training for some managers in the actual handling of this sort of situation.

GETTING READY FOR ACTION

Ideally, estimates of the actions required in the company, to bring about corporate change, should be made initially as soon as the idea of change begins to be acceptable to the top managers and directors of the company. At that point a study must be started of:

1 The new features required in all functions which will be affected
2 The impact of these on organisational, staffing, skill and culture requirements
3 The mechanisms and resources likely to be needed to bring about the changes
4 Whether the resources in 3 are present in the company now in sufficient strength: and whether additional strength has to be in some way brought in from elsewhere.

This preliminary study gives top management an objective overall view of what would have to be done, and what might be the side effects, in the suggested corporate change. The study might be quick and easy to do in cases such as Goodall Ltd. mentioned earlier in the chapter, i.e. a small-medium sized company, on one site, with good managment-employee relations and communications, close working between line, Personnel, and T & D, and a change into 'familiar' processes and organisation. All the items (a) – (i) in the last point of the above list could be considered by the manager of T & D without much difficulty. He knows the site, and the managers, and whether the present practices will cope. He can consult quickly on points on which he is uncertain. He will join the study group, of top managers, and report and discuss his findings with confidence. The same goes for the other top managers – production, planning, sales, personnel and so on.

The preliminary study in a large, multi-centre company, is likely to be much more complex and difficult, particularly if the intended corporate change is into 'unfamiliar' organisation structures and 'unfamiliar' behaviour and relationships. But in this case the work of the study group becomes even more important and critical to ultimate success. The idea that the whole company must become quality minded, or give equal opportunity to minority groups, or that employee empowerment is essential to corporate success, may be a splendid vision for some. But others, set in their ways and in their prejudices, can lack either the will or the skill. Hence a preliminary study may have to be made, of attitudes amongst the managers, supervisors and other employees, at various levels in the present organisation. This study provides information from which to produce additional plans for dealing with unsatisfactory attitudes. All plans need to be tested out and modified through dialogue with managers, supervisors and employees. And so on – through pilot schemes, re-appraisals, and further adjustments as needed, with T & D deeply involved in managing and monitoring the actions, as well as in designing and facilitating courses, seminars and workshops. It can be a mountain of work for T & D: and T & D's role has been shown to be critical for the success of the whole project.

RESOURCES FOR CHANGE

T & D management has therefore to examine the findings of the first studies and in collaboration with line management and other branches of personnel management, estimate:

1 What actions require the involvement of T & D?
2 Has T & D the strength and capability to man these actions?
3 If the answer to 3 is 'no', what extra staff is required in T & D?
4 What training/communication role is to be undertaken by line management and supervision and what back-up will come from T & D?

Further resources may be sought from outside the company, particularly where organisation and attitudinal changes are envisaged. Consultancies, or university departments with special interest and experience, can contribute to every phase of the total programme of corporate change. In fact, today, much of the initial inspiration of top managers and directors has come, at some time earlier in their career, from their attending business school courses or university seminars, and learning about the management of change. The professor has ceased to be a 'mere academic'. The partnership of practical management and academic insights is increasingly welcomed, by both sides, and is to be recommended.

24 Conflicts

As we have said in earlier chapters, the more long term that the manpower development plan is, the less likely that those who are in it and those who operate it know what its objectives are; or even know that a development plan actually exists. It might also be sometimes true to say that the plan drawn up a few years ago has become irrelevant to that company, and in the absence of a current controller of the scheme its irrelevance may escape the attention of management. Hence the main conflicts that we have to observe arise if there is insufficient understanding around the company about the scheme, its objectives and methods. This can lead to the scheme drifting on without proper monitoring and correction, and it can lead to problems for a range of executives whose responsibility it is to undertake, on a day-to-day basis, those actions in recruitment, training and organisation on which the successful running of the scheme and the successful pursuit of agreed objectives, depends. The European seaboard chemical factory case on page 147 described one effect of insufficient understanding.

Let us take a further example, to illustrate how this sort of failure in communications interferes with manpower development. When Astral Company decided to take steps to develop its next group of junior executives, it was agreed that, according to opportunity, each member of a list of eight promising senior assistants was to be offered the chance of working in the field, at a sales or manufacturing centre, to boost his technical or operational ability in the direction which seemed to be most appropriate to his later promotion. One of them, Charles Wilkins, was thus posted to the big warehouse and distribution centre in the West country, to gain close familiarity with packaging, storage, handling and road and rail transport. The decision was made by the senior development committee; they fed their decision to the personnel manager, and to the head of distribution, who was quite pleased that people in his function should be considered for this scheme.

Wilkins was posted by the normal personnel transfer machinery, and was out of sight from then on for some months until he was visited and reported on by the assistant head of distribution. Apparently he was getting on very well; he was well thought of by the manager of the centre, and he himself was enjoying his work on the installation of the new small computer and terminals. The centre manager had discovered that Wilkins had a lot of head office computer experience, and within two weeks had transferred him to that work in the warehouse, to sort out the software.

There was, of course, a slight problem to be resolved. The centre manager regarded Wilkins as his own employee, and used him to the best advantage. The development committee had told no one that Wilkins had to be employed on physical handling and control; they took it for granted that he would be employed in that way. They then insisted that he was taken off the computer development work, but they were very reluctant to say why. The centre manager had to do what he was told, but immediately jumped to his own conclusions, that Wilkins was being groomed to take over management of the centre.

The conflicts are obvious; they are between the long term interests of the manpower developers, and the short term day-to-day interests of the employing manager. These interests would remain different even if a fuller explanation were given to the centre manager at the outset, but at least a number of subsequent upsets would be avoided although with a loss of the confidentiality which the senior development committee thought necessary to maintain.

It is inevitable that the line manager finds himself at times in conflict with the long term development plans. Although they may be drawn up to operate in such a way as to minimise work interference, interference there will be. He has to take apprentices and trainees at undergraduate and graduate level, give them work, instruct them and supervise them, often for a small work output. When they are becoming proficient they are taken away, and replaced by others for whom the treatment starts again. He has to accept people into his work area in order that they gain useful experience; they may or may not work well, but he has little choice. His best assistants are taken away from him for rapid promotion, and his able deputy is sent on a twelve-week course in the USA against his protests.

He may also find that his freedom in recruiting is heavily constrained. In order to balance the overall age structure of the total commercial function he is told that he may only recruit people between 27 and 30 years of age, and preferably from the technical services department which is being reduced in size. What he needs, in his own view, is a 38 year old ex-sales representative.

Line management may fight therefore against development strategies and plans, arguing that they cause a serious loss in day-to-day operational effectiveness. Sometimes they win; and if they win often enough the original plans may crumble, and be abandoned. It is desirable that, in the drawing up of such plans, key line managers should be consulted early, and their advice should be sought as to how the actual objectives could be reached, in practical terms, without a disruption of work, or without throwing an unacceptable load on other people.

It is also necessary that more senior management recognise the possibility of a loss in output in some areas of work, and accept the responsibility themselves for the loss as and when it occurs, having made this clear to the more junior managers at the very beginning. If the junior manager, who is to employ people whose permanence or quality is affected by development plans, is assured by his boss that the occasional inefficiency will not be held against him, he is much more likely to participate readily in such plans. There will still be the possibility of his disliking the decline of standards, for most managers and supervisors have a pride in the quality of their work, and a lowering of this quality can be distasteful, even though it is recognised that they are not responsible for it.

We have seen in an earlier chapter how the organisation specialist, or, if there is no specialisation, those who from time to time design and authorise organisation changes, shares an interest in manpower development with those concerned professionally with training and development, and with line management. The organisation has to be suitable for the development of the capability of people in the company, providing opportunities for work and movement; and, we suggest, the organisation can be developed in such a way as to make best use of the interests, skills and energies of people, according to the heuristic principle. Organisation, in this context, does not mean merely the hierarchy as shown in the organigram, but includes also the distribution of responsibilities, authorities and working relationships.

If there is no partnership between organisation and manpower development, and no common understanding of the interdependence of the two, then organisation changes can be brought about which are to the disadvantage of manpower development, and to the running of particular schemes.

The same can be said of the relationship with efficiency experts, who themselves can promote organisation and manpower changes in a company, which, whilst saving costs on the balance sheet, may make it more difficult to ensure that the right quality of manpower will be produced in the longer term. And the balance sheet of the future will depend on that manpower quality. The efficiency expert is rarely interested in the development of human ability; his attention is turned towards those aspects of organisation, methods and manning which can be made to run at lower cost or to provide greater output at about the same cost. Whilst this is undoubtedly of great importance it is necessary to remember that learning itself contains an element of what, in commercial terms, is regarded as inefficiency. Whether one considers the slow work of a person learning the first stages of an entirely new job, or the loss of productivity incurred in moving Charles Wilkins from what he could do well to something he knew little about, we are faced with some day-to-day inefficiency; but it is necessary in order to provide longer term efficiency and growth.

We can now turn to a further group of people of special importance in the implementation of development plans. Within this group are the manpower planners themselves, the recruiters, the training officers and other personnel officers concerned with internal transfers and promotions. It might be assumed by the reader that, as all of these belong usually to the same personnel function, there is automatic and effective co-ordination of their work. This would be a false assumption about co-ordination, anywhere. There is never any assumption that the work of design engineers and production engineers is automatically co-ordinated; special steps have to be taken by them to bring about the co-ordinating necessary. Without this the rather different professional interests of the two groups would lead to an unacceptable level of conflict, and some inefficiency.

The same can be said of the component parts of the personnel function, but with particular emphasis where manpower development work is concerned. Each specialist, for example the recruiting officer or the training officer, has his own day-to-day work to do. A lot of that work comes from the current requirements of the managers and other personnel for whom the personnel function provides a service. There are always vacancies to be filled and the recruiter is kept busy searching and selecting. The new recruits require induction and training; and this, with every other element of the training opportunity matrix, will keep the training officer occupied. If there were no manpower development strategies and plans at all in the company, there would be a need for basic co-ordination between these parts of the personnel function. With the introduction of such strategies and plans there is a need not only to ensure that such co-ordination exists, but that the total effort produced now supports, and does not conflict with, those plans.

There are two main problems here; the first we have already encountered, that of the difference between day-to-day requirements and the longer term requirements of the manpower strategies. The personnel function, in meeting the needs of management for day-to-day replacement, external recruitment, and internal transfers and promotion, may tackle these challenges with enthusiasm and ability. But it may be just as capable as line management of working in conflict with undeclared longer term manpower policies, or in conflict with plans which have not been explained or worked out in sufficient detail to ensure reasonable harmony with current work.

This brings us straight to the second problem, that of confidentiality. It is not unusual to find that certain company decisions on the future of manpower are regarded by management as demanding some secrecy. For example, if the company is preparing to expand its operations in four years' time beyond the normal growth rate it may have reason, commercially and politically, to keep this information to itself. Hence the increase in recruitment and training which is to start shortly will not be accompanied by a general announcement; perhaps, if the directors like to play most developments close to their chests, there will be only very few people at the most senior level privy to the secret. In a similar manner attempts by the company to adjust the various structures of the company, by adopting new tactics in wastage, redundancy and recruitment, may not be accompanied by general announcements or explanations. There will of course have to be instructions and controls for line management and the personnel function to observe; but where meaningless instructions are given there is a tendency for even the most ardent professional to forget them, or to change them according to his own judgement. This will cause a divergence between what is actually done and what is required to be done.

Confidentiality is very important to top management when, in an attempt to improve company profitability, they are drafting schemes for reduction in employee numbers. If word gets round about this, employees are likely to worry about who will lose their jobs. Management don't want this to happen, for it will cause many people to be hurt unnecessarily. Throughout, the personnel function must offer a service. When management announces its proposals on profitability and on manpower reduction, it must indicate steps that will be taken to ease the problems for employees who will find themselves redundant. Personnel specialists will have thoroughly studied the practical steps to be taken under the headings of natural wastage, early retirement, internal and external transfer, the external job market, redundancy compensation, pension rights and entitlement to unemployment pay.

T & D will have studied the impact of the employee cut-back on existing manpower and succession plans, and on current and future recruitment, promotion and transfer numbers and priorities – and the need to adjust day-to-day recruitment where necessary. In addition, the programmes and agendas of courses and meetings in the company must give room for ample discussion and clarification of 'what is going on in the company'. Management's decision and action produces conflicts at many levels and in many ways, some of it organisational, much of it in the thoughts, feelings and lives of those seriously affected. There is pressure from organised labour that no such plans or decisions concerning employees should be secret, and there is a growing practice of management to discuss in some detail plans that have any implication of reductions or redundancies. In these cases there is opportunity for the personnel specialists to study the integration of the special measures into the normal day-to-day practices, and to find and declare those instances in which there appear to be incompatibilities, so that corrections can be made, hopefully before damage is done.

There are other development activities which deal with the training and career/s of named people, and in these activities we can expect often to find a very high degree of confidentiality, except where the individual is a member of a publicly known scheme, with widely understood objectives. If the Astral Company ran an 'open' executive development scheme Charles Wilkins and men like him would form a group of executive trainees, whose existence would be no secret to anyone; nor would its programme; nor would its objectives of preparing the men for promotion into executive grades. But the company have a closed scheme, about which very few people have knowledge, and only a select committee know the names and the plans.

One can see that the more deterministic the company's development practices, the more one is likely to encounter secrecy; and the more probabilistic the more likely one is to find openness. Deterministic development implies that, where short or long term appointments are concerned, someone's name is already inked in against a future vacancy and no one else is to be seriously considered for it (although there may be one or two second choices). That particular person may not yet know, nor his manager, nor his colleagues, and it is believed that premature announcements, or leakages of information, will produce an upset; it is also correctly recognised that the appointment may never take place, for in the interval of time before the planned promotion there may be changes in the company fortunes or internal affairs that could make it undesirable to go through with the move. Hence, a not unwise decision to keep quiet about the intention to promote; but in the meantime the training and preparation must go on.

25 Managers

Although decisions in a company may be said to be made by management, they are, in fact, made by managers, individually or collectively. Although the training specialist provides a service for management, he actually deals with managers. To understand the management of the company, to work with it, to help it, you have to work with and help managers, individuals, not some faceless amalgam of authority. Hence we have to understand, not merely management and management practices, but also managers.

Managers, of course, are no more than ordinary people who have acquired exceptional responsibilities and some of the special skills needed to enable them to handle those responsibilities. Despite these, they remain the same people, but usually under some pressure or stress, with the same wide range of human attributes, strengths and weaknesses that one finds in the population as a whole. These attributes, strengths and weaknesses affect their working relationships with the training function as much, if not more, than do management skills or the backcloth of management policies against which their day-to-day actions are taken.

So we remind ourselves that these people, in their various ways, advance or retard the progress of every single piece of training undertaken in a company, at every phase, from conception through implementation to evaluation. They may buy it, or reject it; they may do it themselves, with or without help from outside their own functions. They are of the utmost importance to the training manager. They cannot be thought of, satisfactorily, in real life merely by using the term 'the management'; they must be thought of as individuals with individual variations in all attributes. Some of these attributes we shall look at closely, because they influence strongly the sort of manager the person is. We shall also look at management in the impersonal sense, its pattern of skills and responsibilities in particular, into which the person, whatever his own attributes, is expected to fit.

Companies themselves have so many differences between them, in size, wealth, activities, organisation and product, that one is tempted at times to believe that it is not possible to reduce the concepts of 'management' down to simple statements or simple theories. But it has been done. There are books and courses dealing with management that can give rise to the belief that a relatively small core of ideas on management principles will equip a person with what is necessary for him to steer his function or his company successfully into the future.

Now this may well be true: there are, for example, within this core of ideas, general principles of accounting, techniques of forecasting, planning and controlling, on which many managers will draw in dealing with their problems; and in doing so will confirm the value of these principles and techniques. Nevertheless the actual company, the actual situation, within which any one manager has to work, is as unlike the next as chalk is to cheese. He has to deal with the actual, which is unique, not with the theoretical, which is universal. His management principles and techniques are little more than instruments which he will use in a way which suits the situation and the problems with which he is faced.

If he is a good manager, he will, by definition, be able to perceive the actual problems of human relationships, of economics, of technology and so on, and decide what has to be done, and how his instruments can best be used, changed or unchanged from their previous use.

The distinction between a knowledge of instruments and their use in general; and the ability to perceive what is actually happening in the company and the world around, is of fundamental importance to management, and to the *training and development of managers*. This is widely accepted today, although in the early years of management and business training the distinction was often not seen in proper perspective. Theory was too often referred to as 'mere' theory; and people with a lifetime of familiarity with the workplace regarded as 'merely' having 'lots of experience'; a good thing or a bad thing depending on the point of view of the critic. For some years a sort of battle was fought out between those who believed in 'the practical' and those who believed in 'theory'. It was a foolish battle, for the two are not natural enemies, and, happily, reconciliations have been achieved on many fronts.

This has led to an increasing awareness that managers should posses a wide range of knowledge and capabilities if they are to undertake their work properly as managers. First, there is the knowledge of the 'instruments of management', i.e. the techniques relating to finance, planning, progressing and evaluation, and the basic concepts of human relations and organisation. Second, there is the knowledge of the company itself, its processes, its function, its *status quo* and its future, as well as of the social, economic and political environment in which the company operates. Third, there is the specific technology for which the manager carries responsibility, and in which he must remain competent to some professional or near-professional level.

All of the above constitute the body of knowledge, some universal, some specific to the company, which the manager has to digest. But even if he does so, with obvious success, he does not automatically become a good manager. He will merely be a successful student.

To be a good manager demands other things as well. What these other things are is a subject which preoccupies both managers and management analysts. The lists produced by management-potential appraisal experts include characteristics which read well, such as 'determination', 'powers of observation', 'leadership', and others, and which are clearly of importance in management. Although this chapter is not being written with the intention of scrutinising these characteristics, it is, nevertheless, of some importance to refer to them, as a class, because they do create the bridge between the individual manager's 'knowledge' and the environment in which he works, and in which he has to apply that knowledge. They are characteristics which describe the way he performs in and relates to the human and physical environment.

Given that these characteristics are important, which intuitively most would agree with, the questions must be asked

(a) How are they defined, thus enabling reasonably precise observation and appraisal of them to be made?
(b) Who makes the actual observation of them and in which circumstances were they exercised?
(c) Who decides what particular set of attributes is required for any particular management post?
(d) Can they be improved in any individual?

These questions are basic to the methodology and operation of a management selection, training and development scheme. Yet they are very difficult questions to deal with rigorously and satisfactorily. We shall return to them later. In the meantime, we shall look first at the question of variations in style and capability in management, and see exactly how great these can be, with no loss of efficiency, even in one post.

We shall look at the marketing manager's post. David Smith was marketing manager of a manufacturing and marketing company dealing with household equipment, mainly for kitchen and toilet use. It was his habit to deal with his work problems by consulting with his colleagues in other departments and in the service functions. He organised weekly management (trouble-shooting) meetings attended by sales, transport, planning, accounts managers, with invitations to specific meetings, as required, to the managers of personnel and research.

Smith himself was an extrovert ex-salesman who had come up on the selling and the sales planning side of the company, in which he was strong. He was generally capable of appreciating the work of the other functions, but took no initiatives in other functional areas without making absolutely sure that his ideas were fully approved by heads of other functions. During the weekly meetings, which he chaired, he encouraged wide discussion, often proving practical and useful, between those present. He was successful both as a manager and as a marketer, and his departure to become director of an overseas subsidiary was regretted by his seniors, colleagues and juniors.

He was replaced by Walter Cramm. Cramm had been, up to this new appointment, the deputy chief accountant, and had quite often attended the management meetings, as well as dealing in the course of work with the marketing accounts and balance sheets, and forward estimates. He had joined the company 18 years before as a management trainee, worked short periods in sales, planning and research, and had been two years abroad as chief accountant in a subsidiary. He was a good

196

manager and supervisor and unquestionably competent to do the job, as the next few years confirmed.

But he was different, and in some respects the job he moved into, marketing manager, became a different job. He disposed of the weekly trouble-shooting meetings, appointed a personal assistant, and dealt with the problems directly in his own office, phoning or visiting his specialist counterparts only when absolutely necessary.

There were many other changes: he spent more time in the directors' and less in his subordinates' offices. He delegated to his subordinates more 'absolute' authority than did Smith, but asked for much more paperwork, to give evidence of their success or failure to meet targets. He was more difficult to talk with, except by appointment; he never answered his own phone, leaving this to his secretary's discretion.

Yet he was not a hard or unfriendly man: and he, too, was recognised to be a good manager. The differences between him and Smith were not merely in character and temperament; they were ones of detail of day-to-day operational method, and they affected not merely the way his own job was done but how a lot of other jobs were done.

The question we might now ask is which was the 'real' marketing manager's job? That done by Smith or that done by Cramm? If we had to describe the job, as a job analyst, prior to putting a third person in, when Cramm is promoted to the Board of Directors, what should our description contain? Just the details of the work done and systems operated by Cramm, the last holder of the post? Or should we try and produce an ideal synthesis of the Smith and the Cramm versions? Such a synthesis would probably appeal to no one actually put in the post, for should we not expect the next incumbent to remodel the job slightly to suit himself in those aspects in which change is permissible and practical?

The conclusion we have to reach is that there is not only no one way of doing the job, but that it would be foolish to try and establish any one way as an ideal. No two good craftsmen hold and use their tools in exactly the same way, no two machine operators operate in exactly the same way, but in these instances the differences in the way of working are virtually indiscernible to the observer, and have little impact on either product or workmates.

A manager's job is more elusive. He does not work an automatic machine with little flexibility in its operating rules. He works through people, organisation and systems, which all have a higher degree of permissible flexibility. He himself likes changing things (although *he* may object to being changed) and improving systems, and this characteristic, which is one of the characteristics of a progressive manager, demands its expression. There is, of course, a danger that imposing changes on routines may not be progressive from the point of view of either the manager or the routines, but merely the expression of habit and preference without due regard to efficiency.

In the light of management training and, indeed, of management selection, this shows the question 'What is the context of the job?' to be one of great sensitivity, as is the question 'What sort of character do we require to fill the post?'

If the training manager presumes that the same rigidity of job and man descriptions, associated with much other training in the company, can be introduced equally into the selection and preparation of people for management posts, then he may be doing some disservice to the development of managers. The requirement, in the face of necessary and desirable flexibilities, is a different one, and we have to look at this requirement.

The words flexible and flexibility are used often in describing desirable characteristics of a manager. In an age during which changes occur in every aspect of work and society, with great speed, clearly flexibility is a prerequisite of many management jobs. But flexibility is a word which itself requires further definition. What do we mean by it? Some examples will be a useful starting point.

During the final decades of the twentieth century, Europe is undergoing profound political, social and economic changes, which ultimately affect even the smallest branches and work units in companies. Some of the changes are financial and economic in origin – due to inflation and trade depression – and have led to the search for efficiency and productivity in many companies. Some changes are social, based on the liberation of women, on the rising output of graduates from universities, on the new laws defining the rights of the worker and the obligations of the employer. Political changes are removing barriers to Eastern Europe, altering trading agreements and currency controls. Some changes are technological, many brought about by the development of information technology and the introduction of more and more complex mathematical models as a basis for decision-making. In the face of all these pressures the manager is not merely asked to run his job, his office, his function, so as to maintain a reasonable *status quo*; he is from time to time obliged to accept and to introduce new systems, new attitudes, new objectives and make them work well.

Any manager who finds such changes unacceptable for reasons of personal inability to alter his ways, cannot happily survive very long. Those who find them acceptable and who intelligently assist in their implementation, still have a future in management. Those who are able, for themselves, to anticipate the changes, and who are able to think for themselves in realistic terms about adjustments needed in procedures, relationships and organisation, are likely to be amongst the most successful managers of the future.

We need therefore to distinguish between two different manifestations of flexibility. The manager who accepts changes which are announced to him from above, and who can help make them work properly is certainly flexible. The manager who can, in addition, perceive for himself the need for change and who can design or help design those changes, has an additional and valuable management quality, that of creativity. A creative manager is obviously one who is associated with change during his management career, as is the non-creative flexible manager. The creative manager, however, is seen to take initiative, not merely in the implementation of new work arrangmeents but also in their conception and presentation to others.

It must be emphasised that by creativity we are not referring to change for the sake of change, nor to change for mere personal comfort and familiarity. We are talking of change that will keep the enterprise aligned with the environment, that will ensure reasonable objectives, and maintain a satisfactory level of efficiency.

There are further points to make about flexibility/creativity. Given that managers who possess these characteristics also possess and can use the necessary instruments of management, as described earlier, we should hope to find that the senior members of company management are more liberally endowed with creativity than are the junior members. As a general rule the lowest levels of supervision and management are responsible for running the company's operation on a day-to-day basis; flexibility is required of them because of changes imposed on them, albeit with explanation and education, by more senior management. Middle management are concerned, in addition, with the pursuit of design, manufacturing changes, manpower changes, to meet new economic targets, new legal requirements, in the near future. Top management are concerned, in addition, with looking ahead at where the company might be going at the end of the present and planned production runs, at what changes to introduce if there is an introduction of decreased tariffs, if the EEC falls apart, or any other minor or major environmental change.

We might therefore assume that, in the search for the future management at middle and senior levels, we are searching for evidence of this sort of creativity. Some companies do so and nourish it when found. It is valuable at *any* level of management, and essential at the middle and senior levels. Its presence in the existing senior management can be a stimulus to the young professionals and managers; its absence can be a depressant for them. No organised management training and development scheme can expect to operate successfully without drawing on exactly this same creativity in senior management to sponsor, steer, and contribute to such schemes as are designed. Senior managers without creativity may give authority to management training activities, but it takes creativity to nourish them and help them flourish.

What does creativity depend on? Foremost amongst several factors is 'knowledge of the actual and future environment'. The environment contains the elements with which the manager has to deal, which he has to keep in order, which he has in some way to rearrange without loss of efficiency, and to whose changes and demands he in turn has to respond. The environment is virtually limitless. Every interface with every other function in the company is a door to another sector of his *own* environment. He has to know each sector well enough to enable him to understand the meaning of the activities and changes within each one, for the company as a whole and for his own work area in particular.

Some of his knowledge comes through sifted information given to him expressly for the purpose of keeping him informed – through reports, meetings and company seminars, for example. Much, on the other hand, comes from his own perception, within the random information with which he is presented almost every minute of the working day. The power of perception is therefore important and is a management characteristic to be placed high on the list of desirable attributes. Perception we define here as the ability to sense some meaning in what is observed, without it having been previously analysed or arranged before being presented to the manager (or indeed to anyone else). For example, if an array of production and sales cost figures is so analysed and arranged that the projected figures show a net loss in eight months' time, the manager who reads these can hardly be called perceptive when he understands the significance of what he reads. Nor can he be called perceptive if his knowing about the dissatisfaction of his subordinates has arisen from a frank written statement presented by them to him. By our definition, perception relates primarily to things that have not been analysed, prepared and presented. Perception arises from the manager's, the individual's, own view of the situation. It is important because, without it, the manager is no more than a puppet, as it were, dealing in a 'logical' way with all the information which other people organise and send to him. Each piece of information will have its own logic of course, financial, legal, technical, sometimes human.

Perception is the watershed of practical creativity: with it the manager 'knows' the real world around him, and makes better use of the analysed material typically provided for him. The extent to which he is able to bring about effective developments, or changes, or improvements, will then depend on inventiveness or design ability, and on his powers of persuasion or even courage. But if he is not perceptive, cannot see the actual environment for himself and understand what he sees, his conclusion and his design may either come to nought, or produce new problems as acute as those he is attempting to resolve.

26 Managers as learners

We can now envisage the manager as a person undertaking two roles, one of high precision and highly instrumented, and the other more subjective, intuitive and unprecise. These two roles are, in a sense, undertaken in a company and its environment which has two corresponding aspects, one highly structured and systematised; the other changing, uncertain and also very human. Of course there is only one manager and one environment, but the distinction between the certain and the uncertain, the mechanical system and human society, provides a view of the manager and his job that can be helpful in the consideration of selection, training and development of managers.

Company systems and procedures, as well as many of the techniques of management to which we have given the name instruments, may be learnt without a great deal of difficulty by managers or trainee managers who have successfully reached the secondary educational levels typical of Western society. For some there will be difficulty in understanding mathematical concepts, or in manipulating mathematical data; for others, there are, for example, blind spots in accounting or in economic concepts. Everyone has his strengths and weaknesses both as a student of, and as an executive with, the wide array of management instruments. However, two factors have made the weaknesses less likely to be an actual danger. One factor is the existence in most companies of specialist functions which deal with great expertise with the techniques, the instruments, necessary for modern management. Thus we have the accountants and financial experts, the computer and mathematical experts, the operational researchers, economists, and planners, all of whom provide services to management and to individual managers. This removes from the shoulders of the manager, in all but the smallest companies, the burden of having to be an expert in a wide range of subjects, and expert in using all the instruments of management. Total management expertise lies in all the management, in all the managers as a group, backed by their professional specialist staffs.

The second factor, of advantage to the average manager, is the progress which has been made in presenting specialist concepts and techniques, in courses or in books, to managers. It is not necessary to be a mathematics graduate in order to understand statistical methods, to the level needed by most managers. The same is true of finance, of economics, and of a great number of analytical techniques available to managers. Although he may not acquire executive skill, the manager can, in the course of days or weeks, develop an understanding of the concepts, possibilities and limitations, and of the language of any specialisation with which he needs to be conversant.

All of the above represents one large basic area of learning for managers. It is not true to say that anyone can learn it, but it is true to say that most men and women with secondary and tertiary education are able to make progress without undue difficulty, sometimes very much to their own suprise. This is one of the more easily recognisable components of management training, and is composed of a range of subjects, each with its scale of difficulty and progress. It lends itself beautifully to training analysis, and to management training based on that analysis.

Thus a manager, or trainee manager, can be appraised in terms of his capability or understanding under a number of subject headings, and a learning programme stretching over weeks, months or even years, can be designed and implemented to bring him up to a required level in each of the subjects. He will then have acquired all, or most, of the instruments needed up to that date. Some he will be able to use himself; some he will leave to others to use.

The success of management education, in producing rapidly a higher level of understanding in subjects that can be taught analytically, is quite outstanding. This success is partly due to the mutual understanding that has developed between business school teachers and their pupils, i.e. company managers and executives. At one time the teachers tended to see the pupils as somewhat old undergraduates, who had to listen and learn. This illusion was shattered – and continues to be shattered – by the 'pupils' seriously wanting to *know why* they are learning this particular theory, what is the truth and practicality, *how* do you use it, and so on – right through to challenging the teachers' knowledge and experience. The teachers came quickly to see that the class wanted to *understand* the subject matter, and be able to draw on it back in their work, in meetings, in discussion with company specialists: they were not going to take an examination. This mutual understanding, in many instances, has led to professional friendship and consultation between class members and faculty, to the lasting value and pleasure of both sides. In this whole process, as the reader will anticipate, the training officers concerned exercised their 'facilitator' capability, with success – which brought the training function closer in its work to both the business schools and company managers.

Managers have to be good learners, for their jobs demand continual development of knowledge. The ability to learn is today a prerequisite of management, and the sympathetic form that contemporary management education takes not only makes analytical learning easier in the classroom, but also boosts the capability of the manager to learn and to adapt himself rapidly on the job itself.

The acquisition of a number of instruments is only one starting point in the development of the manager. The next step is more difficult, more elusive to the management trainer. All the knowledge, all the instruments, have to be put together to make one body of interrelated knowledge and technique. Much of the subject matter constitutes one universe of concepts, and for ease of understanding, of use, and of teaching, it is broken down into parts, each with its own coherence and logic. This is true of political/sociological/economic subjects and of organisational/financial/technological subjects.

The learner has to put together this subject matter for himself; he has to see for himself how the descriptive components relate, and how the tool subjects relate. It cannot really be done for him, even by the most expert teacher. Moreover, he not only has to see the relationships between different subject matters and different concepts; he also has to see how all of this relates to the actual world in which he lives and works. This world he has to see for himself also, as we have discussed earlier.

Whether one is seeing the relationship between different concepts, or the relationship between concepts and the actual environment, or the relationship between things in the environment, one is engaged in perception, internal or external, although one cannot be divorced from the other. We have noted the importance of perception, for learning and for development, in Chapter 1 and in Chapter 21 on 'Continuous development'. We have referred to how the individual 'perceives, digests, comprehends and later uses...' that which he experiences. In this he 'learns through experience', and perhaps enters into creative, innovative, thinking. It is true of many managers to say that they *need* to enter into creative/innovative thinking, because

(a) they are faced often with situations which contain new features, and which demand new approaches by the managers.
(b) There is a constant need to take a fresh look at well established processes, routines, standards, and organisational relationships, and see ways of improving quality and effectiveness.

Hence, enhancement of perception, and of the creativity that springs from it, is one of the most important objectives of management development. However, it cannot be 'taught,' although it can be improved if there is sufficient capability already in the person concerned. Seminars and workshops can help managers understand the processes of perception/creative thinking and action: self-appraisal and personal target setting will help some to get to grips with self-development: coaching by a perceptive and able boss – perhaps by a colleague – can be valuable. Also important, is that the company culture and boss-subordinate relationships encourage and permit creative thinking and action. Without the satisfaction of seeing their ideas actually working, some managers will stop trying. The training manager, faced with the challenge of improving this aspect of management development, will need to acquire a deep understanding of the processes of perception/creativity and of the the practical steps that can be taken to bring about improvement in individuals or in the company management as a whole. It is easy to set one's sights too high: but it is not difficult to adjust or introduce management workshops, appraisal and coaching systems and bring about worthwhile improvements in performance in the course of time. Fortunately the recent work of Honey, Mumford, Koch and Hardy and others, enable such steps to be taken with a good understanding of principles and practices. Let us turn to some problems that have to be recognised and dealt with.

As with intelligence, creativity seems to have its own early history in the development of the person as a child. The adult who enters a company is already formed in terms of character and personality, within which perception is an important capability. It is in no way easy to determine the level of perceptiveness in an applicant, and all companies must perforce engage people at all levels of capability, and must expect to find that many of their newly recruited swans prove to be geese, and that some geese prove to be swans, in the course of time.

Recent experience confirms this, within industry and in the academic world. There have been very serious efforts to improve both perception and creativity amongst company executives by direct methods. Most well known are sensitivity training techniques. This is not the place to discuss the pros and cons of these, and we confine our attention to the significance of them for the development of perception and of creativity. First let us look at underlying precepts which are germane to the whole question of management development and management performance, with particular reference to creativity.

A manager, or indeed anyone else, in a company, works within a highly structured environment. This includes the processes, systems, standards and objectives which totally surround his job, and very largely determine exactly the what, when and where of what he has to do. All of this produces a constraint on being different, creative, or developmental. For some people this constraint is overwhelming, and no effort is thought to be possible to bring about changes – apart from short cuts introduced by employees to make their work easier, maybe to the disadvantage of others or the consequent lowering of standards.

On the other hand, there is the constraint of the hierarchy of supervision and management. Even if a person does think of improvements that do not appear to imperil some other part of the system, he still has to get permission to act. He even has to get attention from his own manager. He may meet with indifference, delays or negatives, and become eventually frustrated by holdups, and inhibited by the power that others exert on him.

The challenge, therefore has been to find a way to break through or dissolve these organisational constraints – without destroying the organisation itself – and release the creative capability presumed to be present in the managers and executives of the company, either individually or collectively.

Sensitivity training takes the following form. Bearing in mind the effect of organisational constraint, managers are invited to spend time, that is to say days or even weeks, together in rooms away from normal work, in which there is no declared objective, no structure, no hierarchy, no work, no programmes. Just nothing, as it were, but themselves. This totally unstructured situation is provided to enable them to explore freely themselves, each other, and to develop the perception and sensitivity latent in them. Some groups have been, and are, run with a low degree of structuring, e.g. some teaching about personality and relationships, for example, or with a programme to enable progress to be discussed as the days go by.

One early finding, one conclusion, of relevance to this text was that those who were able to deal with the very testing circumstances of these groups, and understood and made something of the elusive opportunities for self-development, seemed to be those who were already perceptive and otherwise mature and competent. These were the people who, in a sense, did not need to attend in the first place. But the more in need a person was, the less perceptive, the less mature and socially competent, the more problems he was likely to encounter, some too severe to deal with successfully, and the greater the chance that he would not benefit.

On returning to work from this very radical experience each person is, it is hoped, in a somewhat better condition to exercise their sensitive, perceptive or creative capabilities. There has been but little evidence to indicate that this is the case. There has been, on the other hand, a confusion of means and ends. No one going through such an experience, or going to any highly moving or motivating course, is likely to forget it and the impact that it has on their thoughts and their feelings then and later. This is an impact of the 'means'. 'Ends' are to be measured or observed in change of behaviour and capability at a later date, not in nostalgic reminiscence.

There is, then, from this some support for the contention that perception and creativity cannot be taught and learnt, as can be mathematics and accounting. There is support for the contention that those who have this capability, although somewhat suppressed by organisational constraints, may blossom if placed in new and more favourable circumstances, e.g. working for a boss with coaching capability. Or in a grass roots project which demands innovation and consultation. One cannot say that some have, and some have not got it, and then proceed to test for its presence or absence. In the development of managers one has to be continually on the watch for its genuine expression, and one has to do whatever is reasonable and possible to create circumstances which will favour its expression and hence its development.

This task becomes, therefore, an organisational one. It is not simply to be regarded as the job of the training manager, or of the management development officer, to arrange special courses, seminars or other events to promote management development. The whole management, and the organisation for which they are responsible, have to recognise that some of the structures and features of the company which present opportunities for up-and-coming managers may, at the same time, inhibit their development as individuals and as learners.

The training manager has to address himself as much to organisational and relationship questions, as he does to questions of learning physical and intellectual skills. This does not mean that complete organisational change has to be striven for: this would become almost certainly an abortive preoccupation for him. It means that his own perception has to be directed towards the day-to-day activities and relationships of managers, and the identification of constraints which are likely to have an inhibiting effect on those managers. The constraints take many forms – lack of communication and information is one of the most common, as is lack of explanation for decisions and new actions. Constraints often arise through imperfection in character: senior managers with a 'closed' and intolerant style can be damaging to their subordinates. Constraints come also in the form of badly thought out procedures and duties, which can produce conflict and fatigue, thus limiting the energy and willingness available for freer thinking.

It is worth noting here that Blake, in his proposals for organisational development, incorporating the use of the managerial grid, offered to any one company a solution of heroic proportions and ambition. This requires intimate involvement of the entire management in a sequence of seminars dealing increasingly, but voluntarily, with company situations and problems, in which the keynote is frankness and mutual understanding. There can be little doubt about the objective. But whether or not a company can sustain the entire long process, which demands a great deal of all managers on top of their daily work, must be open to question. It is a scheme that repays consideration in depth, even if it cannot be fully adopted for practical considerations.

Coverdale works in a similar way, and focuses on the build-up of team work in smaller units that exist in companies. The free and frank discussion which are held by these units, their supervisors and managers, embrace their actual work problems and methods, and in sufficient depth to ferret out attitudes, ideas and improvements, cutting across some of the existing constraints and inhibitions. The natural authority of the unit managers makes it possible for these improvements – in procedures, or methods or organisation – to be implemented. The learning by those involved is through the opportunity to perceive their work situation and environment more fully, and do something to make it better. Their perception and creativity is exercised, in the working world, and to their ultimate satisfaction. These are essential elements in the development process.

The work of Rackham and others in interactive skills is also worth noting here. It focuses heavily on the observation of behaviours in other people, enabling perceptive skill to exercise itself and develop. This exercise can lead to advantageous changes in one's own behaviour, either intuitive or through conscious self correction, and according to one's own outlook on life. Perhaps not surprisingly a notable success in using this development technique is in training people whose job contains regular and definable interpersonal tasks, e.g. counter clerks, aircraft cabin staff, where the job requires definable behaviours in the staff, towards which the training can be directed and structured, and easily understood.

All of the above examples of work to improve sensitivity through heightened perception, tackle the constraints arising from hierarchical as well as other subjective inhibitions. We have to recognise that, for example, habit can be a very powerful personal constraint, as can social shyness and, in some cases, social ineptness, and the fear of conflict.

However, there are many other ways in which organisational constraints can exist; they, too, have to be identified first and their effect on management learning and development considered. Two examples may be helpful.

In an engineering factory making small parts, the sales office and the production control office were next door to each other, separated by no more than a solid partition with a door. About 60 people worked in each office, under George White the sales superintendent and Harry Green the production control superintendent. Both superintendents were middle-aged, of average ability and well experienced. Both were interested in training, for themselves and their staff, and got help and backing from the training officer and from top management. Top management knew the critical importance of these two offices, and knew that the development of capability in the superintendents was to be taken seriously. But despite their attendance at very good and relevant in- and out-company courses, nothing seemed to improve in the men or their offices, where there was a need for greater efficiency.

The official organisation made it clear that the two offices worked together in a closely integrated and co-operative way. But that was not how the two sets of employees felt about it. They virtually fought each other when at work, although not in their free time. The operational relationships of both employees and super-intendents were so poor that development of the superintendents in their present work was an uphill task.

One day, to provide extra deskspace, the wall between the two offices was removed. All the desks were sensibly rearranged, and the two superintendents found themselves, almost by accident, sitting openly side by side. Rivalry and fighting came quickly to be regarded as a bit childish: most people enjoyed the new freedom to communicate. The two superintendents were able to think together about improvements, and together to implement them. The physical, visual, social and psychological constraint had been lifted, and the development of each man could now proceed in a work setting that was more favourable to development.

The wall had been recognised as a constraint on desk space, and perhaps on communications, but it was not realised until later that it had produced a con-straint on human development.

A further example illustrates constraints in communication. In an oil refinery the process superintendent held weekly meetings with his own heads of sections. The agenda for each meeting was simply a list of problems relating to process and process equipment, and the actual output relative to output targets. The meetings were brief, to the point, and almost without discussion. The process superintend-ent would ask, for instance, a brief question on progress towards the start up of the second distillation column, or the repair of the pipeline from No. 3 crude oil storage tank, and receive and answer equally brief. If he was satisfied he would then issue an instruction, agree a date, and make sure that all present had heard and understood. Occasionally there would be a misunderstanding to be cleared up, and occasionally a question demanding a fuller answer and explanation, which were given.

Now this oil refinery, like many others, was a place in which the many super-visors responsible for plant lived almost separate lives. Physically they were separated from one another: they could visit one another's offices to talk, but this was not attractive in extreme heat, or wet or cold. On the plant itself, and amongst the machinery, it was impossible to hold discussions satisfactorily because of the high noise level. There is, moreover, almost nothing that is self evident in a refinery. Hardly anyone ever sees any oil, which is of necessity in pipes, vessels or tanks; the processes are invisible within their columns and reaction chambers; the pumps, compressors and other machinery and equipment carry out their func-tions equally shielded from view by their casing. Although the refinery is alive with activity, virtually nothing can be seen but unmoving inert steel exteriors, and the faces of the instruments.

It struck the process superintendent, one day, that despite the fact that any man working in a refinery was surrounded by the most sensitive instruments, the most powerful machinery, the most complex processes – in fact some of the most sophisticated products of man's intellect – the amount of observation possible, and, indeed, the amount of available information, was the smallest amount deemed necessary for efficiency. Even his own meetings were run like a process unit, he thought: he as chairman, was virtually in the control room, and he got the information he required by talking exclusively with the person who could give it. Working in a technologically rich environment did not seem to be a technologically, or humanly, enriching experience for many of those employed in supervision. The constraint on enrichment lay in the refinery environment and in the traditional procedures of meetings and accountability. Did it matter? And if it did, could he do anything about it?

We shall deal with these particular questions more fully in the next chapter, concerned with 'managers as teachers'. At this moment it is sufficient to say that, with regard to the junior managers 'as learners' they were not only learning the minimum necessary for immediate work, but also learning, unconsciously, a style of management that would tend to carry the minimisation of learning into the future. This has its obvious disadvantages for management development: but it is important to note that the disadvantage does not arise because of decisions concerning management development. It arises because of 'constraints' inherent in the plant, the systems and the organisation. They are not designed for the purpose of human development and inevitably have features which are to some extent antagonistic to that development. These features, or constraints, have to be constantly searched for and brought to management's attention.

27 Managers as teachers

Our process superintendent, in the previous chapter, has some important decisions to make, and it is worth our while looking closely at how he arrives at them, for there are some general principles to be discerned here. He asks himself three questions:

1 'Has there been, and will there be, technical inefficiency as a result of minimum information?'
2 'Can the heads of sections do their jobs well, as supervisors, with minimum information?'
3 'Does minimum information provide a satisfactory diet for developing managers and other people?'

The most trenchant question is, of course, the first in most circumstances and in most companies. It is frequently recognised that the risk of error increases if people work in intellectual blinkers, and the cliché that 'a little knowledge is dangerous' is best answered by giving people a lot of knowledge. The best run companies do their best to analyse all likely errors, faults and emergency situations to a simplistic form so that all people at operator, supervisory and management levels know how to recognise danger signs and what to do when they arise. Beyond this there is an increasing amount of automatic warning and shut-down to deal with problems before any human being is even aware of them. But there can be no question of this systematisation replacing human knowledge and understanding.

In the search for efficiency, companies are organised in cells, so that particular activities of operating, maintaining, accounting, testing and so on are able to be carried out by separate specialists. All of these then have to be brought together again, their work planned and co-ordinated in an integrated way. The search for efficiency produces specialisation, which, if left alone, is highly inefficient, although many people treasure the idea of being 'a specialist'. Absolute specialisation is the enemy of efficiency. Some senior managers know this and spend much time and energy in trying to develop collaboration between production and marketing, accounting and operational research, publicity and personnel management. It is not merely interesting and pleasant for one specialist to know about the work of other colleague specialists. It is an essential step in integration and hence in efficiency, in the avoidance and handling of problems, and in the improvement of the organisation.

The process superintendent knew that nothing was being done to further the knowledge between specialists, and to enlarge the knowledge of individuals of the company as a whole. He knew that he was therefore running a technical risk and that in this he was not fulfilling his own responsibilities. He had reason enough to modify the format of his weekly meetings, which he did. In so doing, and in producing an ambience in which perception and creativity were generally better provided for, he was automatically improving the performance of management and supervision, and improving the prospects of management development. Questions 2 and 3 were dealt with simply by raising the company's management capability, and by reducing the traditional constraints.

Every manager is a teacher. He teaches in a number of different ways; he teaches distinctly different things; and he teaches different sorts of people. Compared with a university lecturer or a school teacher his teaching responsibility is likely to be much more complex. Yet it is not usual to think of industrial managers as teachers, and very many do not think of themselves as such. But if the effective teaching capability of management is poor, then so will be its training and development work.

The teaching capability of management, and of supervision, as a whole is important not only to management development, but also to the whole training effort of the company, to the training of clerks, operators, professionals, to all types of employees. Although it is obvious and logical to check, from time to time, on the whole pattern of training activities in a company, as we have discussed in earlier chapters, it is not so obvious, nor so usual, to check on the teaching capability of the company.

Yet this is an important factor, and warrants, if not an actual audit, some serious consideration from the training manager if he is to understand fully the circumstances in which training schemes are run, and the working circumstances in which people work and learn from day to day. Some of the teaching is deliberate and planned, and some of it is not conscious. This compares exactly with the learning experience of people, of which some is conscious and some, the greater part, is not conscious. We have to consider all aspects if we are to get a fully significant picture.

Let us start by examining the teaching done by the process superintendent in the course of several days at work. Sitting at his desk he dictates a memorandum to his secretary to be sent to the maintenance superintendent, with copies to several people inside and outside process and maintenance. It says that there will be a shut-down planning meeting next week. His secretary, who is new, asks what this means. He briefly describes what a shut-down is, who takes part, and what the meeting will discuss. He has taught; his secretary has learnt. This ordinary event is of the highest significance, although it was unplanned and was informal. It was spontaneous.

He repeats spontaneous teaching many times in a week; sometimes for a junior, sometimes for a colleague or a senior member of another function. He has no idea at all, before the spontaneous teaching, that it is going to take place. Someone asks him a question; or someone looks puzzled; or he realises that a meeting has moved beyond somebody's understanding. His reaction is that he must explain. That is spontaneity. He does not use an overhead projector or a classroom; he does it on the spot. That is informality.

It is also conscious teaching, but on other occasions it may not be consciously done. For example, when he is in the maintenance superintendent's office and discussing the organisation of the repair of the bellows on the catalytic reformer, the two men have different views on the best procedure, and each explains his view to the other. In the room are their junior assistants, who hear it all. The two men teach, unconsciously, a great deal in that 20 minutes to their juniors. Their juniors have learned some technology, some economics of process shut-down, and something of the different approaches to problems, as demonstrated by the two superintendents.

During these several days informal teaching opportunities arise frequently and, despite their high value, pass almost without notice, are taken for granted. We shall return to them shortly, but first we shall extend the picture by looking at the formal teaching undertaken by the superintendent. On the first day he attends an induction course in the company for new graduates, where, in accordance with the programme, he talks about the company's operations. On the third day he attends a luncheon given for the induction course members and speakers, and says a few more words, previously prepared, to those present. On the fourth day he spends an hour in a meeting between the company and the local press, in which emissions and spillages are being explored. He gives a prepared talk for 20 minutes illustrated with slides, deals with questions, develops discussion. It lasts for one hour altogether. After these three formal teaching engagements he is free from further engagements for two weeks.

The formal teaching capability of management, and indeed of supervision and of all others who are called on to give talks in company courses, seminars and meetings, is something which requires constant appraisal and improvement. Fortunately, formal teaching, no matter how difficult it is for some people to do well, is something which can be looked after without undue problem. The teaching is done in public, the teachers are known and can be assessed as to their capability, and training in lecturing or in discussion leading can be provided for them. The efficient organisation of courses, with a good service of audio-visual aids, and with competent management of the programme as a whole, add to the quality of the manager-lecturer, and, it is often found, may even add to his acceptance inside and outside his department. An audit of formal teaching capability in a company, using a framework such as the training opportunity matrix, is relatively straightforward, even if lengthy, to make.

But the informal teaching capability, including the coaching and tutoring and mentoring required by developing managers, is much more difficult to evaluate. Its scope, should one believe it not to be of great importance, ranges from all on-the-job training for new recruits, promotees and transferees to the development and implementation of effective management skills at the highest levels in the company. Most of the informal teaching is out of sight and out of reach of the independent observer. It takes place in the course of a day's work in the offices, on the shop floor, in the corridors, during meal times. It is an integral part of the day's business and the day's communications and cannot be easily distinguished from everything else that is going on, except by those who directly experience it as and when it happens. What is perhaps easier to recognise is the growth, or lack of growth, in capability and confidence of those who are receiving it. If their performance is good, then we may infer that they have been well taught: if it is poor, then perhaps they have been badly taught.

Ideally, one could argue, the managers and all others with supervisory responsibilities in a company, would be technically well informed and skilled, highly perceptive, articulate, and ready and willing to give information to others. To this one would add that there would be no undue organisational or physical barriers to communications; and that there were good traditions and habits already existing in the company, to encourage teaching and communication practice. In this ideal world the employee, whether plant attendant, engineer or accountant, would also be intelligent and articulate, interested in his prospects and, above all, with sufficient initiative to ask lucid questions about his work and fully digest the information given him.

There are, indeed, companies in many parts of the world, in which these ideals appear to be met. The result is a competent manpower; achieved sometimes without much discernible training effort by anyone, although closer study reveals that the quality of the members of the company, and the traditions of communication, enable personal learning and development to take place at the speed which is optimal for both individual and company.

The question of optimal speed is important, and we shall refer to it later in the chapter on routes. The point that has to be made here is that a well run company, in training terms, may have a satisfactory informal training capability as long as the rate of development of organisation and technology remain fairly constant. But if these developments accelerate then, with people changing their jobs faster, and with new technology to be learned, the traditional informal communication and relationships between managers, supervisors and employees may not be able to cope with the new teaching and learning demands on the company manpower. At moments such as this both the formal and informal teaching capabilities of management need to come under review, and decisions need to be taken on the improvement of both.

The actual characteristics of managers and supervisors, and the actual state of the organisation, may be far from ideal. The examples they set, as well as the informal teaching done, may be indifferent or even counter-productive. This inefficiency arises from many causes, and we shall look at some of them.

We have noted above some of the ideal characteristics of all those people with managerial or supervisory responsibilities. The first was that of being well informed and skilled, in things for which they are responsible. No one can be expected to know everything in minute detail and, therefore, it is normal to excuse responsible people if, from time to time, they reveal gaps or errors in their knowledge. Close studies of the actual knowledge levels may, nevertheless, reveal unacceptable ignorance and potential incompetence. Obviously, in a company with a stable manpower, and with little technological change over the years, the risk of damage through ignorance may be slight, and the knowledge levels of all may maintain an acceptable level. But in a very fast-changing company managerial and technical skills may not have time to take root. The teaching and supervisory capabilities will suffer in consequence, and the strength of the informal teaching effort will decline with a loss of confidence between employee and supervisor.

This situation, in extreme cases, can have serious consequences. In European companies undertaking rapid expansion in an expanding market the very fast promotion of young employees into middle management has produced management groups and individuals who have not assimilated or practised the skills which their position normally demands. The most intelligent will find ways to compensate for lack of experience and practice, but many others cannot. The result, for informal teaching, is that such people cannot fully instruct their own staff, and cannot properly instruct or supervise the other junior managers appointed below them.

This phenomenon is seen, perhaps, in its most extreme form in developing countries where, as we have discussed earlier, political or social pressure may bring about the very fast promotion of young nationals into middle and senior technical and administrative management. When done too quickly the company finds itself with too many managers who have not enough technical knowledge to make any great contribution to functional management. In addition to this, sometimes overlooked, is the fact that there is little that they, formally or informally, can teach their employees, their juniors and their colleagues that is of any great use. Extreme cases such as these remind us of the importance of knowledge. Like health, when we have it we don't notice it, but when it is missing we suffer.

Organisational and physical barriers to communication can be of great importance. The introduction of open-plan office design, even if not to everyone's liking, has given frequent evidence of the sensitive relationship between physical layout, hierarchy, and communication. A common practice has been to take a group of offices of conventional type (that is to say each with one or more people, each of closed cubicle type along a corridor in the office block) and replace them with an open-plan office. This is now a familiar layout – all the desks and essential personnel in one large room, and even the most senior manager seated somewhere within that room. The arrangement has advantages and disadvantages, but an interesting finding has been that the inhibition and constraint on communication have often lessened noticeably, and that the supervisor-employee communication has risen, sometimes spectacularly. The same managers, the same supervisors, the same employees, but without the walls which separated them, have crossed not only the physical but also the hierarchical boundaries.

The two factors which this underlines as being of importance to both communication and informal teaching, are those of hierarchy and visibility. Each can be inhibiting on its own. Dealt with together the results may be even more profitable than dealing with each separately.

Is the manager ready and willing to teach informally, spontaneously? And if he is willing, is he articulate enough, and skilled enough in explaining things, to do it well? These factors are also interdependent. A foreman may be willing enough, in principle, to explain things to his employees, but he is bad at explaining. As a result he gives the impression that he doesn't want to explain any more than necessary. This becomes a habit of attitude, and he loses interest in doing something that he doesn't actually enjoy doing. In cases like this involving a lack of skill in speaking and demonstrating fluently, a great deal can be done to improve teaching ability by providing courses for supervisors in techniques of teaching. If the willingness and stamina are there, the techniques can be put to good use, and old negative habits will fade away.

In order to illustrate not only the various factors but also their interdependence and interactions, let us take an extreme example of a company in which management's teaching capability is at a very low level and examine the reasons for this. The company is in a developing country, and processes vegetable oil. It is owned partly by a Western international organisation, and partly by local interests. Its operations are managed by a mixture of Western expatriates and local nationals. The expatriates are in sufficient strength in number and quality to make sure that all managerial and technical decisions are well made. The national managers, although equally numerous, are of far less experience and capability than the expatriates, and their actual contribution to decision-making is small. The supervisors and other employees in the company are also almost entirely nationals, and their standards and work effort are generally recognised as not yet satisfactory.

The complaint made by the local owners and by the national managers, that the national managers, supervisors and employees are not learning and exercising the skills and authority appropriate to their jobs, forces the company to investigate the reasons for this malaise. At first sight, to the outsider, the company looks well equipped with all that is required for successful training and employment. There is a large training department, with courses and schemes provided in basic commerce, science and technology. Many managers and supervisors are sent each year on external courses. There are job descriptions for all manager and supervisor jobs, as well as for all the technical and commercial key posts at a lower level. There is an annual performance appraisal well administered, providing information for training and development purposes.

In addition to these provisions, the company salary and benefits package is very competitive; and the opportunities for promotion are good and everyone knows that they are good. The full personnel administration structure of those things often assumed to be essential to manpower development, i.e. formal training, formal appraisal and planning, formal job description and pay systems, is excellently designed and run. What has gone wrong?

The answer, to a large extent, lies in the almost complete absence of informal teaching, of valuable informal communication in the company. This has come about in two ways. First, the high promotion rate of the nationals, through supervisor and manager posts, has made it almost impossible for, say, a national superintendent to teach his newly appointed assistant the realities of his new job. The job description is fine, but it contains little or nothing that is of value for training in routines or decision-making. The superintendent was himself formerly the assistant superintendent, but for such a short time that successful training, handover and experience never materialised for him. He cannot, therefore, now help his assistant beyond giving broad directives. There prove to be too many people in the company in this condition, in need of job training on a day-to-day informal basis, but not able to get it. The attractive high promotion rates have proved to be an Achilles' heel.

Second, the expatriate managers have not come to the rescue, for various reasons. It is not in the tradition of this expatriate group to exert themselves unduly in training nationals on-the-job. Some feel that it is not even in their interest. Some feel that the national's weakness in management merely confirms that they are not cut out to be managers, or not for a long time. Expatriate management form their own communication network, with its own language, its own internal self dependence for decision-making. They neither teach spontaneously, nor do they set a clear and good example – much of what they say and do is beyond the sight and hearing of the national. Worst, with their speed and ability gained from longer experience they pre-empt the decisions and decision-making of the national manager, and deny him the opportunity of maturing in his management role. The company's operations, meanwhile, continue to run satisfactorily.

In this extreme and somewhat dramatic example, we see that, despite good formal structures, the national is not going to learn very much, or very fast, about his new levels of responsibility. The answer to the question 'how do we improve the performance of the national?' clearly does not lie simply in providing more formal training for him. Something has to be done about the excessive promotion rates – this will be unpopular. Something has to be done to break traditional patterns of isolation, communication and pre-emption in the expatriate group. And this will be unpopular with the expatriates. The many factors which are present must not only be identified but also their interdependence must be recognised. The unwillingness of the expatriate relates to fears of job security, and to the sheer difficulty of intercultural communication; the position of some nationals has its roots in promises made in the annual personnel appraisal and the political pressures to localise the next layer of management in the company. The solution must take the whole situation into account.

In most companies, of course, the situation is neither so dramatic nor so clear as in our example. But in studying how to make training and development progress well, management's ability to teach, both formally and informally, by plan or spontaneously, must be regarded as vital to success. The ability is based on much more than the mere pedagogic skills of the manager, as we have seen, and the improvement of this ability may require adjustments in management communication practices, and in both physical and hierarchical organisation.

28 Places and routes

We now pay attention to the question of whether the place where a job is done is satisfactory for training purposes; whether the job itself is not merely a reasonable job for employment and work purposes, but whether it lends itself to training, learning and development.

The occupant of the job may be there indefinitely or he may be there for a planned shorter period before moving on to another job, in another place, as part of a programme. For the permanent occupant, the suitability of the job for training may not be so critical as for the itinerant, temporary, trainee. For the shorter term trainee-occupant the suitability may be critical, if he is to learn sufficient during a limited time, to meet the objectives of the overall programme and, at the same time, find the interest and occupation necessary for his maturity.

For the shorter term trainee it is also essential that the place is available for him to occupy at a time that fits reasonably into the overall pattern of his own training. If there are insufficient places, or if the organisation of the moves of the trainees is done badly, he may miss essential experience. Hence, in the overall management of training, the management of training places has an importance for some special training schemes. This is also true of training routes, i.e. the sequence of places through which the individual should move. These sequences often have a 'best' order, the first places, for example, providing basic skill and knowledge essential to the work in the later places. Consequently, in planning the moves from place to place, a route is planned with those sequences thought best for training purposes.

Typical training schemes in which places and routes feature prominently are, for example, apprenticeships, operator traineeships, and graduate training. In all of these there will be places of two main types. First, places which are not essential to the manning of the company, sometimes called 'supernumerary' places; second, places which, although used for training purposes, are essential to the manning – we call these 'established' places. Usually one finds that the flexibility of schemes, the speed with which moves can be made, and the confidence with which training-move plans can be made in the supernumerary places are quite different from the established places. The movement of supernumeraries is likely to be at the wise discretion of the training manager and the head of the function concerned. The movement of people in established posts is more likely to be in accordance with the natural manpower flow rates of the company, influenced even by attrition and external recruitment – unless something is done to protect those posts.

In designing, or in updating, a scheme in which either supernumerary or established posts, or both, are needed, a number of agreements have to be reached between training management and functional management. To start with, within the overall objectives of the scheme, there is a target figure, by skill or profession etc., of the number of people who are required for employment on completion of the scheme, year by year – let us say 10 per year total. As, on completion, a percentage will leave the company (unless under contract not to do so) the numbers of scheme 'graduates' required will have to be increased from 10 to, say, 13. Because people leave the company during the training, that number (13), will have to be increased to 18 (say) to give the number to be recruited to start each year. As the programme is 3 years overall, the total number of trainees in the company once it has been running 2 years and more, will be about 42. This final figure may shock those members of management who had no more than the figure 10 in their minds: without doing the arithmetic they had assumed that the company would carry 30 trainees in all. In this example, we have taken only small numbers, in a small company. In a larger company seeking to employ 50 ex-trainees per year from its own training scheme, the comparable total trainee population would be about 210. Although, being a larger company, it would have a greater number of places in which the trainees could work, the sheer size of the trainee force, the annual recruitment of 90 people per year with, perhaps, 200 to 300 short-listed and interviewed – these and other factors of staffing and cost can be daunting.

But the numbers have to be calculated, and the agreement reached on their acceptability, at every phase from recruitment to final posting. Armed with these figures a search for, or check on, quantities and quality of suitable training places can be made. Each place must offer real work with a satisfactory opportunity to develop skill; the supervision needs to be sympathetic, and with adequate teaching ability. These are basic requirements if the quality of the training and experience is to be safeguarded. But they are requirements which are self evident: there is no need to elaborate on the attention that needs to be given to these qualities.

What is less evident, perhaps, are the problems of setting up the right number of training places in the first instance, and the problem of maintaining the flow of people through these places, month after month, and year after year, and of maintaining the places themselves.

Trainees, and training places, may exist at various levels in a company, ranging from very young clerical trainees to middle-aged members of a management development scheme; from engineering craft apprentices to retired army officers starting an industrial career. Although there is no universal rule, it is often the case that supernumerary training places are provided for the trainees who are newcomers to the company, and the established place is used for trainees (whether or not they are so-called) who have been in the company for some time on the payroll. It is also often the case that the programme of moves for the older person has to be consistent with the development of that person's career progression; whereas, for the younger person, moves to places which provide excellent skills and experience but which cannot be seen as promotion are more often used and normally more readily accepted.

The acceptability of a move, i.e. the acceptability to the person moved, is influenced by the personal expectations of that person; and the expectations are often those connected with career and not merely with training and the raising of personal skill levels. Hence, we cannot divorce the discussion of training moves and training routes from the discussion of career development. In this chapter, however, we shall focus on schemes whose main objectives are the improvement of skill and capability. In the next chapter we shall discuss career development.

Let us look at three schemes, all operating in one company, at three different levels. The company designs, manufactures and sells engineering components, and employs all of its 4,800 people on one site, in the factory and the main offices, apart from about 200 people in sales and marketing in 14 sales offices throughout the country and abroad. The three schemes are for student trainees, for university graduates, and for middle management, and we shall take each one in turn, then summarise the similarities and differences between them in their use of places.

The student trainees are studying for degrees or diplomas at the various colleges in the country. They are either fully sponsored and employed by the company, or are independent college-based students who come to the company for practical experience and training. Their courses, of 4 years' duration, are of the familiar sandwich form, allowing either about 6 months each year for practical work, or one full year of practical work, and three years full time in college. There are 80 fully company-sponsored students, with about 40 in the company at any moment; plus 15 further students in the company at any time who are college-based. Thus there have to be 55 places, some in technical work and some in administration and commerce, maintained throughout the year and from year to year, as long as the company continues its present policies.

All the places are supernumerary. That is to say, the work place is not classified as essential to the effort of the office or department where it is located. The trainees are administered continuously by the training department, and their pay and allowances appear as a cost to training department and not to the departments in which they actually work. The philosophy, and tradition, behind this, is that the student trainees are not yet fully employable, not having completed their professional studies; that they come and go too frequently to be considered as a real responsibility for the department in which they work only temporarily.

The problems of managing these places proves to be a serious one. Each place has to offer real day-long work, if the trainee is to benefit, and should offer opportunity, even if only occasionally, for some creativity and responsibility. In the earliest days of the scheme there was much misunderstanding. Supervisors and managers were reluctant to accept such trainees in many cases, as they could not see them as anything other than a nuisance, a burden with no pay-off for the host. However, the trainees were mostly intelligent, hard-working and willing, and supervisors came to find them actually an asset. Within a year or two of the start of the scheme supervisors were talking frankly about how useful these trainees were; and places were confirmed as always available with certain work allocated to those places. There were, of course, a few battles in cases where some supervisors, previously reluctant to take trainees, now refused to release them because they had become so useful. It was perhaps fortunate that their return to college cut short any further dispute.

The management of places now entered a second phase. The real work, done to a good standard, and associated with a place, demanded that that place was always filled otherwise the work of the host department would suffer. Supervisors were now earnestly saying to training department, 'You *must* give me a replacement when young Jones leaves next month'. Thus there had arisen a real need for smooth planning and a supply and flow of trainees to keep these work places filled. The trainees were no longer spectators in the department, observing and questioning as best they could the practices and principles of work; they were fully involved in the work and had full exposure to the processes and problems. Training department, in neglecting the supply of suitable replacements, could undo much of the good that had been done. It could even lose the place altogether: there were cases where because the supervisor did not receive a replacement trainee to fill the supernumerary post at a time of high workload, a case was made and accepted to create an additional established post. This post was then filled by a regular employee. No amount of persuasion would then convince the supervisor that he should, at a later date, accept a further trainee. He had been let down and in any case the work pressure had eased, and there was really nothing that he could give an additional pair of hands to do.

The third phase of management concerned cost. All of the trainees' costs were allocated to the training department, and the annual total caught the attention of the consultants engaged to study and improve company organisation and efficiency. The training department contained staff and all types of trainees numbering about 160 people, which was above average department size for the company, yet it seemed to produce nothing of calculable added value apart from high quality staff for the future.

However, the study of the actual work done by the trainees, and the cost of replacing trainees by full time employees on that work, showed that the replacement of young vigorous trainees by older and higher-paid full time employees would result in higher net costs to the company. The scheme was reprieved.

Such a reprieve was, of course, largely good luck, for in another company, with other types of work and training, comparable calculations might not have favoured the trainees, and a different defence would be sought. But it does underline that the training place must be examined and managed by training management from many points of view. The administrative convenience of supernumerary posts, giving the training department a degree of control and authority over those posts which it might otherwise not have, does at the same time, expose those posts to criticism and risk. They require considerable attention in their initial selection, in their maintenance and in the supply of people to fill them.

The second scheme in this company is for new graduates from colleges and universities. About 35 are taken on each year in technology, marketing and administration. Some are ex-student trainees, and therefore already know their way around the company and have a good idea of what work they would like to do. The rest have everything to learn. Ninety per cent of them arrive in September.

The first year in the company is spent as a graduate trainee, a supernumerary on the books of the training department and administered by that department. After several weeks of induction, orientation and basic courses on company manufacturing methods and organisation, each graduate is placed in a job, as a supernumerary, which gives him initial experience appropriate to his professional interests, and which helps him to learn about surrounding departments and the company as a whole.

Some of these supernumerary posts are 'fixed' e.g. there is one permanently available in quality control as assistant quality engineer; it is not necessary to keep them filled, but there is no difficulty in putting a new graduate in at any time. Some have to be negotiated on each occasion they are required owing to the uneven availability of both work and good supervision. Some are actual establishment vacancies, but to which a graduate is not actually posted during his first year. The rule is that one year must, in normal circumstances, be completed before posting to an established job. During this year the graduate will work in two, perhaps three, supernumerary jobs, selected to suit his and the company's interests, and giving a broad base from which to judge which direction his career should take.

At the end of the year he will be posted if a suitable established job is identified and vacant for him to move into. If there is not, then he will remain as a supernumerary on training department's book until one is available. This rarely requires more than a few more months: company recruitment planning is well done.

Although this is the end of his time as a trainee, and as a supernumerary, it is not the end of the scheme of training. As in many companies, it is considered that the first few years of employment of the young professional, or the new college graduate, must be so arranged that there is a satisfactory build-up of experience and responsibility. This cannot be achieved simply by leaving each person in his first established job until a vacancy arises elsewhere for him. That vacancy may not provide a significant broadening of experience or responsibility; or he may have to wait too long for it, and either go stale or leave the company.

In consequence the company operates a flexible scheme for the first four years which will enable each person to work in two or three jobs in that time. The jobs are the existing established jobs of the lower or junior grades in each professional sector of the company. The content of each job is known and it is possible for centrally planned and controlled moves to be made from job to job at about 18 to 24 month intervals. These moves are not only in the interest of keeping the posts filled and getting the work done; they are also to ensure that each person acquires the skills and knowledge needed within the company in the future, and needed by the person to meet his career ambitions.

The posts are established posts; and the individuals are no longer supernumerary trainees but normal employees. The planning and control of the moves is done by the placement officer of personnel department, who handles all internal placements of normal employees. The consideration of what constitutes the optimum movement pattern or route for any individual is done in committee by the head of the function concerned (e.g. engineering or accountancy), the placement officer and the training officer. There are agreed guidelines on objectives and movements for each function, of which all managers, supervisors and professional employees have a copy.

We have now entered into the consideration of places and routes which are subject to the everyday administration and mechanisms of the company personnel systems. Steps have to be taken to maintain the integrity of the scheme.

The first question asked by the training officer was 'are there enough posts of *the right types*?' There were enough posts in total, of all types, to absorb comfortably the flow of young professionals through each professional sector. But a comparison of the experience required with the experience available, exposed a number of shortcomings. For example, in technical sales, there were sufficient junior technical representative posts available, in both head office and the field offices; but in the technical and design department there was no job at all available for a junior whose destiny was technical sales work. Two posts were therefore created. Another example was that all the personnel administration work by the personnel department for the field sales office was done from the head office. This meant that junior personnel officers could not gain experience in the conditions of field office work. Personnel assistant posts were established in two large field offices.

Getting the balance right, matching the experience provided to the needs of the individuals, did not, and does not, have to expand the total number of jobs at that level in any function. Instead, in this company, some posts were removed to keep, not merely the balance, but the total number of posts right. This can *only* be done successfully through the full involvement and commitment of the head of the function.

Moving from one post to another may be intended to provide a person with a widening experience and interest, but does it satisfy his wish for career and salary advancement? This question has to be treated with respect. The designers and administrators of schemes may be very satisfied that a particular move proposal meets the scheme's objectives, but the person to be moved may not be impressed by either the work or the pay prospects of the new job. A set of jobs may have a grade and salary structure which, although satisfactory for normal employment purposes, is unsuitable for the flexible movement of people in this type of training scheme, and the members of the scheme will be quick to see this weakness.

Basically, a person expects his salary to go up and to receive promotion over a period of years. When an individual moves, say, after 18 months in operations, to the vacancy in technical development, will it be a promotion, lateral transfer, or a demotion? He will want the first. He may not accept even a lateral transfer, having seen his friend lucky enough to get a promotion through a more favourable move, in the same scheme, last week. He would regard a demotion as a joke.

The salary and grade structure needs to be made suitable for the new purpose. Personal grades, temporary grades and double grades are amongst the methods used by companies. As the jobs are occupied not only by people within the scheme but also by others, perhaps older, perhaps without much potential, or nearing the end of their careers, the company has to be fair to all in any restructuring it undertakes.

Once the balance of jobs, and the salary/grade structures are satisfactory and the scheme in capable hands, the places and the routes have to be safeguarded. For internal reorganisation may take place without taking into account the training scheme. Places may disappear, or job contents change in a way that is disadvantageous. A manager may fill a post with a middle-aged external recruit and block its use in the scheme indefinitely. To minimise the eroding away of places there not only has to be a clear statement as to which places are of significance to any training scheme; there also has to be a warning sign on the job description and other documents relating to the jobs and their pay scales, obliging those who are about to make changes to consult with the authors of the schemes which use those places.

We now move to the third scheme in our company, middle management training. The middle managers of this company, whose ages are mainly between 38 and 56, all receive training, as a matter of policy, in the form of courses, seminars and conferences, inside and outside the company. It is held that they need to be kept up to date in techniques and company and environmental knowledge, and to be kept mentally alert. In any year each manager will attend up to three short courses or seminars, each less than three days in length; and each will attend a longer course or conference every two years or so.

There is a management development committee, of the managing directors and function heads, i.e. the most senior management, which concerns itself with, amongst other things, identifying the most suitable people for senior management posts in the future; and with providing the prior education and experience that will help those people fill those posts well. The committee is therefore very much concerned with management succcession planning for the short, medium and longer term future, and makes use of the management succession charts which its well organised personnel department keeps under lock and key. The middle managers of highest quality and potential appear on these charts as candidates for senior posts. For some there are plans that they should work in a preliminary job before they are finally promoted, in a few years' time, into the later job against which their name appears.

The purpose of the preliminary job is to give them the wider, specific experience that the ultimate job demands, but which their present work cannot provide. An example would be to give a senior works engineer experience in labour relations before he becomes works manager, or to give the senior product designer a post in operations and maintenance before he is made chief engineer. In each case the man is put into work that is outside what one might call his natural line of promotion, in order to learn in depth about matters which are important in a later job. There are, of course, also moves inside the natural line of promotion, i.e. natural succession, of great importance; the senior works engineer, above, might be given the job of assistant works manager, or assistant to the works manager, before final promotion to works manager, also as a deliberate training move. Such moves would be regarded as conventional in most companies; but whether the move is inside or outside the natural line of promotion, if it is for some purpose other than simply to fill the vacancy with the best man available there are likely to be problems. Let us examine this more closely.

There are several criteria to be met if a post is to be used satisfactorily, by a particular individual, for training purposes. Amongst these are

1   The post should be vacant and available for him to move into
2   It contains sufficient real work
3   He is able to do the work, or quickly learn it
4   He wants to go into the post

That the post should be vacant and available is obvious enough; yet it is often not the case. It is a happy coincidence if, for example, at the time that the senior works engineer should be given the preliminary job of assistant works manager, the post of assistant works manager is vacant. It is likely to be filled already by someone doing the job very satisfactorily. What is to be done, if the senior works engineer is to get the preliminary experience needed prior to becoming full works manager? There are many possibilities: the creation of a second post of assistant works manager, or of the post of assistant to the works manager, or of deputy works manager are amongst them.

But here the second question has to be asked, i.e. does a post so created contain enough real work? Will the incumbent carry the responsibility for operational, financial and labour decisions so necessary for him to gain on his way to the top? Or will he be little more than an interested onlooker contributing opinion only to the decision-making of the management team? It can be argued, in principle, that the creation of extra posts such as these always runs the risk of their being unsatisfactory. The responsibilities for all day-to-day management are already carried by the existing managers. The new post will, in these circumstances, either overlap with, or take away from their responsibilities. Neither is satisfactory, unless it can be shown that there is an advantage in removing some of an excessive load from the existing managers and putting it into the new job. In this case we are witnessing a reorganisation for other than training purposes.

If there is not enough real work, the move into that job can be counter-productive. Not only is the opportunity to learn weakened by the lack of responsibility but there can be easily a decline in morale in the individual or, if the experience is repeated too often, an erroneous view built up by him as to what constitutes management responsibility.

A move into a preliminary post in the line of natural succession is not likely to produce problems of capability – our third point – greater than for other in-line promotions. But where the individual is taken from a senior position in one function and put into a post of comparable seniority in another function, the question 'is he able to do, or to learn to do, the work' becomes more important. One factor, of clear significance, is the extent to which a post requires specific and sophisticated skills, and previous unique experience, if it is to be filled adequately. If it is a 'skill-specific' post (and the skill may derive either from knowledge of technology or unique personal experience) then the post is available only to those with that type of skill, knowledge and experience. On the other hand, if the job is regarded as 'non-skill-specific' it may be open to members of other functions who will be assumed to be capable of learning it quickly enough to carry responsibility in a relatively short time. There can, though, be misjudgements made, despite the general truth of the above, particularly in designating a post as 'non-skill-specific': jobs may require more skill and knowledge than is apparent to the outsider.

No one would seriously question that the senior employee relations officer (who is likely to become employee relations superintendent and then industrial relations manager several years from now) would be very much better at his work if he had closer knowledge of operations, operator and supervisor responsibilities and activities, and the shop floor origins of labour demands and disputes. Yet no one would seriously suggest that he should be given a responsible post in operations department at the same level as he occupies in employee relations; for that would put him in direct charge of plant and people. The plant and the operations would be at risk; and the people, the operators and their supervisors, would not accept the move. He could be made administrative assistant to the operations superintendent; or become a member of a productivity project team studying operations efficiency, provided there was genuine work; but the 'skill-specific' nature of operations responsibilities, and the risk and cost of error, preclude him, at his level, from undertaking serious operations work. If he were more junior he could work directly in operations: he could be trained and work in plant operations, or quality control. But at his age and level such a move would constitute a demotion: and it would largely preclude constant contact with the supervisors and managers of operations from whom he has also much to learn. He will have to learn about operations through a mixture of personal visits and observation, discussions, reading, and by attending courses.

On the other hand the operations manager designate, John Smith, who needs to understand industrial relations policies and practices in considerable depth, is given, as a preliminary post, the job of assistant manager, industrial relations, with special responsibility for steering the work in re-evaluating the jobs of supervisors on the manufacturing side of the company. This is familiar ground for him, although he has no personal skill in evaluation techniques. Like most men with years of operating experience he has already a working familiarity – a user's experience – of most of the activities of industrial relations. He is already sensitive to those things in IR which require careful handling, or require consultation with such people as legal and trade union specialists, or with manpower analysts. He finds that there is still much to learn and there is little that he can do in direct decision-making on his own, but he has the support of his colleagues and his days are spent generally supervising and chairing the job-evaluation work, reading and commenting on drafts as they are prepared by colleagues and specialists in the job-evaluation work.

He is fully occupied and is learning a lot from his own work and from his colleagues. He has some authority, which he exercises cautiously. The post he occupies, he knows, is not a full senior post, but it has enough work and interest to stretch him and to satisfy him – and to satisfy those around him who might be otherwise critical of such a post providing an 'easy life' for a privileged person'. Risks and costs of error are low.

In contrast with the post in operations, which we considered above, unfavourably, as a possible training post for a non-technical person, this post meets the four requirements which we have listed for success. Availability, real work, ability to learn quickly are the first three, which need no further elaboration. The fourth, i.e. 'He wants to go into the post' raises the question of why a person should want to make a lateral move of this type and how management (for example the management development committee) handle the announcement of the move. This can be a critical moment for the individual – in this case John Smith – who, as an ambitious man, requires explanations for job changes which appear to affect his career adversely.

Should management tell John Smith that his move into industrial relations is intended to be for training prior to his later promotion in operations? Or should they tell him only that there is a need for an operations man to head the new job-evaluation work in the manufacturing workshops, in order to focus on practical day-to-day job requirements and organisation during the analysis? If they tell him neither, John Smith will refuse the new post, for he is very interested in technical work and wants promotion in that line. He may leave the company as he will believe that his technical potential is very much undervalued by management, who now want to make an IR man of him against his wishes.

If he is told simply that the post needs a technical man to look after shop floor interests during the re-evaluation of jobs, he will accept the good sense of this, and then ask 'what do I do when that is finished?' If no satisfactory answer can be given he may then decline the offer; or, if he accepts, spend some time worrying about where it is going to lead him, which will increasingly interfere with his work and demotivate him. Unless, of course, he has great confidence in his management. Confidence can arise from favourable personal past experiences, and from the observation of how well and fairly other people are treated.

John Smith is actually told that the lateral move is to provide him with IR capability which will equip him to carry more senior operations management positions; and that if he does as well as expected in the IR post then the present intention is that he will, at a later date, be promoted into the job of operations manager, probably in nine months' time. He has to do well in the preliminary post, he is told, in supervising the work, the meetings, the production of recommendations, the presentation to employees, the handling of complaints.

He recognises much, in this briefing, that is pertinent to more senior management posts, and accepts the offer with interest, and with pleasure in the future prospects. However, he is also told that the objective beyond the preliminary post should be treated with strict confidentiality; he should not tell anyone about the company's later plans for him, for no announcement is to be made until much nearer the retirement date of the present operations manager, in nine months' time.

The reasons for management's secrecy were that, first, it was a company rule and tradition that promotion announcements were made as late as possible – thus minimising the chances of an upset in plans between the date of announcement and the date of the actual move; and, second, that they had not yet reconciled the present operations manager to what was to be, in effect, an early retirement. The management development committee had come to recognise that there was hardly ever a straightforward move of a person from one job to another. There were problems of logistics and timing, which called for constant adjustments of the plans on paper. There were also the problems of communications and announcements, of employee ambition, interpretation and misinterpretation. These problems could never be fully solved, or handled immaculately, and they often had to make decisions that incorporated a minimum of upset in the company, as well as meeting the succession objectives.

We can now summarise and contrast the more usual use of places for training within a company, that is to say places, or jobs or posts, which are selected or created in order to provide the training opportunity for people in training schemes. These schemes, as we have seen, have various degrees of rigidity and flexibility in their structure, and can be at various levels of seniority in the company, as well as at junior levels. Many of these places are used for preliminary moves, prior to the individual going into a target job, or a type of work, for which he is being prepared. The individual could be promoted without these preliminary moves, but they enable him to gain skills and knowledge of value, sometimes absolutely necessary for later work, and which it may be difficult, or too late, to acquire in that later work.

We should add here that people moved in this way sometimes discover interest in and ability for types of work that they may never have otherwise encountered, and their careers may from then on be changed to their advantage and to the advantage of the company. This point we have dealt with as the 'heuristic principle' earlier in this book.

If real work is to be used, then, once the place where it is available has been identified, close attention has to be given by the scheme organisers, e.g. in our company the apprentice superintendent, the training manager and the management development committee, to two interconnected questions in deciding on work content and status. They are

1 What is the organisational fit of the post?
2 What is the acceptability of the post?

Organisational fit

This covers such matters as whether or not an established post can be used; whether a new permanent or temporary post has to be created; whether supernumerary posts should be created. In addition to these is the question of how the 'real work' is to be apportioned to these posts, and whether the apportionment of work, plus some responsibility, to the training post will produce an overlap with, or dilution of, the work of neighbouring jobs and colleagues.

Generally speaking the problems of organisational fit are less at the bottom of the company than at the top: apprentices and graduates for example, are known to be people who require training and first-time experience for which special provision has to be made. At this end of the company, the presence of a trainee in a trainee's supernumerary post is commonplace, and the use of first established posts explicitly for training graduates is a common practice. Even so there remain problems. Supernumerary trainees may carry a significant percentage of the workload: this may not always be acceptable to other employees particularly if their own jobs are at risk; or it may pass unnoticed until, in the search for lower costs, management cuts the numbers of trainees and reduces the output of the areas affected by the reduction.

The movement of junior trainees, according to some sort of timetable, so that the prescribed training jobs, supernumerary or established, are kept full – and hence the work effort maintained – always presents some planning problems, but it is practical and is a feature of training officers' work in many companies. On the whole its successful operation depends on having a reasonably uniform and satisfactory standard of trainee, so that one can replace another without undue problem, and a range of jobs that are well chosen for suitable content, i.e. matching the needs and capabilities of the trainees, and for suitable supervision, i.e. good instructors able to allocate and teach work with some flexibility and imagination. These schemes are mostly 'open' in that the trainee is known to be a trainee, or a young professional or an apprentice, and the places they occupy are known to be reserved for such trainees. There is no secrecy, and most problems of work content, performance standard, and the next move of the trainee can be discussed openly amongst all those concerned.

At the top of the company the problems of organisational fit are more difficult to deal with. The right established job for a training move may not be vacant when required, and there can be no question of taking the present incumbent and moving him, and then others, just to suit one person's training requirement. The creation of a new and special post may not be needed organisationally; all the work is being done satisfactorily by the present post holders, and an additional post would be clearly artificial and lead to dilution or overlap of responsibilities, or to conflicts. How does one explain such a post if there is some secrecy or confidentiality about the training and promotion plans? Of course, if the right post is vacant at the right time then the move can be made without organisational problems.

Acceptability

The acceptability of a training post, and of the trainee himself, to the other employees and supervisors in that work area, is a prerequisite of success. Equally the acceptance by the trainee, of that place, the work and the status, is an important requirement. This mutual acceptance is frequently met as far as junior trainees and training schemes are concerned, but it must never be taken for granted by management. The permanent employees may feel strongly against any indiscipline, idleness or undue privilege shown by trainees in their midst, and object to their presence. The employees may object to a poor scheme being operated by the company and express their objection either individually or in an organised fashion. The training officer may believe that he knows all about his trainees, but he doesn't know anything like as much, in certain respects, as the employees who work alongside them. The employees will react to anything they don't like, with action ranging from friendly advice to a strike. They will react to anything they do like by being supportive. Their attitudes and actions are like the iceberg, largely unseen but not to be under-estimated.

The junior trainee is sensitive to where he works as a trainee: he has his technical and work interests and his preferences as to physical location. He will also be aware of the relationship between his training and his career, and has his own ideas as to where he might work next, and where he might get his first posting. Provided he is confident that the company and its training scheme is going to move him in the general direction in which he is interested, he may find it equally acceptable to train first in the foundry and then in quality control, rather than the other way round, for either way he will end up as a production engineer. The sequence is not critical, and both places he knows to be important. As the specific places and the sequence of places assume greater importance, and become more critical, in relationship to the person's ideas about his career and status, so the acceptability to the trainee of moves and places becomes a more prominent factor in planning moves, and, indeed, in designing training schemes as a whole.

The very young apprentice, the finishing apprentice, the professional acquiring field experience, and the middle manager hoping for promotion, are at points on a scale of increasing sensitivity on questions of 'what do I do next?' In the open schemes for younger trainees, with many years of career still ahead of them, a

227

move for training purposes may not please an individual at first sight. But it is possible to discuss its value for professional broadening, for increasing the width of his promotion possibilities in the future, or to confirm that a later move will take him into the special work he has fixed his mind on. There can be real room for manoeuvre, real flexibility in future moves, and these make it possible for the trainee to accept training moves that do not exactly match his present interests.

The older man has much the same interests and has the same anxieties, but he is at a different stage in his career and in his life as a whole. He probably believes that his future in the company must lie in a certain direction, and that departure from that direction may put his career at risk. He is becoming too old to switch to something different, too old to get a good job in another company, too old to retrain – so he believes and fears. Anything that destabilises his career, or reduces his chances of promotion, is not only a personal threat but probably a menace to the stability of the family, home and possessions for which he is responsible.

However, anything that promises to advance his status, income and career, will receive very close and interested attention from him. A murmured suggestion from his manager that he might be in the running for a promotion, can easily become the basis of some fantasy discussion with his wife on how to spend the extra income. He wants it to happen and believes it will happen, whereas he may refuse to believe that he is *not* going to be promoted or get a good salary raise next time round.

If, therefore, he is moved laterally in his organisation, for training purposes, and does not know the purpose of this move, he is likely to find it worrying and perhaps unacceptable. He would perhaps try to persuade himself that management 'have something in mind' for him later, but it is difficult to sustain such optimism without some evidence in its favour. If he were a younger trainee, within an open scheme, he could ask for, and get, an explanation in a comparable move situation. As long as his management believe in caution and confidentiality concerning future promotions and management succession, the mood of uncertainty amongst all managers and potential managers, and with the uncertainty increased by lateral moves, will continue to produce the undercurrent of anxiety often discernible in the middle and upper levels of a company.

Sooner or later, of course, the individual and colleagues have to learn about preliminary moves. In some companies where there are many such moves followed by in-line promotions, there is open speculation amongst executives about the meaning of the move, and there develops, over the years, a recognition that such moves are tacit announcements of unspecified promotions. If the morale and general career prospects in the company are good then this speculation, and some leaking of information, becomes almost an executive pastime, enjoyable and interesting for most, although distasteful for the frustrated few. Where, however, the morale and career prospects are not good, training moves amongst the more senior levels may gain some reputation of being privileges, and not be seen as an action by an unprejudiced management.

It is now the moment to turn our attention to career development.

29 Career development

The successful management of training and of development schemes demands an understanding of other parts of the manpower system, and of the relationship between training and those other parts. Mention has been made, in earlier chapters, of recruitment, resourcing, and manpower analysis and planning. In this chapter, we shall start with a brief résumé of those parts, and then define and discuss the place of career development in relationship to them.

As we have seen, a company can produce *manpower forecasts*, for each of the years ahead. The forecast is of the number of people required, overall and function by function, and at all levels and occupations. The forecast takes account of planned and likely growth of the company, of organisational developments, and changes in technology. The forecast is viewed with less and less confidence the further into the future one looks, from the short term, to the medium term, to the long term.

The company then has to plan the way it will get the numbers and types indicated by the forecast. This is the activity of *manpower planning*, which will make use of *manpower analysis* in order to estimate how many of the present company will still be in the company in the various years ahead. It is possible for the analysts to estimate future wastage from the company, from causes such as death, retirement and resignation on an actuarial and statistical basis. It is possible also to take into account the potential of people for doing higher jobs (i.e. for promotion) and estimate how far the present population will be able to fill the more senior jobs in the future, when they are (calculably) older and more experienced. This is part of the study of *manpower resources*.

Another part of the study of resources is to be found in looking at the external labour market, from which experienced people can be recruited, and in looking into the recruitment of inexperienced people, mostly young, as trainees.

When the future manpower needs are sufficiently defined, then the manpower plan will be drawn up showing the pattern of external recruitment for replacement and growth, the pattern of internal promotions and movements to fill vacancies and new posts, and the types of training which will be needed to produce ability in individuals and groups. These in turn lead to new or modified policies and action, for recruitment, promotions, transfers and training schemes; some of these actions such as new apprenticeship schemes, may be entirely new and spectacular, and others may be no more than the continued implementation of existing practices, such as internal promotions as and when vacancies appear, but with new targets to be met.

A study of the future 'flows' of manpower upwards through the company structure may reveal that there are bottlenecks, produced by the structure. Bottlenecks can restrict upper flow and

(a) starve the upper layer of the company of the numbers of able people needed in the future
(b) restrict the realisation of career prospects of people lower down in the company.

The analytical methods for identifying problems of manpower flows, such as developed by the Institute of Manpower Studies, makes it possible to make structural changes earlier, and more gently, than would otherwise be the case.

All of this is planning and action to meet, broadly speaking, the company's requirements. Is anything more needed? Every likely vacancy in the short, medium or long term is identified and examined, either individually or collectively and statistically, and the human resources which will be needed to fill those vacancies are also identified either individually or collectively, or both. By means of recruitment, training and progressive moves the right numbers and quality of people will arrive in the jobs at the right moments in the future. There will, of course, be failures of individuals, failures in recruitment, and there will be changes in the company's operations, which will upset the company's manpower plans and make it necessary to review these plans. Good planners and managers can look after these problems, if they are small, and if extra or flexible manpower resources are built into the plans to cover the likely contingencies of the future.

But when we consider planning and vacancy filling *from the point of view of the individual*, and of all the individuals, we get a different picture from that seen by the planner. Although there are people who are pleased to stay in their present jobs indefinitely (and in times of high unemployment there are many such people) it is fair to say that the following factors are important to the individual employee:

1 To make progress in terms of interesting work, responsibility and seniority in his company.
2 To improve his income.

Together, these two constitute promotion for the individual, and promotion is a goal and a motivator for most people in management, supervision and professional and executive work, in which there are hierarchies which permit promotion. Where there is no such hierarchy with promotion possibilities as, for example, in some unskilled and semi-skilled workforces, the improvement of income and benefit may become the dominant and explicit preoccupation of those workforces. It would, it must be added, be untrue to suggest that the unskilled man is only motivated by money and benefits, and equally untrue that the professional seeking more responsibility does so only because of the money attached to greater responsibility. The exact relationships are complex, and we cannot deal with them here.

To continue our generalisation. The individual who is interested in promotion is also likely to be interested in 'career'. A career is defined by

(a) The field of activity in which the person works, e.g. engineering or accountancy and in the iron and steel industry; or in the stock market as a broker.
(b) The end-point job of that person, at the end of, or near the end of, his working life.
(c) The succession of jobs held in reaching that end-point.

This is a simplified picture, and is illustrated satisfactorily by the career of the engineering apprentice who remains in the one company until he retires as production manager 40 years later. When he looks back he can see the sequence of jobs and training, of promotions and transfers, which he experienced on his way to the top. Everything is crystal clear: each job, its pay rise, his increasing seniority, and the contribution which each job made to his growing expertise and management capability. Another man may look back and see that he has had two careers, one as an accountant until the age of 38, followed by a later career as systems analyst and computer manager up to retirement. There are many variations in career pattern in a life time in one company only. In addition to the one-company man, many look back and see their careers as having taken them through several companies, and in cases like this they recall having had to make decisions to move from one company to another. Young mothers often give up work completely to look after their babies and the growing family. When the children are in their school-years, some mothers enter into part-time work and later go back into full-time work. At that moment they may resume their earlier career or go into a different type of work altogether.

Clear though the 'historic' view of career may be, in looking back at the past, there can be no such clarity in looking at the future. For every person who knows, or who is determined, that he will end up as the chief engineer, or the chief accountant, there are vastly more who do not have any clear picture of where they will end their career, in which company and at what level – except, of course, those who are approaching the end of their careers.

The forward look which a person takes at his career will contain both his ambitions, wishes and preferences, on the one hand, and, on the other hand, his expectations or his view of what life in the future is going to offer him. He has an idea of what he would like to do; and he has his idea of whether it is realistic to expect it to happen. He may be accurate or fantasising on both counts.

The forward look into career is clearer the nearer into the future the individual looks, and he will think of promotions, or getting a job somewhere else, over the next few years, as distinct from concerning himself with ultimate career fulfilment. He will want to see that in his company there are jobs into which he could be promoted which are in the right field of activity, in the right professional sector, and he will want to see that there is a *good* chance of getting that promotion in the not-too-distant future. In this forward look he depends on his own perception of the company. On what is that perception based? On gossip, published organisation charts, announcements of future appointments – and many more snippets of reliable and unreliable information. He does not have, however, the highly sophisticated and detailed picture which the manpower specialists have.

If we take a step back, we see that the individual employees are very much concerned with their own promotion and careers, and speculate about and build up expectations on information of doubtful accuracy and sufficiency. We see that the manpower specialists are concerned with the anticipation and filling of actual vacancies in the future, and use data of almost intimate detail about individuals, and forecasting and planning techniques which are comprehensive and sophisticated. They are not primarily concerned, however, with careers for company employees.

This may sound strange, for many companies do offer careers, and with sincerity and success. We must remember, however, that in most companies careers, for many people, are simply inevitable. The passage of time will ensure that vacancies occur and that promotions occur. We must also remember that within companies such as we have discussed in our chapter on Places and routes, some people, whose potential is assessed as high, who are in development schemes, or whose names appear favourably on long term management succession charts, will enjoy some years of planned career, and a sequence of moves and promotions. This is all creditable, and is necessary. It is not the same, though, as the company being generally concerned about the careers of its employees, irrespective of whether they are earmarked for greater responsibilities or not, and planning and taking reasonable steps to safeguard, in some way, their careers.

Has a company a responsibility for the careers of all the individuals in the company – a social responsibility? Are there advantages to the company in assuming some responsibility? And if it does, what practical and effective steps can it take? These are three important questions. To the first question, the most difficult one, the answer must be positive. The company holds the individual's future in its hands. It has elaborate manpower machinery to try and ensure that its future manning is adequate. The individual appears in these future plans, with or without development and promotion, but the individual normally does not know what the future plan holds for him partly because he is not told; for even the planners cannot predict the future accurately and are very reluctant to disclose their plans. There is, therefore, a critical relationship between the individual and the company: if the individual wishes to plan his own future career he cannot confidently take into account his future route in his own company. No one will tell him – unless he is a rare high flyer – what lies in the plans, and he has to guess.

How much it seems to be right and reasonable to tell all employees will depend on the confidence of management in their forward forecasts and plans, and in their assessment of employee reaction and behaviour individually and collectively. As a minimum it would seem that an individual should be advised about the likely limits of his future in the company, so that he knows that there is, for example, little chance of his ever becoming section leader, or of becoming head of his function, or of reaching a grade two levels above his present level. With this information, provided it is given when he is sufficiently young to take action, he can decide whether to stay or leave. He may be reasonably pleased at what he is told and feel that the longer term future prospects are satisfactory. The estimate of his future limitation in the company may, in the event, prove to be wrong. He may go further, or he may stop well short of the predicted limit.

The estimate of how far an individual can go in his company career has two distinct components. One is the assessment of his future capability, his potential. The other is the likelihood of a vacancy being available at the right time. Three managing directors of about the same age may all have the potential for company chairmanship, but only one will become chairman. The other two will not get promotion to match their potential. This sort of impasse happens at all levels in a company, sometimes predictable, and predicted well in advance; sometimes predictable but not predicted in advance. If managements counsel their employees about their future careers and use only the information on individual's potential and capability as a basis for prediction, then they may be misleading their employees. Management's view of future careers should take into account not only the quality of the individual, but also the predicted future vacancy probabilities. These probabilities can be calculated by using computer models, but it is not likely that such models will be used by other than the larger companies for some years to come. The alternative is to scan the succession charts and count the numbers of eligible candidates for predicted vacancies in the future at various levels. This only gives information on the present queues for promotion, and does not take into account uncharted wastages, opportunities or constraints on company growth; but it does add some realism to the thoughts of the counselling manager, a key figure in advising the individual on his career.

What are the advantages to the company in assuming some career development role, and what can it do that is practicable and realistic? These two questions are closely linked and we shall deal with them together. The advantages are to be found in the maintenance of morale and quality of the employees in their work. If there is sufficient movement and promotion of people, and if it is seen by those people and their colleagues to be taking place, then this can produce a mixture of confidence and expectation, concerning careers, in that company. The skill of management therefore is not merely to fill vacancies with the best people and hence to get the work done. It is also to keep an optimum tempo of promotions and transfers which not only brings satisfaction and incentive to those immediately benefiting, but in addition encourages many more people to believe, rightly, that opportunities do occur in the company with a frequency commensurate with their ambitions, provided trading conditions are favourable.

This skill of management must be such as to deal with problems arising from major upsets which make it impossible to maintain the frequency and pattern of promotions which previously has been operating by design or good fortune. These problems can be great, and companies may find themselves with morale as low as it was high, following an upset or organisational change which appears to weaken the career prospects of employees. The fact is, that the high morale, high expectations, arising from the individual's favourable perception of the future, can be quickly replaced by low morale when that perception becomes unfavourable. The deliberate interference by management with what otherwise might be deemed good 'natural' career patterns, is as risky as their ignoring the significance, origins and stability of those natural career patterns.

30 Managing career development

Whatever the best definition of career development may be, one thing appears to be becoming clearer as the years pass by – it is not easy to do it well, it has a variety of recurrent problems, and some of these problems are serious ones. Many are rooted in what we might call control. But, instead of attempting to define control in an abstract way, let us look at one company's experience: a true story, true of many companies and not merely of the one now described.

This company, successful and growing, took its promotions very seriously, as any good company should. It preferred to fill vacancies by internal promotion. It had a management committee which considered vacancies and suitable internal candidates, and it took account of appraisal reports on performance and on potential, and was very sensitive to the declared interests and ambitions of its staff. All of this threw a considerable burden on the personnel department, but personnel management seemed to welcome it, and to enjoy the new and important responsibility. They kept things tidy and the whole activity went well: vacancies were reasonably well anticipated, succession lists were drawn up and the best people selected, promoted and trained.

Perhaps the most rewarding aspect of the whole activity was a sort of collective satisfaction expressed by the employees, in that their careers were receiving very reasonable attention from management. Management was flattered by this employee attitude.

One day one of the bright young personnel officers did some arithmetic, and the personnel manager reported it to the management committee. He said that the average length of time spent in jobs of a particular grade, by junior and some middle managers, was one year seven months. This at first shocked the management committee – who confessed to having spent years and years in each job on their way up the company – but they soon got used to it. They then started to use it as a yardstick; and then as the expected length of time in their planning of jobs and moves in the future.

Moreover, the middle and junior managers and the employees in the grades just below, soon got to know about this and quickly adopted the idea – which confirmed their own experience – that about one year and seven months was long enough in any job. Management now made a virtue of a necessity, and produced a career development policy in which one year and seven months, or thereabouts, featured, and which spelt out the objectives and the advantages from the point of view of the company and of the employees. Everyone was happy. The employees had prospects of a fast moving career; the management had policies and practices which fitted the situation; the personnel function enjoyed a new power. It went well for just a few years.

The reader will have guessed what had happened. The high frequency of promotion opportunities was due to two main factors. First the economy of the country was improving fast and expanding. There were vacanices, well paid, in other companies, and some men left this company to get on faster, in larger numbers than previously. Hence there were more vacancies and promotion opportunities in the company. Also the company itself was expanding: new functions, factories and departments require a lot of entirely new jobs at the top and in the middle. New jobs are promotion opportunities not merely for one man but often for several men below.

The management committee had said that one year seven months was a policy, but that was naive. It was the consequence of growth, and not a policy decision. When the president proudly said that 'we move our people on average about every 19 months', he should have said 'our people are moved by the force of circumstances every 19 months'.

One day it was realised that the growth had stopped. The national economy had flattened out, and the company's growth programme was complete. The abundance of promotion opportunities disappeared. Management, of course, took it philosophically at first. They were quick to see the reasons for the change in promotion rates. The personnel officer estimated the average length of time in a job in the near future: it would rise to four and a half years. That was 'more like what it used to be. No harm done', management said.

But there was a lot of harm done. The career development policy had to be rewritten, and this had to be explained to the employees. Some didn't believe what they had heard; some did believe. Many thought that management was incompetent, and management became discredited in the eyes of its employees. There was demotivation: some people now decided to leave at the first good opportunity outside, and take their career development into their own hands.

The company is still there, of course. It is doing quite well. The mishap was not a disaster, but it did set the company back. They don't talk about career development now. They do it, but they don't use the expression.

This sort of thing has happened to many companies in Europe and in USA. It has also happened to companies in the Middle East and other fast developing areas of the world where there are most certainly additional special circumstances. The lessons learned from economic growth and decline in Europe and USA have led to research and to an understanding of career development that was rare ten years or more ago. Although many good managers have had an intuitive feel for the factors and concepts which are important to career development schemes, there has been neither the time nor the motivation necessary to research and develop a valid body of knowledge and techniques, until recently. In the meantime, the education system, the media, the social and political pressures are making more and more people career conscious and not merely job conscious. Companies which attract career conscious employees have been under pressure to produce policies and practices which will satisfy the ambitions of the employees. The employee's own self-consciousness, his hunger for career, is reinforced through learning of the company's policies; and the company and employees become locked in an uneasy relationship in which disappointment and frustration are too frequent occurrences. A better understanding of the structures and dynamics of a company manpower system suddenly becomes an urgent need.

Individuals can only get career satisfaction if the vacancies which occur match, in frequency and level, their expectations. If there is an imbalance, then there will be problems of frustration and lack of personal growth. This must not only be true for today and tomorrow, but also well forward into the future. A career is a long time and the expression "career development" is inappropriate if applied merely to the short term, ignoring the problems of the medium and long term.

Understanding the relationship between the vacancies of the future – that is to say, the promotion opportunities of the future – and the needs and expectations of the employees in the future is therefore basic to the design of a career development scheme. One would like to know how many vacancies are likely to arise each year in each level of job and how many suitable people are available to fill them. From this we can work out the chances of promotion, and compare them with employee's expectations which can also be estimated.

This is no more than common sense, but it is difficult to do. Management often resort to 'talking-out' manpower problems of this complexity. There are so many factors to take into account. The expansion or contraction of the organisation, actual rate of growth, internal reorganisation, labour market pressures, and the age distribution are all important. They influence the wastage, the creation of vacancies, as well as of redundancies, and the expectation. We can think about them, most successfully, only for the very short term and for the smaller company.

Fortunately mathematical models, and the computer, come to the rescue, and programmes available today enable the company's manpower in the future, and its career opportunities, to be examined and various policy options to be considered. The effect of recruitment policies and promotion policies, which are options open to management, on the actual chances of promotion can be assessed, and career development policies can be selected which minimise the future imbalances. They also throw up into sharp relief potential manpower problems which might otherwise not be noticed, and which can be studied and dealt with early; or sometimes avoided completely. These might be problems of skills shortages, grade drift, payroll cost, as well as of career blockage.

This all requires professional personnel capability in the company, co-operation with corporate planning, manpower planning and others, and the education of management in the use and understanding of these new methods and ideas. It does not replace manpower planning, or management succession planning, or individual or group training and development activities. It is complementary to them. Some would say that it has already become a prerequisite of responsible manpower management.

Manpower models are particularly helpful on the quantitative side of career development, on the analysis of numbers of promotion opportunities, the numbers of people, and the chances of promotion. What of the quality of the individual? How is this to be developed during his career, how is he to become a good manager or a good technologist? How, indeed, is he to become good enough to do his job well? A man may have a successful management career; but at the same time he may not be a successful manager despite his attendance at top management courses. It is at this point that there can be a divergence or incompatibility in objectives, as between training and career development.

Researches into European career development discovered, not surprisingly, that although fast corporate and national economic growth produced fast career development, it also produced two unwelcome consequences. These were that the executives and managers who were promoted fast often did not reach the standards normally reached. They did not become as good as the others despite their good potential. However, these men thought that they were above standard, better than average. They overvalued themselves.

How familiar a picture this is; easy to understand, but difficult to correct once it has begun. The fast rate of promotion, the quick achievement of personal ambition, is flattering and satisfying to the man. But the short length of time spent in any job, the lack of exposure to much ultimate responsibility, the lack of training and of decision-making, produce a person who is not as good as he otherwise would have been, and who has not enough experience to judge himself.

How, then, does he do his job? The answer is that, as often as not, he doesn't. He does a part of it. Other people do the rest: and the other people tell him what decisions to make, or correct his decision if they are in a position to intervene. The weaker executive in a well organised company has around him colleagues, subordinates and service functions working so well that sometimes they can almost do without him. How many weak executives can a company afford to have, one might ask? Well, one answer is 'as many as the remaining management structure can tolerate'. This is most clearly illustrated by the special circumstances of the developing countries, where the training and career development problems are most acute.

In case the reader believes that this chapter is devoted solely to the question of how to get into difficulties, let us briefly consider the steps in career development which will help a company avoid difficulties, as far as this is possible, of its own making.

First, on the quantitative side, one can use or develop the data and the resources which one uses for manpower forecasting and planning, to produce information on the promotion opportunities in the future in the company. These are linked with the growth of the company and wastage from the company, and are influenced by recruitment policies, the national and international economy and the labour market. From these one can come to some conclusions about both longer term practical career opportunities, and the optimum policies to adopt in the short and medium term. An optimum policy is not the fastest or the slowest, or the maximum or the minimum. It is the one that works best for both now and the predictable future. It takes into account, amongst other factors, what time is needed to become proficient in a job. Proficiency is a question of standards, and of quality.

So, on the qualitative side we have to look into the jobs that people are doing, and may do in the future, and decide what skills must be developed, what leadership, what decision-making; and how long this actually takes to achieve. It takes quite a bit longer than most inexperienced people believe, and often less than the elderly are inclined to accept; but it produces good managers and technologists.

One now has the main elements for an optimum career development policy. The short and medium term decisions may be significantly influenced by predictions of long-term outcomes. And one has to defend this against adverse pressures from employees, and sometimes from persuasion by governments, to go faster or to over-dilute the jobs. This can be the toughest part. It may be easier to defend a position and a policy with data and facts, rather than merely with opinions.

Finally, a word about the day-to-day management of career development. If there has been no satisfactory look into the future, no adequate thinking about actual and ideal promotion rates and about employee expectation, then there is likely to be an increasing amount of crisis in the day-to-day management. This usually leads to short term crisis decisions which lead to further crises. If the qualities and standards are allowed to slip, then organisation problems arise, undue external specialist recruitment may take place, and self confidence and pride are hurt.

With the groundwork covered in the way suggested above, and with six months or yearly re-runs of the manpower analysis on a continuing basis, crises are minimised, although not completely avoided. The present is always examined in the context of the future, to ensure that today's career promotions and expectations do not lead to unforeseen conflicts and problems in the future. Vacancies are filled, promotion and training are provided, and standards are maintained. There is steady advancement for the majority and faster advancement for the gifted – not all according to plan, but all within both the bounds of possibility, and the boundaries of the economy.

The past years have shown that career development has to be treated with caution and respect. It need not bring automatically the happy fulfilment that it appears, to many, to promise. Personnel management has to adopt the techniques now becoming available which help to identify, and then to minimise, the imbalances between promotion opportunities and employee expectation; to minimise the occurrence of either over-acceleration or stagnation. For these may lead not only to individual frustration for many, but also to an increasing difficulty in achieving qualities and standards needed and hoped for in companies. Are there any other ways of handling career development, ways of reducing the effect of bottlenecks and frustrations? The answer is 'yes', it lies in:

1   Vigorously adopting policies and practices of continuous development, so that people's capabilities can grow in accordance with their potential; and their work responsibilities and contribution grow with their capabilities.

2   Recognising and rewarding the development and contributions of individuals by means of personal up-grading and salary increases; making people responsible for particular projects or areas of work, as they develop, beyond the present scope of their job.

3   Modify the classic pyramidal organisation structure with its tight formation of branches, divisions, departments; with its multitude of career and promo-

tion ladders converging towards the top of the pyramid. Introduce more horizontal structure to enable people to move without promotion, but with increased responsibility, work challenge, and personal interest and growth, and appropriate rewards.

Some companies are already moving in this direction: some have for many years incorporated these ideas, as far as is practicable, into their practices. The proposal is *not* to do away altogether with organisation structure, or hierachy, or promotions, but to complement them by providing opportunity for experience and growth, increased responsibility and stature, and recognition and reward. There are examples of this way of working and living outside of industry and other comparable organisations.

For example, many university lecturers may remain as lecturers for the greater part of their careers: most of them do. But the challenges of work, research, the achievements of pupils, can be a source of ultimate satisfaction. The same can be true of the medical general-practitioner, who starts and finishes his 'career' as a GP, but whose work and the possibility of restoring health to patients, bring challenge and satisfaction. For these two, the traditions and structures of their position and work are favourable to the exercise of personal skill and potential. In industry the traditions and structure often are not favourable, and need to be improved.

During the next many years the continuing political, economic and industrial developments, upheavals and depressions will produce new forces of circumstances which will have a great influence on company manpower and manpower policies. Career development requires that we seek the clearest possible vision of what the future will look like, how it will behave, inside and outside our companies; what will be the consequences of the policies, structure and traditions which we have today? Without this vision we are sailing our ship into uncharted waters over the horizon. If the seas prove to be friendly, we may then congratulate ourselves on our good luck.

It would be better to congratulate ourselves on our good management as well.

31 The international context

1 THE DEVELOPED COUNTRIES

From place to place in this book there are examples drawn from overseas experiences in training and development. The examples have been chosen because they happen to illustrate the application of a management principle, and not in order to illustrate similarities or differences between practices in one country and another. We now turn our attention to the impact of international operation on training and development.

First, we need a few definitions, for it is not sufficient to refer to a company, or any other organisation, merely as working or trading 'internationally'. The scale and complexity of operation can vary considerably. A small organisation may sell its produce to a foreign country, where the local sales are looked after by totally independent, foreign organisations. That is relatively simple. Much more complex are world-wide organisations with offices, operations, and employees in many countries, and with the international movement of raw materials, products and people. Between these two extremes there are a range of complexities, varying from one organisation to the next.

All such companies are 'international' in their operations and their trading interest. All are likely to retain a head office in the home country, the country of the original enterprise, although occasionally a headquarters may move to another country. The overseas countries, where operations/sales are established, are likely to contain subsidiary companies or joint ventures or partnerships shared by head office and an overseas company or partner. All of these options are typical of the 'multinational', within which it is not unusual to refer to the whole collection of companies and headquarters as 'the group'. One further distinction will be made, i.e. between international operations which are between developed countries, and international operations embracing underdeveloped or developing countries.

The staffing of all of these centres of employment, in the home country and

240

overseas, and, in particular the managing of each subsidiary, is as important an issue as the operations and trading for which the company exists. There are a number of factors in the international situation which produce problems in addition to those typical of purely home country companies and operations – and which call for special attention from the T & D function.

Starting up abroad

When the owner of a small printshop thinks of selling postcards abroad: or the directors of a car-hire outfit want to move into intercountry hiring: or a new supermarket chain believes that it should go international – they all have to ask and get the answers to a similar set of questions. These questions are under such headings as the overseas economy, market, consumers, competition, government regulations, and available professional and other manpower; and the rights of employees and the obligations of the employer. Similar questions would be asked in the case of an expansion in the home country; but the feeling might well be one of confidence in dealing with home affairs with which everyone is familiar. Abroad, it's different: guessing, or extrapolating from past experience in other countries is not good enough. The decision makers have to seek information, *and they have to learn,* if they are going to make the 'right' decision. Where does this information come from? Fortunately there are government agencies and departments, chambers of commerce, trade organisations, university departments and many other institutions which can give up-to-date commercial, political and social information. This is the beginning of a very long period of learning, about the foreign, the distant and the unfamiliar, which can extend throughout the group or company at many levels and will continue after the initial management decision-making. This will become one of the preoccupations of T & D, whose work will come through a range of tasks, as follows:

1 The establishment of *ab initio* training, for new overseas operations. This training will be for head office functions which are going to be affected by the new operation; for head office and other staff who are going to be transferred to the new operation; and for those people recruited in the overseas country to work in the new operation.
2 The establishment overseas of a training and development unit to service the needs of the new operations/company; and developing its capability as the new company progresses.
3 The maintenance and enhancement of international working relationships and understanding, between head office and overseas.
4 The review and correction of manpower and career development plans in order to take full account of the requirements of the overseas operation, and the personnel development opportunities it provides.

These four areas will be very familiar to the managements of the long established multinational companies, in which traditions and practices are well established, and, which have learned to adjust to changing political, economic and social demands. But even the most experienced companies experience, and expect, problems and difficulties in these areas. Let us look at some of the more typical start-up needs, problems and actions, in detail. We shall not discuss the learning and exploratory thinking which leads to the decision to go ahead with the new overseas venture: but we must remember that this exploration uses information on skill availability, recruitment possibilities, employment and training obligations, and other matters, all characteristic of that foreign country. This same information forms part of the baseline for the planning of Manpower, recruitment, and training and development, and the design of the Personnel/Training/Development unit which will be required.

We distinguish the developed world from the developing (or undeveloped) countries because, overseas in the developed world, the education levels, professional skills, and industrial, commercial and other sophistications may be as well rooted as in the home country – perhaps better. This means that the home country head office will expect to recruit managers and other staff in that overseas area, capable of running the new operation, on a day-to-day basis, once an initial settling-in and learning period has taken place. This does not exclude, of course, some home country managers and/or specialists working in that operation for an extended period. This would be in order to maintain personal head office/subsidiary contact and control, or to give field and operations experience to younger managers and specialists from the home country. Similarly, experience might be offered to local staff of the overseas company, by enabling them to work in an established post on a special project in head office or elsewhere in the home country operation.

If the new overseas operation is based on the acquisition of existing operations which are already fully manned and managed, then the exercise is simpler, on paper. There may be an additional problem involved in shifting an existing foreign management, workforce, product pattern and work quality, from its present standards to the *new* requirements of the new owners. This can be a tremendous undertaking, involving a re-education and retraining of many people who intuitively resist and perhaps resent changing their ways. There are ways of approaching this, and the chapters on 'Organisation development' and 'Corporate change' discuss some of these.

Initial training for the overseas operation

There are several groups of employees whose needs are critical:

1 *Home country/head office management and staff* who interface with the overseas operation, *but who are to remain in the home country*. For these people decision-making, and day-to-day work will be extended and modified. The overseas company will have its own local culture – its 'foreignness' – which will show in its dealings with head office, and this needs to be grasped and understood as much as technical and administrative changes in head office work. Time alone will not create harmonious working between home and abroad. Communication must be developed both formally and informally. International visits can be arranged for key people in each function not merely to talk with their opposite numbers in the other country, but to meet a range of staff individually and collectively, and generate a feeling of confidence, collaboration and goodwill, and resolve 'technical' and procedural misunderstandings.

2   *Home country management and staff who are to work in the overseas operation.* These may be appointed for a period of weeks or months to assist with the start-up of the company, helping to ensure that, where necessary, organisation, staffing, operation/administration methods, and basic manpower and personnel systems are established to standards typical of the group, or otherwise agreed by head office. Here the size of the task confronting the expatriates from head office depends on several factors as follows:

(a) *If the new operation is based on an existing company*, which has management, staff, processes/procedures and products which correspond closely to the requirements of head office, then the main work of the expatriates is likely to be:

   (i) To make a close appraisal of the main function and structures of the overseas company, identifying major or minor departures from required standards. To gain an understanding of how that company works. To recommend changes.
   (ii) To help develop systems and practices, and the collaboration needed for co-ordination and communication with head office and with other parts of the group.
   (iii) To act generally as ambassadors.

(b) If the new operation is based on an existing company in which one or more of the factors listed above, such as management, processes/procedures etc., is inappropriate and has to be radically modified, then the head office task will add to the above (a) (i) – (a) (iii) the redesign and the installation of new practices in that overseas company. Depending on the nature of the new practice, one expects to find some of the redesign carried out in the overseas company, and some carried out in head office by technical specialists.

(c) If the new operation is totally 'grass roots', establishing a new company, premises, plant, management and staff, then to (a) (ii)–(iii) and (b)–all of which will now be on a greater scale – there has to be added recruitment and training on a large scale.

For the company which is already *a multinational, and which already has operating centres in a particular overseas country*, the problems of developing a new operation in that country are diminished. This is because of

(a) The existence of experienced group staff in that country who are of that nationality, who can be called on to help start up and to run the new operation in its many departments.
(b) Up-to-date knowledge in head office and in the existing centres in that country, of local regulations, laws, the employment market etc.

One can see that with the advantages of (a) and (b) above, many of the problems of new ventures in overseas countries become no more severe than the problems of opening a new office or factory 100 miles from head office in the home country. In fact, in the multinationals it is often the case that new French operations are developed by the French, new German operations by the Germans, and so on, with the group head office mainly concerned with the integration of that new operation into the group, with ensuring that the highest expertise is available in the design and launch phases, as well as with financing the development.

For the company with no existing operations in that foreign country, the problems and risks, right from the start, are more acute. This is not because of incompetence, but because of the occasional difficulties in getting reliable information about that country. Fortunately, some of this information is available through institutions and agencies, and the training manager in head office can use these services to great advantage.

The role of T & D

We are now in a position to look at the specific interests and role of the Training and Development function in the international context. The principle areas of interests of T & D will be as follows: the amount of involvement will depend on status of the overseas company as in 2(a), 2(b), or 2(c) above.

(i) Head office management education to improve international economic, commercial and political understanding and decision-making. This is important in the very first phases of exploration of overseas trading possibilities, and will continue indefinitely after that phase.

(ii) Assessing and developing the consultative and teaching capability of head office and home country staff who go abroad to explore and negotiate the setting up of the new operation: and those who are to do whatever teaching-training is needed when the new operation is being launched.

(iii) The education and some re-training of head office staff at various levels, whose work is affected both directly and indirectly by the overseas development. Much of this will be undertaken 'automatically' by the head office departments such as marketing, accounts, production and so on, if they are working on the new operation. Other parts of head office and other home country centres, will 'want to know' more than the lunchtime gossip tells them.

(iv) The establishment of a T & D unit in the new operation. The size of this unit, and the part played by head office's T & D function, will depend on the size and complexity and newness of the new operation.

An already well established overseas company with an experienced T & D function, will nevertheless require some auditing from head office. This is to ensure that head office knows how the T & D function operates, to what standards, and whether it is able to look after whatever operational and organisational changes lie in the foreseeable future. Also, as is the case with the Marketing, Accounting, Production functions in head office, the T & D head office function needs to establish rapport with the T & D function overseas. This is the beginning of a collaborative working relationship.

At the other extreme, *an overseas grass-roots company* needs to have its T & D function built up from scratch, to deal with initial recruitment and training, through commissioning to the full operation of the company. *If there are other Group operating centres* in that country it is likely that T & D expertise will be transferred in from those centres – as far as it is available. It may be a little or a lot. In either case head office will need to participate in the build-up of the new unit. It will act either as a consultant; or it will provide management or senior staff, and perhaps other staff for the new unit.

If there is no other group operating centre in that country, then head office will provide manager and staff from head office, from home-country centres, and from other overseas group centres, preferably those with grass-roots training experience. If possible local people with T & D experience will be recruited also, as will be the case in manning any of the functions of the new company.

(v) *Career planning and development.* The new T & D unit, with the Personnel function, will pay attention to manpower planning and to career planning, right from the start. Forecasting wastage rates can be of great importance in new operations. These may lead to modifications of earlier recruitment plans, and of plans for the repatriation of the expatriate staff at the time of start-up of a new company.

The new company may have the local expertise to undertake all aspects of career planning and development. If not, it will have to be supplied and taught by head office. Head office will have the additional task of presenting to the new company management the policies and strategies of career planning and development favoured by head office. This does not mean that head office dictates exactly what has to be adopted by the new company for its employees. The new company is in a different country where the people, the traditions and expectations differ from those in the home country. The new company's T & D/Personnel management, together with other managers need to work towards policies and plans suitable for that company in that country.

International transfers can be seen as possible employment opportunities for head office individuals who require that sort of operational experience for their own development. And, it is argued, in working in the overseas centre the individual from head office takes with him expertise to pass on to others, makes friendships, and increases the sense of comradeship within the group, particularly if he does a good job out there. The same is true in reverse. The management of the overseas company see a virtue in having one of their capable and promising staff working in the group head office in an appropriate job, for long enough to get thoroughly into his job responsibilities, and into the head office culture.

The idea of international movements of individuals, not merely to transfer expertise, but also to enhance career development, has some popularity. But it needs to be handled well. The work and responsibilities offered to the 'foreigner' need to be real and significant, and the length of time in that job has to be adequate to allow real achievement – otherwise a well-designed visit or visits might achieve a better result.

245

On the other hand, a long transfer from your home to a foreign city can produce social and domestic problems. These problems, of separation from spouse, home and children, from local interest, from ageing parents, may be overcome happily. But they can cause stress and unhappiness in the family and at work. Such transfers should not be entered into lightly, and should be designed as far as possible with consideration for social factors.

Some companies, particularly the multinational, depend on having a significant number of their staff, at any one time, working and living abroad. It may be a clause in the initial employment contract, that the employee is 'prepared to work overseas'. These companies may make special financial provision as compensation for the social disruption of overseas work, which help to make it 'all worthwhile' to the otherwise disturbed individual. The companies also keep an eye on the transferred staff, to make sure that things are working out well, both at work and at play. All of these measures have been developed over the last few decades, and are regarded helpful in reducing stress and dissatisfaction amongst transferred staff. More will be said about this in the section on developing countries to follow later.

(vi) *Inter-centre rapport.* Everyone goes to company conferences nowadays. Some of the speeches are interesting: the speakers themselves may be more interesting than what they said, because the conference members see the head of department in the flesh and put a face and a style to a name. Discussion groups, mealtime chat, evenings at the bar are likely to be much more rewarding. The sales manager from Manchester branch meets his opposite number from Grenoble. They both learn a lot, some of it surprising and impressive. They end up as friends. The Swiss accountant finds himself at the bar talking to the head office tax expert with whom he had a difference of opinion on the 'phone only the week before. Eye to eye they continue their talk – and begin to see eye to eye.

All of this is commonplace experience. The conference, or the group management course, brings people together to meet one another, and this is fruitful, in both intellectual and emotional terms. The well designed international meeting/conference/course *aims* at fostering questions, discussions, frankness, and hopefully – mutual confidence. International operations can improve as the result of the openness which follows the establishment of such confidence.

In the larger company it is fairly common practice for annual, or more frequent, meetings of multinational groups to take place. Some will be 'strictly business', others may be more general, designed for personal development, and for understanding of group business and relationships, for managers, and for other employees. The T & D function will be concerned with more general meetings, but it can also be concerned with the 'business' meetings. The style of chairmanship and discussion leading: the use of small group discussions within larger meetings: the availability of free time for members to meet informally are things that may be improved This is within T & D's proper interest and capability.

2   THE DEVELOPING COUNTRIES

What are the developing countries? It is important to know the answer to this question when considering and planning operations in any so-called 'developing country'. We have referred to the differences between countries in the industrialised western world. These differences have to be understood by anyone in the home country who deals extensively with an overseas western centre. The differences are not always easy to understand or adjust to. The probability of cultural misunderstandings between home and abroad is significant. But the cultural gap between home-in-the-west and the developing countries is much greater, and much more demanding on managements and individuals.

Basically, the developing countries are those with a very small share of the world's industry. Although they contain some 75 per cent of the world's population they total only 10 per cent of the world's manufacturing capacity. Low education levels, and but little local capability in science and technology, slow down their development towards the economic status of the West and of Japan. The per capita income and purchasing power of most developing countries is, by western standards, very low. There are exceptions, such as the oil-rich countries, where the income from oil has made it possible to develop rapidly education, hospitals, housing, as well as trading on a broad front.

From the point of view of the T & D manager, operations in a developing country present a challenge far greater than operations abroad in a developed country. Let us look more closely at some of the questions and problems he is faced with.

1.   Staffing

(a) How is the operation to be staffed through commissioning and start up – whether of a bank, a plantation, supermarket, mine or chemical works?

(b) What is the availability of skill in that country amongst local people – in clerical, technical, supervisory and managerial work? What are the normal methods of recruitment of local skills and labour? What is the education system and its standards?

(c) What essential technical staff and managers must be sent out from the home country?

(d) What staff must be recruited from other countries, where skills are more readily available?

(e) What staffing obligations are imposed on the company by the government of that country? Do they specify levels, ratios or numbers of local people to be employed: do they put a limit on the number of foreign expatriates who may be brought in, or the length of time they may stay by contract?

(f) Has the local government set targets of any description for the 'localisation' of the staffing? These may be 'open ended', and ask that every effort must be made to recruit, train and develop nationals to replace foreign expatriates at all levels but no dates or percentages would be included. On the other hand they may be much more precise, giving dates and percentages and levels to aim at, and identifying some senior positions to be immediately occupied by qualified and experienced local people.

All of the above items contribute to the building up of a manpower model and manpower plans. All the items demand information, not just guesswork. Some very important information comes from the training manager's colleagues in head office, who form the project design team and who are responsible for the new overseas operation. They will, in the normal course of work specify the staffing required for the overseas operations. They may have previous experience of similar overseas situations and be already fully aware of the likely skill levels in that country. If they have no previous experience in developing countries then their plans for manning the operation will merely form a start point, on western lines, from which to develop more appropriate future plans, when they have more information.

Where does the additional information about the developing country's manpower resources come from? If you are going into a joint venture or partnership with a company already operating out there, or with an agency of the government of that country, then your new partner can provide information, or point the way, in that country, to other companies or institutions which can give help. Closer to home there are the embassies, trade attaches and other representatives of that developing country who are appointed to give information to western industry: and there are trade organisation and teaching centres in the west such as the Centre for Overseas Briefing at Farnham Castle in the UK with a great deal of knowledge about specific developing countries. From this information, estimates can be made of initial local employment, loss rates, and recruitment into full employment and training schemes.

Training and development

When the T & D manager is in possession of the recruitment plans, and the forecast of losses and of growth of the new operation he would be, in normal circumstances, in a position to identify the T & D activities needed and the T & D organisation needed to service the training. For a home country project he would probably be able to plan his staff and facilities fairly near to the mark, and make the small adjustments needed later on, without much difficulty. One instructor more or less, an extra room for seminars (lent by Computer Department), more induction programmes and so on. However, in starting up and consolidating training and development in an operation – particularly a new grass roots operation – in a developing country one is faced with uncertainty and upsets that call often for a rethink. Let us look at some of the more frequent and severe of these.

Expatriate staff

These will come from the company's existing home country operating centres, and from other companies in the home country. There will also be 'other nationality' expatriates, from Europe or America, Australia or the Philippines. Each person will be looked at closely on recruitment to ensure that he is competent at his trade or profession, with adequate experience and qualification. These same people will also carry responsibility for supervising and training the locals in the new company. How good are they as supervisors and as trainers? The recruiting officer or agency may ask no more than 'Have you had training experience?' The

THE INTERNATIONAL CONTEXT

answer will be 'Yes', and in some instances the wrong man is recruited. This will show up later, out on the job, perhaps through objections voiced by the trainees who complain that they aren't being told anything.

Moreover, at the time of recruitment of expatriate staff, how can the recruiting officer test the expatriate's reaction to local people in the developing country. It has often been the experience that some expatriates undergo a sort of social withdrawal when confronted with a local employee. Some have confessed to a mild nervousness: some to increased aggressiveness: some to unusual impatience. There is a risk therefore that a significant amount of job instruction, and of moment-to-moment communication and supervision, will be fluffed. The training manager together with all other managers will need to take positive steps to raise the capability of expatriates in instruction, communicating and in working with locals. This last point is referred to again later in this chapter.

There is a further 'risk' implicit in employing expatriates. In some poor developing countries there is a considerable capability in those people who have had education, and experience in industrial and commercial companies. Their country may lack minerals, oil or other wealth, and they and their family are poor. They gain employment in another, richer, developing country where a new project is looking for scarce skills. The pay is good and can make a lot of difference to their family back at home. Some are likely to be reluctant to put much effort into training a local person and, they fear, thereby do themselves out of a job. They need to be confident that they will be able to complete their current contract period: and they need to understand clearly what the chances are of extending that contract.

Local recruits

There can be a very wide range of standards, of education and capability, amongst local recruits. Standards differ from country to country: and standards can differ within any one country very much more than is the case in Western/developed countries. The reason for this is, mainly, that the developing country is developing its education system, developing its industry and commerce, and changing some aspects of its culture. None of these developments can be achieved quickly. They take years and generations to install, operate, and to produce a raised level of capability generally throughout the population.

Hence recruitment, at the start up of operations, and from then on, has its unique problems. An American company starting up in Italy will be able to specify recruits, by number, capability and experience, that correspond to recruitment schedules in the USA. These will have to be modified somewhat as recruitment proceeds – but so would the schedules for a start in the USA. In the developing country recruits may have to be accepted at much lower standards, and the job-structure and training adjusted to suit.

One may ask, 'Why not recruit more expatriates of the required standard?' The main reasons frequently encountered are:

(i) By recruiting local people the company will establish rapport with local people and the local authorities, and contribute to what may be called 'the education of the environment'.

(ii) The company may be obliged to recruit a percentage of its workforce locally, provided it is possible to train them to an adequate minimum standard.

(iii) The company may be obliged, in addition to (ii), to develop the careers of local and other nationals; and to provide promotion with a view to local participation in the running and management of the company in the longer term.

(iv) Expatriate staff, particularly if drawn from the home country and the West, can be very expensive. Travel, housing and other allowances, put up their cost: if their wives and children accompany them it goes up further. Head office will quickly see virtue in training local people for the new operation, even if there is little return for the first few years, because of the ultimate financial savings.

The problems produced by (i) – (iv) above are likely to be much less for a small scale operation than for a large operation. If for example, the operation is no more than setting up a sales office to accommodate three senior and two junior staff, then somewhere in that developing country, perhaps locally, one might find a promising senior and a good junior, both with appropriate education and useful experience. They will work directly with the three expatriates from head office. If, on the other hand, the operation is technically complex, and requires scores or hundreds of people to operate plant, work in maintenance, laboratories, security, transport and other services, then the chances of finding a large number of people well educated and with useful experience, can be remote.

In this latter case the company is faced with a large-scale training and development commitment. The company may, of course, have large-scale T & D activities in the home country, and in other countries. This is an advantage in that it knows about managing the T & D function, and has staff and instructors who can be transferred to the new operation. But they, like all other expatriates, need also to learn about the history, culture and expectations of the new country, and the way that these will affect the organisation and conduct of training in the new operation. Let us look at some of the more typical demands made on T & D management in these operations; produced by a developing economy, and a changing culture for expatriates *and* locals.

The initial training of recruits

This may have to include *preliminary weeks, months or a year in schooling,* to raise linguistic, writing, science, mechanics and other elementary levels of the younger school leavers and perhaps of some adults. The company may be able to persuade the local authority to provide this schooling on a full-time or part-time basis. This, in some countries, or in some regions of a country, may be a step in developing secondary, tertiary or further education for local people. If this sort of collaboration is not possible then the company will have to consider setting up its own schooling facilities. This means providing premises, teachers, timetables, syllabuses and materials and equipment. The training manager may be faced with problems of teaching methods, standards, and the measurement of progress. The subject matter of teaching must be relevant to the future employment of the trainees, as well as contributing to their general social development.

There is nothing unusual in the above steps. There are very many examples in western industrial companies, in the home country. Overseas, however, in a developing country, there are problems which can arise from differences in culture and in language; incompatability of instructors and trainees; and in a failure of the instructors to interest the trainees or to have necessary patience with them.

At this level of training it is valuable for the company to search for and recruit or transfer a suitable local person, or persons, into the training unit. The local person will do some teaching, will help the trainees adjust to the new environment of industrial/commercial training and employment; and he will help the expatriate staff, wherever they come from, understand better the local people and local recruits. In fact, it has been found often the case that the locally recruited assistant, if encouraged and helped in his new role, can grow in stature and within a few years assume increasing responsibility in the T & D function.

Learning the first job

Now the local recruits, either as recent school leavers, or adults or college graduates, are ready *to learn their first jobs*, ready perhaps to start their company career. A training centre, large or small, may be needed for the teaching of the basic skills which cannot easily be taught and learned on-the-job. Again the training manager must recruit instructors who are able to gain and sustain interest amongst the trainees, and able to identify skill and potential. The training manager and his staff can be seen as a link between the trainees and the company, and an important link between the company and the outside world. He and his staff must recognise this fact and must not merely see themselves as trainers.

The trainers in the training centre (and elsewhere in the company) need to bear in mind that in many undeveloped regions the people know almost nothing about industry and commerce, and that *trainees can find the instructions they are given almost meaningless*. It doesn't relate to anything else they know about. So the training manager and his staff have a further challenge – to search for ways to give meaning, interest and motivation to instruction and learning off-the-job in the training centre; and on-the-job in the offices and on the plant. A world-wide educational problem, but potentially acute in these situations.

An international company with operations in the home country and other countries has an opportunity for *sending trainees* from the new operation in the developing country *to an established operation elsewhere*.

In the 'established operation elsewhere' the trainee will be able, it is presumed, to learn quickly from experienced people on well tuned processes and plant procedures. Sometimes this is successful; sometimes it is not. The reasons for failure are likely to be:

(i) The trainee is a foreigner and his language ability is weak and taxes the patience of those who are supposed to employ and train him.

(ii) The receiving centres are not properly prepared for this type of exercise. It is an interference with their work routines.

(iii) The trainee knows nothing about the work he is supposed to learn; he has to be taught from scratch, and this places an unacceptable burden on the supervisors and staff of the receiving centre.

If the receiving centre is fully prepared and equipped for handling *ab initio* trainees from abroad, then there is a better chance of success. But the trainee will then have to adjust himself to the somewhat different circumstances of work in the developing country when he goes back home. A mature person will have but little difficulty: an immature person will need some help. This is a T & D responsibility.

A good general rule is that trainees sent away to another centre to learn or improve their skills – in no matter what – should have learned the rudiments of those skills and their use beforehand. The receiving centre, in its Training Department and in its operating departments, will then be able to handle the visiting trainee much more comfortably, even find pleasure and interest in someone with whom they can communicate and work without undue difficulty. The receiving centre will need to take responsibility, particularly with young trainees, for their social life – where they live, how they spend their spare time, if they are attending classes, and so on. The failure to give sufficient attention to trainees' social life can have unhappy consequences.

Doing the first job

And now the new recruit, of whatever age or level in the company, is in his first job. He is a local person relatively inexperienced, working in an office, or a workshop, or manufacturing plant. Around him are other local people, mainly inexperienced, and expatriates. The expatriates are experienced, carry more responsibility, have to do more work; and some are supervisors, some are managers.

It is often the case that the local people, who have initially least experience and the least to offer, are intended to have a future, a career, in the company. The expatriates, who run almost everything, have no personal future or career in that particular company. Some of the expatriates have a job waiting for them when they return to the home country. Some do not, but they will find a job somewhere. Between the expatriates and the locals there is a culture and communication gap. How do the local employees, some of them ex-trainees, get on in these circumstances? Another question for T & D management.

Back home, line managers and their training managers would be working and training according to practices, and to quality standards, which are traditional and agreed. In the developing country, the traditions have yet to be established, and the quality standards of work have yet to be set or attained. People hired from different places may have different ideas, different standards. Given local, freshly recruited, employees with relatively little experience, the standards of work for those recruits are likely to slip. The expatriate manager will be tempted to offer less work to, or offer less demanding work to, the local recruit. He may also put up with a higher error rate and accept that the local person does not really understand the meaning of his work – how could he be expected to?

Reducing and simplifying the work for local people is reasonable if it is an introductory step towards greater responsibility. Tolerating a higher error rate is only acceptable if it is followed by efforts to increase employee understanding, skills and accuracy. It is unlikely that many expatriate employers, of whatever nationality, will see this type of situation as an agreeable challenge. They will more likely see it as nuisance that they have to put up with. So, it is not only the locals who need training. The expatriates also need to learn how to handle their own training responsibilities, how to understand, relate to, and supervise the local employees. It is not unreasonable to say also that the local people need to understand how to work for foreign supervisors. The whole of this area is a responsibility of the T & D function, and is shared with line management.

Career development and localisation

Career development, for the Western expatriate, has meant being given reasonable opportunities for promotion or transfer, as and when vacancies occur. He knows that he may not be head of the queue, that he may have to wait a year, or several years, for a promotion he would like to get. He knows that he has to be good enough for the promotion, and has his own fair idea of what that means in terms of skills and responsibilities. He *may* expect to receive promotion as part of planned career development in this overseas job. Promotion will hinge on whether there is acceptance in principle, by local partners or by local government, of career development of foreigners taking place in that particular developing country.

But, from the point of view of the local government, or local partners, *career development and promotion for local people will be seen as the way of bringing about localisation.* Localisation means manning the company with local people, i.e. with nationals. It cannot be done all at once: it takes time for people to acquire skills and experience, to develop to the various technical, supervisory and management levels which have to be occupied. Helping such a transition to take place successfully is an ethical responsibility of the international company. *It is, in some cases, an explicit obligation,* a part of the agreement between the international company and the overseas partners and the government. How long localisation is supposed to take, in its various stages, will depend on the sophistication and development of the country, on the size and complexity of the operation, and the experience to date of both the company and the local authority. Often no completion dates are specified: but there will be a requirement for *visible recruitment, training and development schemes,* and these may be closely monitored by the local authority or by a local senior manager or director whom they have introduced into the company.

The obligation to "localise" the company may include the requirement that a local employee must be promoted into an expatriate's job *when he is ready* and able to do it. In the West the promotion of a suitable person takes *place when there is a vacancy* for him to fill. But according to the above requirement, the vacancy has to be created – by removing the expatriate altogether, or by retaining the expatriate as an adviser, or by creating an extra job for the local at that level in the organisation.

This is the background against which the company conducts its manpower planning, its recruitment and training, and against which local recruits at all levels enter the company and learn to do a job. It is a background which alters the entire pattern of employee expectation and motivation, and which produces a preoccupation for the Employee Relations and the T & D function.

253

In the developing country performance appraisal for the locally recruited individual brings additional problems, not merely of assessment but of what to put on the form, how to conduct the usual interviews with the local employee. The expatriate supervisor, and his staff, may have provided inappropriate job training for the employee, and the employee's performance in western terms is still poor. But the supervisor may then write 'satisfactory' on the performance assessment form, and 'promising' as his potential. The supervisor and the manager may have together discussed their dilemma and agreed on a comprise. This, perhaps, is understood and condoned by more senior management. What else, they say, can they do? Does it matter all that much?

The consequence of inadequate training, accompanied by favourable appraisals, is that in the course of time the company can acquire two work cultures, that of the expatriate and that of the local people. The local people may well enjoy a sequence of promotions at a fast rate, but during that rise through lower and middle to senior levels, too many of them may not have acquired the necessary technology and understanding of its use, too many may not be making, or contributing significantly to, major decisions. They will be agreeing or disagreeing, of course, with proposals, and signing the final version. This is a long way from doing the full job which they hold; but for many of them it is a first experience ever of this sort of life, and can be rewarding and pleasing. The company is still largely run by the expatriates, who have had to learn a new form of management diplomacy in order to make the company work successfully. And, indeed, some of the senior local managers will appreciate more and more the service given by the skilled expatriates, and may even find them indispensable.

Dependence on the expatriate in the developing company and country must not be played out at the expense of the local people. Their training and development will demand much greater effort than back in the home country and will demand higher standards of trainer capability than is typical in the western countries. Manpower and promotion planning and appraisal must be conducted with integrity. The most senior local people inside and outside the company must be helped to understand the facts of life in connection with employee development and localisation programmes, and must be involved in passing on this understanding to more junior employees, and to recruits. They must resist the temptation to spread misleading beliefs such as 'because the company belongs to us. . .we should be promoted. . .and soon'. It is a frequent experience that the talented local person can be of immense value in helping locals and expatriates keep the company's growth in perspective in the local and international context. Such a person is often found a senior place in Local Relations, Government Relations, Employee Relations, and can be of great use in T & D. He may, on the other hand, be a talented member of operations management, with a sound view of the capabilities needed to do a job well, and can contribute authoritatively to the examination of training standards and of employee promotability.

3 LANGUAGE AND CULTURE

International business brings staff from head office in the home country into contact with staff, and other people, in the overseas company in the foreign country. The differences in language, culture, and social and business conventions may seem to be slight and unimportant when a visitor from Belgium comes to London for a discussion on pricing. His English is good: he knows his business: he enjoys his overnight stay at the sales manager's house: he is naturally courteous. Everyone thought him a good person. 'Are they all like that?' asked someone. 'No', said the sales manager, who had worked in Belgium, 'he lived in England for a few years as a boy, with his uncle. He learnt his way around early on. That's why they chose him to come to the meeting'. If he hadn't spoken good English, he wouldn't have gone to London. Someone else would have been chosen. If there had been no-one else strong in English, what would have happened? Hold the meeting in French? No one in the Sales/Pricing unit spoke 'business French'. The Londoners took for granted the linguistic skill of the foreigner. The reader will forgive the above parable. Today, the need for people to take foreign languages seriously has become widely recognised. Industry and commerce, and other institutions, increasingly recognise that they must not simply expect the foreigner to be good at languages.

For some years the *lingua franca* of international dialogue has been English. This is due originally to the movement of English speaking people into various parts of the world, establishing colonies and obliging the indigenous people to speak English. Then came a massive American international influence, to deepen this English-speaking tradition. But this is only one side of the coin. The other side of the coin is that some countries recognised the importance of being able to actually use English as a working language, and *developed their culture and schooling methods* to embrace, successfully, this additional language, as in Holland, Denmark and Scandinavia. In a few countries two or three languages, apart from English, may be commonplace. Switzerland, Belgium and the Lebanon are well known examples.

The English have missed out on this sort of upbringing – although it is not true of the Welsh and some Scots and Irish who also have another language. The English, moreover, have the 'advantage' of finding that so many people abroad speak English. So why make any effort? With the opening up of an increasing range of trading competition and opportunities, not only in Europe, companies are becoming much more aware of the advantages, even if only marginal, of language skills that can be used in negotiation, work and socially overseas. Fortunately there are enough examples of company success in learning languages to encourage other companies to invest it.

A good example of company investment is provided by British Petroleum. Before World War II, when BP was known as Anglo-Iranian, all expatriate British working in Iran learnt Farsi, the Iranian language, in courses provided by the company. This pattern of learning was then adopted in the 1950s when BP's operations moved into the Arabian Middle East. All expatriates were expected to learn Arabic, through classes and discussion groups provided in and out of work time. The starting level was called compulsory Arabic, to be followed by intermediate and advanced levels. Those who reached the higher levels were awarded a bonus. As operations spread into other countries all or some of the expatriate staff would be taught the new language, or selected for the job because of some capability in the language. This was backed by company Further Education policies, which encouraged employees to learn languages irrespective of any immediate need for them in their work. Head office, in co-operation with a local institute, staged lunchtime language courses with annual enrolments of some 300 members of staff, on a voluntary basis. Language learning was virtually part of the company culture, and the Training function maintained a constant service to the many learning requirements.

A number of insights, dos and don'ts, have been gained over the years in connection with language teaching and learning. These are of importance to the T & D function in recommending and organising whatever action has to be taken, and we list below some of these. Although the purpose of this book is not to go into details of training methods, the general weakness in language skills amongst the English justifies some comment on language learning at this point.

1 The traditional English schoolroom approach to language teaching is not very effective as a way of introducing the language, or of developing learner interest. A class of adults is likely to waste away quickly if it is subject to working its way line by line through a text book, week after week, taking turns in reading a few lines and in answering questions. In such classes most of each person's time is spent inactively, awaiting his or her turn. The classroom teacher must be able to produce opportunities for a high level of involvement in talking and listening, as well as in writing and translating.

2 The vocabulary must be, or quickly become, relevant to the interests and needs of the pupils, as must be the phrases and sentences and the situations to which they refer. This has been recognised for some time by the well established language schools, whose tourist books and tapes contain sections on hotels, restaurants, travel etc. It has to be recognised also by the teachers of company staff: it means that the teachers will often have to learn new words and phrases, and understand something of new situations, to suit their clients. This is an area for T & D interest and action in setting up classes: and for pupils to contribute to as learning progresses.

3 Skill in listening and understanding, is as important as skill in talking and writing. There is little point in going to a meeting in France and eloquently reading out your proposition, if you can't understand what the replies are. Listening practice can be provided both formally and informally – both are important.

4 Fourth, one-to-one sessions of teacher and one pupil can be very valuable. Not only is the half hour or so solely for the one person's benefit, with continuous 'conversation', plenty of talking and listening, but the vocabulary and expressions can be chosen to suit the specific needs of that individual. One or more sessions of this type can be planned and used as a rehearsal for a meeting in the near future. The teacher has to learn his part – acting as a member of a meeting, and teaching as is found necessary. After the real meeting the pupil and teacher may choose to spend time on a post-mortem. More will be learnt, with both pupil and teacher gaining satisfaction.

5 Both courage and discretion must be cultivated. Many adults are a little embarassed when they try to speak a foreign language. Well run discussion classes will produce an increasing confidence. But if the new language is to be used in critical business discussion, care has to be taken not to enter into agreements solely in a language in which one is imperfect.

Companies will use both internal and external resources for language teaching, sometime using a blend of both, plus the use of tapes and discs. Private language schools and local colleges and universities may provide the courses and teachers, using either their own premises or using rooms inside the company. Some members of the company's own staff may be excellent linguists, and used full time or part time as teachers. Whatever the arrangement is, the training manager must recognise his responsibility for good design and adequate monitoring of the classes and their progress. Handing over to an outside agency does not automatically solve the problems of language learning or meet the company's needs. Close co-operation and monitoring is called for.

BRIDGING THE CULTURAL GAP

The expatriate may note that there are differences in social custom and personal style but it is very unlikely that he will see the full depth and the importance of these differences without help from others; and it is unlikely that he will successfully adjust his behaviour, if that is needed, without guidance from others. For the tourist, holiday maker, and the infrequent business visitor, the differences that can be easily seen will add interest to the trip, and little harm will be done by failing to understand their meaning and their depth. For the expatriate living abroad, working with and perhaps supervising local people, there is a need to understand something about the way the local people live, the way they look at things, what is acceptable and unacceptable, and how they use authority and respond to authority. It is true to say that not only will this understanding reduce the risk of poor communication, of poor co-operation, but it will increase the interest and pleasure in living in that country. The same will be true, perhaps even more so, for the accompanying spouse.

Clearly, the training function has the task of providing education/information for expatriates, and their spouses, well in advance of their departure for abroad. This will need to be followed by further information given on arrival in the new country: and there will be a need for a mentor to whom the expatriate will turn for further advice in his early weeks of employment. The people who give all this information must be competent and carefully chosen. In the home country, before departure, there may be people in, say, head office, recently returned from that overseas operation, with up-to-date and accurate information about social/domestic matters, public behaviour, money, shopping – and many other matters. They could be valuable. There is little point in using someone who is now out of touch with the place, the company, the local facilities. Inaccurate information is misleading, and can cause resentment. If no one is available inside the company it may be necessary to use outside agencies who specialise in preparing people for work overseas. For companies with little or no experience of this sort of education an outside agency could be used to help design the education strategy in the first place, to accept the company's staff onto agency courses or to provide tailor-made courses for the company.

The above brief look at preparation for social life in a foreign country has touched on questions of behaviour and authority. These are of great importance in the company itself, in which the expatriate is working for weeks, months or years. What qualities should *he* have, how should *he* behave? He will have colleagues drawn from

   (i)   local people
  (ii) expatriates from the home country
 (iii) expatriates from other countries.

Generally speaking they may occupy positions at any levels in the hierachy. The variations are almost limitless today in multinational businesses, both in the developing countries and, to a lesser extent, in the western developed countries. To work most successfully in these circumstances does call for particular qualities in the expatriate. These qualities should be noted in the job specification: they should be searched for and noted in performance and potential appraisals in international companies where the search for suitable people for overseas work is almost continuous. What are these qualities? They fall into three groups:

(a) General social and interpersonal qualities. These include the ability to communicate, and to understand other peoples' position: curiosity and a sense of humour: tolerance and flexibility: and a high degree of self-reliance.

(b) Perseverence in the face of ambiguities and changes to goals, that is necessary to achieve ultimately the objectives towards which he is working.

(c) A suitable 'style' in his approach to problems and to decision making. A person's style will be a blend of (i) fact seeking, (ii) intuition, (iii) analysis, and (iv) conforming to acceptable standards and values in the action ultimately to be taken. This is h's style of thinking-and-feeling his way through a problem. The balance of the four factors (i), (ii), (iii) and (iv) will vary from person to person, and hence styles vary from person to person but all four factors must be active.

It is possible to assess, an executive's standing in all of the three main groups (a), (b) and (c) above: and indeed to assess his suitability for employment in different sorts of work which make different demands on personal capability and style. It is possible to create 'profiles' of desirable attributes for, say, middle management jobs, and search for those candidates amongst executives and junior managers whose personal profiles match those of the jobs. Some of these jobs may be wholly or partly overseas, and these assessments help to select the most suitable people, and help to identify potential weaknesses in whoever is selected. No one is going to get a high rating in all three of (a), (b) and (c). No one is perfect, no one will perform 'perfectly' in a new appointment, even in the home country.

When, a person has to visit or reside in, another country for negotiations or for work he can make cultural 'mistakes'. These arise from the differences between his own attitudes, behaviour and expression, and those of his foreign hosts, differences not foreseen by the head office selectors who appointed him. The hosts may see him as a bit obstinate, or hasty, or rude, aggresive, illogical or insensitive; but he may never know how his hosts see him. If he is negotiating a deal, his performance may tip the balance against him. If he is working out there in a day-to-day job, on a two year contract, he may be creating tension in his work area and amongst colleagues that diminishes collaboration and good work relationships.

With luck his foreign colleagues will understand the visitor's behaviour and accept it as unavoidable and forgivable: but there is a risk. What can be done about it?

Until recent years there had been very little serious comparative analysis of the details of cultures of the various countries and societies of the world. Seen from any one country each and every other country looked different to the outsider. But the outsider might never get more than a glimpse of the inner man in another country. Moreover, the outsider may never seriously consider that he himself has characteristics of attitude and behaviour, that he himself is the product of his home-country culture, that he is so habit-ridden that he cannot look critically at himself or change his ways.

For those who are to work overseas, in developed or undeveloped countries, or work in companies with colleagues of different ethnic origin, there is a need for education that will enable them to handle their working relationships better. Hopefully candidates for international work will have been identified by their open-mindedness, tolerance and curiosity in addition to their business skills. Beyond this lies the need to understand something of cultural differences. Geert Holstede, a Dutch academic, is one of a small number of researchers to have studied national characteristics and to have published their findings.

Making use of these findings can present problems. There is value in the 'intelligent reader' reading the published material simply to sharpen the mind, to make him aware of the fact of cultural and social differences. From then on he may become more perceptive and learn more from his own experiences in a foreign country. There is a risk, though, that this reading may replace the reader's existing beliefs and stereotypes by a new set of beliefs and stereotypes which could lead to equally faulty observation of his new foreign hosts and colleagues.

Some companies who have made use of these findings hold the view that the best results, the best understanding, is obtained through the services of a skilled tutor as well as through reading published literature. The tutor understands the general cultural characteristics of a country, and the more frequently met variations from the general characteristics due to sex, age, region, religion etc., as well as those due to individuality. Most important, perhaps, is the understanding of the likely style of management in that foreign company, and of the likely variation in that style. This is of value to the negotiating team and to those who take up residence and work abroad. Of equal value to the latter group is an understanding, in cultural and interpersonal terms, of how employees expect to be treated by their supervisors and managers, of what is acceptable and what is unacceptable.

If one looks for alternatives to sophisticated education through skilled tutors, there is much more which can be done in and by the company in its overseas operations. It calls for *close observation, by line management, of how employee/ management relations are developing*, and it calls for creative thinking, at least by the training function. One western company, operating in a developing country, ran induction and information courses for expatriates. In these courses the expatriates learnt about the local national employees and managers and supervisors, about their cultural background and the country's industrial commercial history. The same was done in reverse for local national employees, at any level, with some emphasis on the technical and managerial presence and role of the expatriates in the company.

All of this was appreciated, but there still was friction from time to time between the expatriate and the local nationals, for reasons that were difficult to diagnose. Someone had a bright idea – why not have a seminar for western supervisors and local supervisors, to discuss, under a suitable title, workplace relationships in the company? The western managers thought this was brilliant, but the local managers were hesitant. Why? Because, they said, 'this is not the sort of thing that we do here', but they agreed. This was the first step to success. They got together and worked out a formula 'acceptable to both sides'. A pilot seminar was run with suitable title, subject matter and discussion method for westerners and locals together. It was in the gentle joint-control of a senior westerner and a local manager. A number of home truths came out, heard and now believed by both westerners and locals. There was a significant adjustment in knowledge and attitude – and in some supervisory habits – from that day on. This adjustment was reinforced by follow-up seminars, by the modification of induction and information programmes, and by putting 'intercultural' matters high on the list of priorities of anything in the company that had an intercultural aspect – which meant almost everything.

32 Auditing the training and development function

The word audit, with its connotations of rigour and objectivity, is not a bad one to use when a study of manpower assets and systems is undertaken. But, of course, depending on circumstances, such an audit might equally well be called an investigation or enquiry, or a study or appraisal. The actual word does not matter greatly. What does matter, apart from the skill with which the audit is done, is what it sets out to present to management. Is it merely to present an accurate statement of present manpower assets and systems? Is it to look into the future? Is it to evaluate these assets and compare them with present and future requirements? Should it point out strengths and weaknesses? If it is to go this far, should it be indicating what and where changes should be made, and, one step further, how those changes can be made? The answer to any one of these questions can, in the case of manpower audits, be yes, depending on who asks for the audit to be done and on other circumstances inside the company.

Audits, by whatever name, may be requested by totally different people and be brought about by totally different pressures as we see in three cases to follow. The directors of the VAK Company are unhappy about the activities and achievements of the Training and Development department and ask the head of that department to produce a statement of what the department is doing, how this matches the needs of the company, and what the achievements are. The head of training and development might produce a list of current and planned activities and some simple and perhaps suave statements about 'meeting needs', and how many people are going through his courses. This does not really constitute an audit. An audit would contain the sort of manpower and operational evidence that we have referred to in earlier chapters in this book, suitably arranged. He might, indeed, do this, but will need co-operation from manpower colleagues, and evidence from operations managers.

In the second company, All Systems Unlimited, there has arisen an agreed practice whereby an annual statement is prepared by selected suitable people in the manpower function, showing with some thoroughness the present and projected manpower characteristics, both actual and required, for each of the employee and management groups of the company. The statement also suggests what current and future recruitment, transfer, promotion and training strategies are best suited to the company, and what changes are needed in those presently in use. Statistical career prospects are also present with warnings of likely future upsets.

In the third company, the Zelba Corporation, the audit is somewhat different in purpose. Zelba has just acquired control of the nearby Towest Company, with which it will integrate. There is a need for some compatibility in manpower policies between the two, and for developing some common practices. So Zelba undertakes an audit of Towest manpower, and includes in this a study of the manpower function itself, its practices, policies, staff, and the efficiency and effectiveness with which their work is done. Zelba has, naturally, to audit its own function in the same way in order to put together a satisfactory picture of the two companies prior to making decisions on the future of them.

Who is the auditor? It might be anyone, provided that that person had functional knowledge, investigatory capability and analytical skill appropriate to the purpose of the audit. Internal financial audits are not unusual in large companies, and this means that accountants employed in, say, the audit section of the accounts department examine the accounts and assets in areas managed by anyone and everyone in the company at any level. They probably show no fear and no favour, and they are likely to be professionally competent in auditing. It cannot always be assumed that the same is true of the courage and capability of those employed in the manpower function, and the more a company is unable to produce its own manpower auditor of genuine professional quality, the more it is likely to depend on an outsider to undertake this work.

In the case of the Zelba Company, above, the newly acquired Towest Company was audited by the training manager and the planning manager of the manpower function in Zelba; both were technically competent, neither was inhibited by friendships or hierarchical pressures when looking critically and objectively into the organisation of the new company, Towest, but found themselves justifying many of the manpower practices in their own company, Zelba, and not being equally critical.

If a company has not the technical strength to undertake its own audit, it will require the technical strength of any external professional consultant it may choose to invite to undertake the auditing. In this case, being technically weak, it may not be in the best position to choose a suitable and competent consultant for itself, and will, quite reasonably, depend on reliable recommendations. On the other hand a company may have the technical strength itself, but, because of internal politics, or other work pressures, or personality problems, decide to bring in an outsider. In this case the company is able to choose, to work with, and, whenever necessary, to challenge the consultant, and probably to learn a great deal from him.

Often a consultant is brought in to a company not so much as an auditor; but as someone who is to rectify a problem; or to undertake a task in an area of manpower development, sometimes real and sometimes cosmetic, to which a top manager has taken a liking. It might be 'our training and development department is in need of some sort of improvement'. Now, in a case such as this, there may be some powerful single reason for inefficiency, that can be dealt with relatively speedily. The training manager and his staff may prove to be uninterested and unalterably incompetent; they need replacing. But it may not be that way. The reason for ineffectiveness may be organisational and structural, and the consultant must be prepared to undertake a partial audit, or to use existing internal audits, as far as this enables him to understand the reasons for ineffectiveness. When he is examining things to do with the training and development of manpower he will use one or more of the various approaches and concepts as presented earlier in this book, which we can now consider as auditing techniques. He will also use his own commonsense and power of perception to spot and deal with those things, not to be found by using techniques, which influence company life, which may produce problems, or which may help future progress.

AUDITING GUIDELINES

As we have said, an audit may be requested for a part of the training/development/manpower activities of a company, or for the entire system of manpower activities. Because of the integrated nature of that system, even if a partial audit is requested, the auditor will need to keep in mind the whole of the system and the company which it serves. This does not mean that, for example, the person auditing the induction and initial training of new entrants to the company has to examine in equal depth everything in the manpower system, and everything in the company organisation and activities.

What would be required, is a selective examination, in decreasing depth, of those things with greater and lesser presumed impact on the matter under audit. The examination of induction and initial training would, in average circumstances, contain a close study of the methods, contents and administration of existing induction and training courses, counselling, on-the-job instruction. It would look at the quality of the employing supervisors; at the first job performance and effectiveness of the new entrants after initial training; and the acceptability of the induction and training procedures to both supervisors and new recruits. It would ask for the current and future recruitment rates into the company. It would take into account rates of pay, career prospects, terms and conditions, shift arrangements. Unless something highly significant arose, the amount of time and effort, data collection and analysis, interviews etc. would decrease as the auditor moves from what he has to audit to matters which he has also to understand because they, in some way, give meaning or measure to what is being audited. He therefore has to be able to put together everything that he sees into a cohesive whole picture with interrelated parts; and he has to have, *a priori*, some sort of conceptual map which he takes with him always on company audits in order that he can find his way around and create the whole picture out of the bits that he sees.

We have offered some maps of this type in the earlier chapters. The training opportunity matrix (Figure 5.1) lays a grid over the entire company, useful for systematic company-wide examination, or for helping to get into place, in the total of company training, the elements of training under consideration. The distinction on that matrix between notifiable training and non-notifiable training enables one to separate out the training (notifiable) for which regular administrative measures may be operated by training and personnel functions; and the training which is the result of other training opportunity generators. These generators, occupying an important place on our total map, need to be identified at conception, as it were, before any new developments materialise in the company. In this latter case there are, somewhere, corporate plans for the future to which the auditor needs access. Equally important, but even less visible to the eye, are the maintenance areas of the training opportunity matrix, concerning standards and personal flexibility.

A second map that we have offered is that of the manpower plans and structures of the company. This cannot be looked at with the same ease as the training opportunity matrix, for it is a dynamic picture, a set of pictures, showing the ways in which the manpower will change from its present state through various states in the middle and longer term future. On these hinge a number of matters of importance to the company such as recruitment policies, the size and purpose of training and development schemes, management and supervisor succession. Much more elusive, but an equally important matter, is career development, which is very much dependent on structures and routes: for this, vision is required as much as are maps. These can become out-of-date with the smallest change in company fortunes, leaving some employees unhappily stranded and the career specialist happily occupied drawing a new map. If structured manpower information does not exist the auditor will require basic manpower and planning data from which to make his own approximations.

A third map, or representation of the company, which is of value in manpower auditing, is to envisage the company as comprising three separate groups, but with total interdependence. The three groups are

1   The manpower function
2   The management and supervisory group
3   The employee group

The internal organisation, manning, and main tasks can easily be appreciated for each of these groups. An audit of almost any manpower matter will take the auditor into all these of them, i.e. the manpower function, which provides the policies and services; management and supervision, who observe these policies and use the service; the employees, under the control of management and supervision, who are also subject to the policies and can make some direct use of services. The whole manpower picture and process cannot be understood without recognising that to a large extent the ultimate effectiveness of manpower policies depends on the interaction and interdependence of these three groups.

Distinction must, therefore, be made between, on the one hand, the role, capability and actual work of each group; and, on the other hand, the relationships, communication and confidence which exists between them. An appraisal of the manpower function, or of a part of it, must include sufficient appraisal of the two other groups, and relationships. An overall appraisal of any aspect of manpower in the company must also make some reference to the contribution, and perhaps the strengths and weakness, of each of the three groups.

THE LIMITS AND SCOPE OF THE AUDIT

In the chapter on Intentions and Objectives we saw how the training manager achieves his own objectives by producing a person, or persons, trained to a particular level of capability. That is the end point of his direct responsibility and of his authority. That trained person, or persons, from then on works for a supervisor or manager, using that new capability and producing an output to a required good standard. It is now out of the training manager's hands, but he has an interest still, and will require feedback on post-training performance of the one-time trainees. The auditor may require the same information.

If the trainee were a typist from the typist's training school it would be obvious and acceptable that an audit of the school should include an examination of the capability and progress of ex-trainees. This might even include those who had left the company. Such an examination is relatively easy to do: typing is visible, measurable and to agreed standards of speed and error rate. Moreover the typist is used to, and not likely to complain about, performance measurement.

If the trainee were a manager, having completed a course, it would be less obvious and more difficult to do any serious examination of post-training performance. Was the course intended to give specific day-to-day *skill*; was it to *increase his familiarity* with some aspect of management: was it *to explore* the possibility of introducing a new technique into the company? Depending on the purpose behind his going on the course, one would have to decide what sort of performance improvement to look for. Who would then give the information about his performance? The man himself? His boss? A relevant department – e.g. Finance Department, who might have observed an improvement in budgeting; or Computer Department who are now pleased with better use of PCs in that manager's offices?

This type of auditing is the sort of thing that the training manager would expect to do, almost as a routine. He would encourage careful course selection, with a clear purpose; a full briefing of the 'trainee manager'; and reporting back on return. Then, a reflection in the next weeks on the extent to which the course content and experience are proving directly useful, or illuminating, or giving confidence, and so on. His boss will be observing his performance, either directly or indirectly, and trying to establish whether there are changes.

The ease with which performance changes can be observed depends to a large extent on what has been learnt. Specific skills e.g. in budgeting, use of information technology, and chairmanship, are easy to see in action and their value will be immediately apparent. The line managers and the training manager will maintain a 'continuous audit', with little formality.

There are other skills, and behaviours, which are not easy to see in action, not easy to audit, and for which formal auditing *may* be thought necessary. If a company is taking seriously its policies of non-discrimination or of continuous development, or of employee empowerment, it will take steps to educate, its managers, supervisors and staff so that they understand the purpose and virtue of the new policy, the new responsibilities of company management, and what *things managers and supervisors have to do*. Will the managers and supervisors then actually do these new things, change their behaviour, use the new skills? Experience shows that if it is then simply left to the managers and supervisors, nothing much will change. Even occasional reminders make little difference. There needs to be rigorous examination of what is being done and not being done, function by function, area by area: target setting for future action: and workshops then to examine individual achievements and difficulties.

In the above extreme circumstances, which may become less rare in the near future, teams – with an auditing function – may be set up to review and energise company action, with the T & D staff playing a major role in planning, co-ordinating and facilitating, as well as in monitoring and auditing.

If we look at the recruitment, transfer, promotion, selection, appraisal, forecasting, planning phases of manpower work, is it possible to examine, to audit, any point down the chain of intentions beyond the point at which the manpower function itself carries all executive responsibility? How do we know if the recruitment is good? Do we distinguish between the administration of recruitment, and the quality of the people recruited and how they work? Is it possible to look beyond the processes of management succession planning and management development, and see whether those people developed and promoted *are actually doing a good job to an acceptable standard?*

These are vital questions, and particularly to the auditor, be he an outside consultant or a resident manager or specialist in the manpower function, if a grass roots examination of manpower is undertaken. The benefits which accrue to the company from the manpower function do not lie in that function itself; they lie in the company outside. The function's skill, and costs and efficiency, can probably always be improved internally, but to assess its effectiveness in meeting the company's actual and future requirements the audit cannot be confined to the function.

This means that the audit must focus on the products of the training and developments activities and systems. It must not confine itself to examining the activities and systems, and their suitability in meeting the company's needs. The ultimate evaluation is whether the individual can do the job well: and how the programme and experiences which that individual has been through have contributed to his present peformance. We have discussed earlier that a great part of learning does not come simply from instruction and courses, but through experience. For experience to be most beneficial the learner must be able to turn to a colleague and to his boss, to interpret fully that experience and make it meaningful and useful. This is important from the top to the bottom of the organisation: it is critical in some jobs, where understanding and personal development depends on getting to grips with complex problems of plant, organisation, of people, of plans and so on – and then trying to solve those problems. The 'learner' must turn to colleagues and his boss for information and to try out ideas.

So managers, as 'teachers', are an essential part of the training and development. Are they playing their part? Do they listen, answer questions, and discuss things? Do they encourage initiative and responsibility? Some management development programmes, which appear to be very good on paper, have foundered because of inability or unwillingness of managers to fill this teaching role. If an audit can reveal such weaknesses, as experience has shown, then action can be taken to improve the teaching capability of those managers and the development of the learners. This is particularly important in companies which have people of high potential on 'fast-track' programmes, moving quickly from one job to another. This demands great teaching and coaching ability and sympathy from the resident bosses of those jobs if superficial learning and experience is to be avoided. It is also important in developing countries where development programmes for promising local managers may include a series of fast moves and promotions to get them to the top quickly. As in the West some may turn out to be first class, but there is a greater risk that they will miss out on real work experience in their moves. The question for the auditor and the T & D manager, is not 'where have they worked?', but 'what have they actually done and learnt, what responsibility have they personally carried?' And, as a final question, 'do *they* make decisions now, or do they agree with other people's decisions?' Whatever the answers to these questions, they will be useful, either to indicate the success of current practices, or the need for improvement in practices.

The auditor must therefore be prepared to move physically across the company, and not to remain simply in happy contemplation and analysis of reports, charts and data, valuable though these are. Getting information down the chain of intentions is best done by visiting and talking with supervisors and managers along the chain, in the place where they work, if possible. No matter how much the consultant, or the training manager, may know about machine shops, the next one and its foreman is different, perhaps in some important respect, and this has to be experienced. It is there that attitudes, qualities, side effects, and the unexpected, will be encountered, and that valuable confidence and rapport will be established. It is not merely interesting to visit the workshops, or the refinery, or the offshore platform; for the auditor, and particularly for members of the manpower function, it is essential continuous education, helping to maintain communication and understanding.

This, of course, is well understood by experienced visiting consultants, but it so often appears to be forgotten by the residents.

Subject bibliography

CONTENTS

INTRODUCTORY NOTE

The books listed in the following pages are about the many subjects to which reference is made in the main text, and about which the reader may wish to learn more through further reading. Although some of the books appear also in the recommended reading for courses and examinations in personnel and other studies, the actual titles have not been selected with such studies in mind, for which lists already exist. Instead, the aim has been to suggest books many of which, whilst providing further useful technical and practical information, also offer comments on the systems and situations within which people have to make their way, a matter of equal concern to all members of management and management services.

The lists cannot claim to be the best possible, for that depends also on the experience and interest of each reader in turn, and our readership is of widely varied composition. Nor are they exhaustive. There are very many more books available, some well known, than are shown in this selection. The fact that the library of the Institute of Personnel Management at Wimbledon carries a stock of some 13,000 publications, plus 21,000 articles from periodicals, all on related subjects, gives an idea of the additional depth of reading now available.

A   THE TRAINING & DEVELOPMENT FUNCTION

A Good Start – Effective Employee Induction
A. Fowler   IPM   1990

Training & Development
R. Harrison   IPM   1988
Looks at the company as a whole, as a learning system, with individual and organisational responsibility for employee development. Many helpful case studies: good introductory reading.

Training Interventions
J. Kenney, M. Reid   IPM   1989
The assessment of organisational and individual needs, and the planning and
evaluation strategies, plus the initiatives and role of the training function.

35 Checklists for Human Resource Development
I. MacKay   Gower   1990
Good food for thought, and action, on virtually every human need and provision
from recruiting, coaching and learning, to stress, succession planning and Training
& Development strategy.

Approaches to Training & Development
D. Laird   Addison Wesley   1985
Everything that the function has to deal with, and how to do it; easy style with
practical examples. Some emphasis on evaluation in the corporate and organisational sense.

Management Development & Training Handbook
Taylor, Lippit   McGraw-Hill   1983
Many experienced contributors cover in detail methods, programmes and organisation development, with useful articles also on the economics and manning of the
development function itself. A big book, with plenty of illustration.

The Management of Interpersonal Skills Training
K. Phillips, T. Fraser   Gower   1982
The choice of the most suitable technique, the organisation of training, its evalu-
ation, and ethical considerations, are compactly presented.

Encyclopedia of Management Development Methods
Andrzej Huczynski   Gower   1990
Describes and helps you choose from the many learning methods, old and new.
Must be a welcome addition to the department bookshelf, with 300 entries in its
directory section, cross referencing and including a guide to the selection of best
methods.

Training by Objectives – an Economic Approach to Management Training
G. S. Odiorne   Macmillan   1970

B   THE TRAINING OFFICER'S SKILLS

(a) *Analysis*

The Identification of Training Needs
T. H. Boydell   BACIE   1976
Origins and types of present and future needs. Manpower planning, Training Officer
and management roles and working methods. Compact, practical, full of information
and tips on 'how to do it'.

The Skills of Training
Leslie Rae   Gower   Second edition 1991
The main methods used in training and development, their best use and advantages
and disadvantages.

(b) *Instruction & Learning*

A Training Officer's Giude to Discussion Leading
A. Devenham   BACIE   1976
Practical introduction to preparation for and handling of discussions, including
physical arrangements, syndicates and handouts, but not visual aids. Brief and to
the point.

Action Learning in Practice
Mike Pedler (ed.)   Gower   Second edition 1991
What it is, how it is used, and how to get it started. Articles and case studies by
experienced practitioners. Particularly interesting for management developers.

Creative Thinking and Brainstorming
T. Geoffrey Rawlinson   Gower   1981
Simple, brief and useful principles and applications.

Experiential Learning
T. H. Boydell   Manchester Monographs   1976

The Origins & Growth of Action Learning
R. W. Revans   Bromley, Chartwell-Brott   1982

Experiential Learning
D. A. Kolb   Prentice-Hall   1984

Interview Skills Training
Practice packs for trainers
P. Hocket   IPM   1981
Has a text on interview skills training and the training methods available, as well as
packs of exercises.

(c) *Interpersonal & Group Relationships*

Improving Interpersonal Relations
C. L. Cooper (ed.)   Gower   1986
Introduces the language, concepts and techniques of four prominent types of social
skills training, i.e. transactional analysis, interaction analysis, assertiveness training
and T-Groups, with applications and a comparative review and evaluation.

Developing Interactive Skills
N. Rackham, P. Honey et al.   Wellens   1971

Management Teams: Why they Succeed or Fail
R. M. Belbin   Heinemann   1984

Team Development Manual
M. Woodcock   Gower   Second edition 1990
Contains basic teamwork theory, groundrules for team development, and selecting
teambuilding activities. Highly practical.

C   THE PERSONNEL FUNCTION & SYSTEMS

(a) *The Personnel Function*

Economics in Personnel Management
J. Bridge   IPM   1981
Teaches and discusses the contribution of personnel and manpower decisions and
factors to the economy of the firm as a whole. Good way for personnel people to
learn about economics, and for others to appreciate this significant aspect of the
personnel function.

Personnel and the Bottom Line
M. Armstrong   IPM   1989
Personnel managers should not remain as administrators, but must become active
in developing human resources and contributing, as business partners, to overall
corporate excellence.

Personnel Management Handbook
S. Harper (ed.)   Gower   1987
Comprehensive reference book; resourcing, performance, rewards, employee rela-
tions – and the personnel department and administration.

(b) *Personnel Records and Data Analysis*

Computers in Personnel
Terry Page (ed.)   IMS Report No. 53   1982
Sections on practical experience in computerisation of recruitment, job evaluation,
negotiation, manpower control, payroll; and on implementation, costs and other
aspects of computer use.

Computerising Personnel Systems: A basic guide
A. Evans   IPM   1986
Introduction to computing, its application and benefits. Offers a systematic
approach to computerising the personnel function.

Computers in Personnel – Your system: Develop or Die
T. Page (C1P90) (ed.)   IMS   1990
The experiences and recommendations of many contributors.

(c) *Assessment & Appraisal*

Psychological Testing in Personnel Assessment
K. M. Miller (ed.)   Gower   1975
Discusses and illustrates aptitude, intelligence and other mainly paper tests for
employment and promotion. Chapter detailing experiences in several companies
showing how reliability can be improved. A little statistics which can be skipped.

Identifying Managerial Potential
R. F. Holdsworth   BIM   1975

Staff Appraisal – a first step to effective leadership
G. Randall, P. Packard, J. Slater   IPM   1984
The skills and training needed to develop managers' ability in monitoring perfor-
mance and developing employees potential.

Performance Appraisal & Career Development
C. Fletcher, R. Williams   Hutchinson   1985

Assessment Centres
C. Woodruffe   IPM   1990
For those who are considering using ACs. Discusses their purposes, design and
proper management.

Psychological Testing – a practical guide to aptitude and other tests
J. Toplis, V. Dulewicz, C. Fletcher   IPM   1987

D MANPOWER FORECASTING, PLANNING AND CONTROL

(a) *Forecasting*

Relating Manpower to an Organisation's Objectives
C. Richards-Carpenter   IMS Report No. 56   1983
A practical and thorough study of essential factors such as objectives, external
social/economic influences, corporate ageing, entered into a coherent easy-to-
understand model, fully explained and discussed. Data needed, analysis and practical steps to be taken in the company, are also dealt with. Includes some mathematical concepts but the text is almost totally 'non-mathematical'.

Forcasting the Size of the Company Labour Force
C. Purkiss   IMS Report No. 6   1981
A short basic introduction to the assessment of manpower needs in terms of
business objectives, future manpower requirements, present manpower and its
future employment.

Changing Output – Employment Relationships
A. Anderson   IMS Report No. 11   1981
A brief study of actual changing output-employment relationships stemming from

factors such as market shock, price shock, overmanning and failure by companies to adjust.

(b) Planning & Control

The Manpower Planning Handbook
M. Bennison, J. Casson   IMS   1984
Everything needed to design and run planning systems to meet present and future corporate needs, including data needs, market information, use of models, planning careers, short and long term thinking.

Practical Manpower Planning
J. Bramham   IPM   1988
Grass roots conceptual and practical approach to forecasting and planning. No mathematical difficulties. Should suit both students and personnel officers.

Corporate Manpower Planning
A. R. Smith (ed.)   Gower   1980
For the more experienced reader. Collection of articles on planning as a whole, with sections on wastage, recruitment, promotion. Excellent on staff-succession analysis. Mathematics an advantage for the reader, but there are good 'non-mathematical' pages that clarify both concepts and methods.

Manpower Planning Workbook
B. O. Pittman, G. Tavernier   Gower   Second edition 1984
Some concepts and principles, but mainly masses of samples of data, forms, analyses and applications. Includes costing and cost-control applications.

Human Resources Planning
J. Bramham   IPM   1989
Planning of human resources must not be only to meet economic and operational needs of the company: it has to take human needs into account.

E   MANPOWER COSTING, EVALUATION, AUDITING & RESEARCH

(a) *Costing*

Cost-Benefit Analysis in Industrial Training
N. Hall   Manchester Monograph 6   1976

Cost Effective Personnel Decisions
J. Cannon   IPM   1979
Analysing costs associated with employing and motivating people and making better decisions about workforce deployment.

(b) *Evaluation, Auditing & Research*

The Evaluation of Organisational Change
C. A. Carnall   Gower   1982
The views and relationships of various interest-groups in a company: what they gain
and what they lose. Includes real-life case studies, focusing on social rather than
financial outcomes. UK and overseas examples.

Evaluation: Relating Training to Business Performance
T. Jackson   Kogan Page   1989
How to calculate the value of training in terms of financial saving or gain, or
increased efficiency and productivity.

Evaluation of Management Education, Training and Development
M. Easterby-Smith   Gower   1986
Aims and purposes, methods and application, as well as the organisational politics
of evaluations.

F   CAREER PLANNING AND DEVELOPMENT

Career Dynamics; Matching Individual and Organisational Needs
E. H. Schein   Addison Wesley   1978
Deals with requirements, expectations and problems, in a practical approach to
career development of individuals. Research evidence and theory provides a nice
balance in the writing.

Manpower Planning – Policy, Careers & Individuals
M. Bennison   IMS Report No. 2   1981
A succinct examination of the relationship between career/career prospects of the
individual, and the dynamics of the organisation and its manpower as a whole.
Discusses how policies may not be supportable by the actual state of the company;
how personnel development and career prospects can be more accurately estimated; and perhaps how realistic policies can be arrived at.

The Management of Career Structures
M. Bennison, R. Morgan   IMS Report No. 24   1981
Based on experiences in a number of companies it describes the principles and
practices of identifying and establishing career structures, analysing their future
changes and stability, and identifying, dealing with, and avoiding excessive
problems.

Using Personnel Research
A. P. O. Williams (ed.)   Gower   1983

G   THE BOARD'S RESPONSIBILITIES

On the Board
G. Mills   Unwin Hyman   Second edition 1986

275

Defines and discusses, with some humour, the board's and the board members' responsibilities. Useful for non-board members to understand what a board actually is, and what its preoccupations are likely to be. Manpower and personnel hardly feature.

Developing Directors: using experience
A. Mumford, P. Honey, G. Robinson   Institute of Directors   1989

Professional Development for the Board
                              Institute of Directors   1990
A survey by Adaptation Ltd for the IOD, showing the changing awareness of the need for the development of specific skills amongst board members. Must be useful reading for existing directors and for those who identify and develop future directors.

H   MANAGEMENT METHODS AND SKILLS

(a) *General*

The Skills of Management
A. N. Welsh   Gower   1982
Emphasis on self-management and people management, with some personnel management techniques. Valuable for line management as a self-instruction guide.

Learning about Management
H. A. Barrington   McGraw-Hill   1984

Management Processes and Functions
M. Armstrong   IPM   1990
Detailed study of the use of interpersonal skills in planning, organising, and controlling, and creating motivation and teamwork.

Defining Managerial Skills
W. Hirsch   IMS   1990
Tackles the problem of identifying the skills needed in management jobs, and establishing a useful language for these skills. A quick résumé for all concerned with selection, appraisal, promotion and career development.

What Makes a Manager?
W. Hirsch, S. Bevan   IMS   1988
A full presentation of skill classifications, and the use made of these in selection, appraisal and promotion, etc. Case studies and research findings. Very practical.

(b) *Financing and Costing*

Management Accounting for Non-Financial Managers
D. M. C. Jones   BIM   1978
Simple illustrated chapters on financial information, costing, budgets and investment appraisal.

Finance and Accountancy for Managers
D. Davies   IPM   1990
Introductory text, from basic accounting to planning and control, including detailed examples.

Management Accounting
G. Mott   Gower   1987
Jargon-free text: costing, planning, decision-making and control.

(c) *Forecasting & Planning*

Forecasting and Planning
R. Fildes, D. Wood (eds)   Gower   1978
Series of practical articles on macro and micro economic forecasting and planning; examines the reliability of forecasts. Chapter on organisational adjustment to uncertainty. Some maths which can be skipped.

Systematic Corporate Planning
J. Argenti   Van Nostrand Reinhold   1982
Covers the whole range of forecasting and planning principles and methods with only little mathematics. Manpower aspects not dealt with.

Long Range Planning for your Business – an Operating Manual
M. L. Kastens   AMACOM   1976

Management Training & Corporate Strategy
D. Hussey   Pergamon   1988

Training Needs & Corporate Strategy: the Relationship between Business & Management Training Strategies.
J. Elliot   IMS   1989

I   A MANAGER'S PERSONAL SKILLS

(a) *Managing Yourself*

The Unblocked Manager
M. Woodcock, D. Francis   Gower   1982
Many management capabilities are inhibited by one or more of eleven possible internal personal 'blockages'. What these blockages are, how they can be identified, and then overcome, is presented in a practical commonsense way. A do-it-yourself book.

Managers and their job – a study of the similarities and differences in ways managers spend their time
R. Stewart   Macmillan   1988

A Manager's Guide to Self-Development
M. Pedler, J. G. Burgoyne, T. Boydell   McGraw-Hill   1986

Management Development – Strategies for Action
A. Mumford   IPM   1989
A very thorough exposition of the processes of learning and developing, both informally and formally, and the resources that can be of help.

Turning People On
A. Sargent   IPM   1990
A study of theory and practice in developing motivation, and of the situations in which there is a demand for this sort of management and skill.

Improve Your People Skills
P. Honey   IPM   1988
Jargon-free A–Z guide.

20 Ways to Manage Better
A. Leigh   IPM   1984
A wide range of management competences, each in a short chapter.

(b) *Teaching*

A Manager's Guide to Coaching
D. Megginson, T. Boydell   BACIE   1979
Deals with many types and applications of coaching, preparation, skills needed and problems. Brief and to the point.

Counselling People at Work
R. de Board   Gower   1983

The Skills of Training – a Guide for Managers and Practitioners
W. Leslie Rae   Gower   Second edition 1991

J   MANAGING CHANGE

The New Managerial Grid
R. Blake, J. Mouton   Gulf Publishing Co. (Kogan Page)   1978

Changing Culture
A. Williams, P. Dobson, M. Walters   IPM   1989
General principles, all the steps to be taken, and many detailed case studies. Includes useful details of the role of the personnel function.

Teaching the Elephant to Dance – Empowering Change in your Organisation
J. A. Belasco   Hutchinson   1990
Organisations are like elephants, particularly old ones, slow to change. This is about how to bring about change, in the right direction, and with employee collaboration.

Understanding Organisations
C. Handy   Penguin   1981

Equal Opportunities – the way ahead
J. Straw   IPM   1989
How to introduce equal opportunity practices for women, minority ethnic groups,
the disabled and older workers. Looks at the future influence of Europe on the UK.

Organisational Behaviour: An introductory text
D. A. Buchanan, A Huezynski   Prentice-Hall   1986
Helps the newcomer to this field to see the organisation, its managers and
employers, through the eyes of the social scientist, with no problems of jargon.

All Change at Work
The human dimension
T. Wilkinson (ed.)   IPM   1989
The role of managers and the personnel function in bringing about humane major
change in the organisation. Many case studies illustrate the upsets and problems,
and the need for new management capabilities and systems.

New Work Patterns: Putting Policy into Practice
P. Leighton, M. Syrett   Pitman   1989
The effective use and management of the 'flexible' workforce including job sharers,
part-timers, temporary and casual staff. For personnel and line managers.

Unblocking Your Organisation
M. Woodcock, D. Francis   Gower   1990
Describes 14 blockages that prevent an organisation from reaching full potential,
and how to overcome them. Covers aims, values, management development, organisation structure, rewards, training, communication, teamwork, motivation and
creativity.

K   THE EMPLOYEE AS A LEARNER

Managing the Poor Performer
V. Stewart, A. Stewart   Gower   1982
Analyses and discusses the causes of poor performance, of physical, medical and
organisational origin. Suggests means of detection and possible remedies, of which
training is one of many. Gives useful perspective to the supervisors view of subordinates, colleagues – and supervisors.

The Right People in the Right Jobs
John Finnigan   Gower   1983
Presents the 'employee' as an under-used resource, right through selection, induction, training, promotion, development and redundancy; and what the manager
should do about it.

Management & The Worker
F. J. Roethlisberger, W. J. Dickson   Harvard University Press   1941

Continuous Development – the Pattern to Improved Performance
S. Wood (ed.)   IPM   1988
Emphasises the importance of learning and creativity in the industrial life of the employee, and its value to the company. Ways of enhancing these are explored, as well as the role of management and the personnel function. Twelve contemporary case studies give strong practical meaning to the text.

L   THE INTERNATIONAL CONTEXT

The Arab Executive
Farid Muna   Macmillan   1980
A research-based study of how the Arab performs, and expects to perform, as an executive and as a manager. The relationship between culture and 'management style' is discussed in this definitive work, written with insight, and must be read by responsible people working in the Middle East, whether of Arab or non-Arab origins.

Breaking Down Barriers
Bob Garratt, John Stopford (eds)   Gower   1980
Written for the Association of Teachers of Management, this book provides generally useful comparisons of managers from different cultures, and discussion on management development in multinationals. Examples are provided of management training and education practices in some well-known companies, with problems and possible remedies.

The World of the International Manager
J. Hutton   Philip Allen   1988
Comprehensive introduction to the development of international business, its impact on economics, people, cultures and countries. Ranges from pricing to cultural adjustment. Valuable for both business and personnel management.

International Management – a Review of Strategies and Operations
M. Z. Brooke   Hutchinson Education   1987
Looks closely at company operations, and points to the problems arising from a globally extended organisation structure with inherent instabilities.

Human Resource Management in International Firms
P. Evans, Y. Doz, A. Laurent   Macmillan   1989
Practices and findings of experienced companies in managing cultural change, and in building a more innovative organisation.

European Management Guides
Institute of Personnel Management   IPM   1990/1/2
Five separate guides on Recruitment, Terms and Conditions of Employment, Industrial Relations, Pay and Benefits, and Training and Development. Outlines of EEC legislation, country-by-country analysis, and pointers to sources of further information.

Sources of European Economic and Business Information
University of Warwick B.I.S.   Gower   Fifth edition 1990
Covers eastern and western Europe on a wide range of topics.

Women Overseas – A practical guide
N. Piet-Pelon, B. Hornby   IPM   1986
Useful for those considering going abroad to work or as spouse. Gives insights into culture differences, handling stress, running the house, helping children, and staying healthy.

European Community Social Policy: Its impact on the UK
C. Brewster, P. Teague   IPM   1989
Examines organisational, legal and administrative links between the EC and the UK, and the effect of the EC social policies on UK organisations, today and in the future.

European Law: Its Impact on UK Employment
P. Leighton   IMS   1990
Differences between UK law, practices and enforcement, and other EEC members. Covers recruitment; health, safety and welfare; working hours; part-time staff; cross border sub-contracting.

The European Labour Market Review
R. Pearson, F. Andreutti, S. Holby   IMS   1990
International comparisons of many aspects of labour including demographic trends, unemployment, industrial change, professional structures, skills shortages, education systems and supply. Comparisons also with US and Japan.

M   ETHICS AND ALL THAT

Counselling – A practical guide for employers
M. Megranahan   IPM   1989
Practical and human approach to helping people in need of redundancy, retirement or career counselling.

Being Me and Also Us
A. Stallibrass   SAP   1989
The social aspects of human biology, as revealed by the research projects of Dr Scott Williamson. Stallibrass underlines the fact that continuous development is a prerequisite for optimum health throughout life, and that individuals have an inherent potential for co-operation.

The Nice Company
T. Lloyd   Bloomsbury   1990
Companies often do not behave like normal caring human beings, although they are composed of human beings. By examining the development of company behaviour in evolutionary terms, it may be possible to understand more fully the forces which favour survival, and to consider the place of niceness amongst survival factors.

Publishers' details

Addison-Wesley	Addison-Wesley Publishers Ltd Finchampstead Road Wokingham Berks RG11 2NZ
AMACOM	American Management Association Distrib. Kogan Page
BACIE	British Association for Commercial & Industrial Education 16 Park Crescent London W1N 4AP
BIM	British Institute of Management Management House Cottingham Road Corby, Northants NN17 1TT
Bloomsbury	Bloomsbury Publishing Ltd 2 Soho Square London W1V 5DE
(US) Bureau of National Affairs	Bureau of National Affairs, Inc. 1231 25th Street NW Washington DC, USA
Business Books	Business Books Ltd 20 Vauxhall Bridge Road London SW1V 2SA

Butterworths	Butterworth & Co (Oub.) Ltd Borough Green Sevenoaks, Kent TN15 8PH
Coverdale	Coverdale Educational Publishers 23 Maddox Street London W1R 9LE
Dept. of Employment Training Information Papers	Training Research Information & Publications Training Agency 613 Moorfoot Sheffield S1 4PQ
Dow-Jones Inc., US	Charles Letts & Co Diary House 77 Borough Road London SE1 1DW
Gower	Gower Publishing Co. Ltd Gower House Croft Road Aldershot Hants GU11 3HR
Grant McIntyre	Basil Blackwell 108 Cowley Road Oxford OX4 1JF
Gulf Publishing Co	Kogan Page Ltd 120 Pentonville Road London N1 9JN
Heinemann	Butterworth–Heinemann Halley Court Jordan Hill Oxford OX2 8EJ
Holt, Rinehart & Winston	Distrib. Holt-Saunders Ltd 24–28 Oval Road London NW1 7DX
IMS	Institute of Manpower Studies Mantell Building University of Sussex Falmer Brighton BN1 9RF

IPM	Institute of Personnel Management IPM House Camp Road London SW19 4UW
IOD	Institute of Directors 116 Pall Mall London SW1Y 5ED
Kogan Page	Kogan Page Ltd 120 Pentonville Road London N1 9JN
MacDonald & Evans	Pitman Publishing Ltd 128 Long Acre Long Acre London WC2E 9AN
Macmillan	Macmillan Publishers Ltd Little Essex Street London WC2R 3LF
Management Games	Management Games Ltd Methwold House Methwold Thetford Norfolk IP26 4PF
Manchester	Dept of Adult & Higher Education Manchester University Oxford Road Manchester M13 9PL
McGraw-Hill	McGraw-Hill Book Co. (UK) Ltd McGraw-Hill House Shoppenhangers Road Maidenhead Berks SL6 2QL
MCB	MCB Publications Ltd 198/200 Keighley Road Bradford West Yorkshire BD9 4JQ
MSC Training Division	Training Research Information & Publications Training Agency 613 Moorfoot Sheffield S1 4PQ

Nelson	Nelson (Thomas) & Sons Ltd Nelson House Mayfield Road Walton-on-Thames Surrey KT12 5PL
Pergamon	Pergamon Press Ltd Headington Hill Hall Oxford OX3 0BW
Pitman	Pitman Publishing 128 Long Acre London WCE 9AN
Prentice-Hall	Prentice-Hall International Inc 66 Wood Lane End Hemel Hempstead HP2 4RG
SAP	Scottish Academic Press 139 Leith Walk Edingburgh EH6 8NS
Van Nostrand Reinhold	Van Nostrand Reinhold Co Ltd 2–6 Boundary Row London SE1 8HN
Vantage	Vantage Press Inc 516 West 34th Street New York NY 10001 USA
Wellens	Wellens Publishing The Sun High Street Guilsborough Northampton NN6 8PY
Wiley	Wiley (John) & Sons Ltd Baffins Lane Chichester W. Sussex PO19 1UD
Unwin Hyman	Unwin Hyman Publishers Ltd 15–17 Broadwick Street London W1Y 1FP

Index